BOARDERLANDS

Rob 1

BOARDERLANDS

The Snowboarder's Guide to the West Coast

Jim Humes and Sean Wagstaff

HarperCollins*West*

An Imprint of HarperCollins*Publishers*

For my parents, for Steve and Tom,
and Will, Bryan, David, and Chris

—J.H.

For Dorit

—S.W.

A TREE CLAUSE BOOK

HarperCollins West and the authors, in association with The Basic Foundation, a not-for-profit organization, will facilitate the planting of ten trees to contribute to the reforestation of our planet.

FIRST EDITION

Library of Congress Cataloging-in-Publication Data

Humes, James.
    Boarderlands : the snowboarder's guide to the West Coast / James Humes and
    Sean Wagstaff. — 1st ed.
    ISBN 0–06–258587–8 (pbk.)
    1. Snowboarding—Northwest, Pacific—Guidebooks. 2. Snowboarding—
    Alaska—Guidebooks. 3. Northwest, Pacific—Guidebooks. 4. Alaska—
    Guidebooks. I. Wagstaff, Sean. II. Title.
GV857.S57H85 1995
796.9—dc20   95–31583

95 96 97 98 99 ❖ RRD (H) 10 9 8 7 6 5 4 3 2 1

Contents

Preface

Snowboarders are different. They have their own way of going down a mountain. They like to explore the areas between runs, and they're not averse to hiking in order to get some fresh snow. They like to fly, to bonk, to point straight downhill and forget about turning. The black diamonds, blue rectangles, and green circles don't mean as much to a snowboarder.

The trail maps weren't telling the snowboarders' story of the mountains, so during the winter of 1994–95, we went to more than fifty resorts on the West Coast to discover where the boarders were riding. We wanted to know where all the juicy hits and pockets of trees were hidden. There were spots out there that only local riders, who had spent years at a single mountain, would be able to show us. So we went on a roadtrip that took us from Alaska to Southern California. We talked to the locals about their favorite spots to ride, where to hang out at night, and what board shops in the vicinity would be able to help out with a binding strap. We explored each mountain, looking for the terrain features that no snowboarder should miss and also discovering places that someone with a resort-issued trail map might not think to ride.

Our objective was to save fellow snowboarders time. Not everyone can be a local, and when you're at a mountain you don't know that well, many times you'll discover the choice terrain just minutes before the lifts stop operating. This book will point you to the places that best suit your riding style: the trees where skiers don't dare, the snowfields where you can find fresh turns a week after the last dump, the hidden gully by the slow chair where the hits line up like ducks on a pond.

We also hope that you'll visit some of the more out-of-the-way mountains, or places you don't normally think to ride. We found some great mountains that, while they're not monuments to the high-speed quad, offer some great terrain and snowboarding scenes with truly distinct flavors.

The West Coast has the highest concentration of snowboarders in the world, and the sport has found its most widespread acceptance here. We hope this guide will be a useful tool as you head out to explore the spectacular mountains on the West Coast, and all the creative ways to descend them.

Happy riding.

Acknowledgments

This book could not have been completed without a great deal of help. We especially owe our thanks to Scott and Jeanine Menezes, Michael Hayes, Nina Schuyler and Po Bronson, Mark Morehouse and Heather Candy. To all of the guides that gave us endless tips on sticking fat airs while revealing prized secret spots, rest assured that we didn't give away all the goods. Each of the resorts in this guide contributed generously by giving us the run of their mountains. Burton Snowboards, Mervin Manufacturing (Lib Tech), and Tubbs Snowshoes helped us with truly outstanding equipment. On behalf of the entire snowboarding community we thank the National Ski Areas Association (NSAA) and Ski Industries America (SIA) for advancing the cause of snowboarding. Finally, for moral support as well as rigorous physical training, we extend our thanks to the morning Hoopsters, including Sam and Kirsten Neff, Mike and Michelle Jumper, Ethan Watters, Larry Gallagher, Scott Ludeke, Ben Prince, Pete Liske, Al Marchi, Jeff Davis, and Gerard McCann.

How to Use This Book

Since Aristotle, classification has been a topic of human existence. Aristotle had little to do with snowboarding, but organization has a lot to do with how to make sense of this book. We've broken down the mountains and their terrain into sections for freeriders, cruisers, freestylers, and grommets (beginners). While it's possible to be all of those at the same time, the sections will identify the best terrain for each style of riding. Our hope is that it will save boarders from spending their valuable time searching for goods, instead of getting into them.

Freeriders

This section is geared toward riders who like to explore the mountain. We've included the steeps, deeps, extremes, and glade runs that will take you away from the crowds. Because freeriding is an act of spontaneity, we've talked about specific rocks, chutes, or terrain features, but for the most part you're on your own once you get to a particular part of the mountain. It's freeriding after all.

Cruisers

Although Euro-carvers aren't an everyday sight at quite a few mountains, their numbers are increasing as more skiers cross over to snowboarding but don't want to buy a new pair of boots. The Cruisers section talks about where you can find groomed steeps, fall-line pitches, or just some wide-open turning. If you are a speed merchant, you'll want to read this section. Intermediates who are looking for good spots on the mountain to practice their turning will also want to check out some of these runs.

Freestylers

It's really not fair to separate freeriders and freestylers, because we've seen all the tricks performed in a snowboard park happening off big rock jumps and other sick situations. So this section for freestyling is more like a section for "predictable landings." We've talked about a mountain's terrain or snowboard park if it has one, as well as its hit runs, where a series of hits will line up on the shoulders of a groomed run. Read this section if you're looking for the hits and landings that will allow you to go out and session a few moves.

Grommets

Every mountain that allows snowboarding is encouraging it by offering lessons and rental packages. Instead of discussing the intricacies of the learning slopes, we've given information on what kind of deals you can find on beginner packages, and discussed the truly fine beginners' meadows.

Nonbelievers

These are folks who don't believe that snowboarding is the path to enlightenment. They wear skis and are commonly the parents of snowboarders. They are also responsible for the existence of ski resorts, and in a roundabout way, the existence of snowboarding. We've given a summary of skier/snowboarder harmony and listed the additional offerings for the nonsnowboarding types.

The chapters also contain some information that we think snowboarders either need or might be interested in knowing:

Vital Information

This includes the resort's address and phone number, the snowphone number that you can call to get information on conditions, the number of lifts, and base and peak elevation. We've included directions to get you to the mountain and information regarding lifts, when its season begins, and what hours the lifts run.

The Local Scene

A quick rundown on where to eat, drink, and hang out after a day of boarding, as well as what you can expect to find by way of a vibe out on the mountain. This section talks about the particular feel of a place, and all the elements that contribute to it.

Where to Stay

We've tried to always include at least one bargain-basement listing in the lodging section. Many times, the local chamber of commerce is the best source of information regarding where to stay for cheap, or for lift and lodging packages, and we've included those numbers as well.

The Mountain

This section talks about the mountain's general characteristics, layout, and some specific terrain features. It's an overview of what you can expect to find by way of terrain. It's a good one to read to find out about a mountain's overall steepness, the average length of runs, or to predict exactly how far over your head you can go.

LÉGEND

 BEGINNING

 CRUISING

 FREERIDING

 RACECOURSE

 STEEPS

 TERRAIN PARK

 TRAVERSE

 TREE RIDING

 FOREST

 ROCKS & CLIFFS

CHAIR 1   LIFT

 AREA BOUNDARY

Chapter 1

Alaska is king when it comes to un-
tracked snow, steep descents, and a season that ends only when
you want it to. The state is home to six ski areas but offers more
backcountry than you can shake a stick at. The terrain exerts its in-
fluence on the snowboarding scene: the boards are longer and
you'll find a higher percentage of freeriders in the state than anywhere else.

Every snowboarder who's opened the pages of a magazine knows
about Alaska—the sixty-foot cliff jumps, sick chute drops, and ex-
pansive powder fields. And every snowboarder dreams about taking
a heli trip up to Thompson Pass to glide through some untracked
snow. There's all sorts of extreme riding in Alaska, and in many ways
this clouds some of the simple truths about the state. It is a place of
extremities, but there are also terrain and conditions for every type
of rider.

Backcountry Opportunities

Before you go storming out for fresh tracks, make sure you know what you're doing in the backcountry. Check with the locals on recent snowfall, winds, and other weather conditions. Ask them how you might find some of the peaks that are good hikes in the area. Near Girdwood you'll find Winter Creek, Wolverine, Fish Breath, and Crow Pass. Closer to Anchorage there's O'Mally Peak, Ptarmigan, and Flat Top. Juneau has its own set of peaks and some heli operations to boot, so check in with them to see where their rates are hanging.

The most famous backcountry is found in the Chugach Mountains at Thompson Pass near Valdez. Snowboarders and skiers come from around the world for the heli drops in this range. The scene is best exemplified by the legendary King of the Hill Contest, an annual extreme snowboarding spectacle that features the sickest descents known to the sport. The good thing is that you can ride Thompson Pass without putting yourself on a fifty-degree slope. Just tell your pilot what you're up for.

Tall Tales

After we arrived in Alaska we realized we had brought with us some assumptions about life there that were pretty far from reality:

Alaskan Myth: Minus forty degrees, permafrost, calving glaciers, death from eating polar bear liver or from exposure, at least loss of extremities due to frostbite.

Alaskan Reality: It's a big state, bigger than Texas, with a lot of different weather patterns. It's darn cold in the interior, but near the southern coast the daytime temperature during the winter averages in the mid-twenties. The Rockies are colder than that. The Japanese currents that move through the Gulf of Alaska lend their warmth to the coastal regions.

Alaskan Myth: It's dark. So dark in fact that all you can do is hunker down in a bar and drink; so dark that you go mad during the winter, that you start honing the edges on your board, and then your ax, and then . . .

Alaskan Reality: Again, it's a big state and the days grow shorter by five minutes a day in Juneau to eight or nine minutes up toward Nome. At the winter solstice, functional light in Anchorage begins around 10:15 A.M. and lasts past 4:00 P.M. Herein lies the excuse for staying out late at night and sleeping in. After a cup of coffee and a big breakfast, you can ride straight through the day without stopping for lunch. By March you've got fourteen-hour days, which should allow you to get in all the vert you can handle.

Alaskan Myth: Everyone shoots guns.

Alaskan Reality: It's hard to read an account of Alaska without the writer at some point firing a gun at something. But we didn't see a single gun while we were there. The bears were sleeping, which might have had something to do with it, but we got the feeling that Alaska is home to

Here are some snowcat, Cessna, snowmachine, and heli operations you can contact when you know you're tired of postholing after fresh:

Alaska Backcountry, Heli Operation, P.O. Box 8448 NRB, Kenai, AK 99635. Phone: (907) 776-5147; fax: (907) 776-5623. Average runs per day: six to eight. Packages, $350 a day with guided runs (six runs); nonguided prices: airplane lifts, $30; heli, $50 per lift.

Tom Moe Alaskan Extremes, P.O. Box 3687, Valdez, AK 99686. Phone or fax: (800) 556-SNOW. Offers snowcat, heli drops, and snowmachine rental, guided and unguided descents. Operates from March through May.

When you're in Valdez, the place to stay is the **Village Inn,** (907) 835-4445. Book well ahead if you're going to attend the King of the Hill. If the rooms are sold out, your best bet is to dig a snow cave on the side of the road by Thompson Pass. Also, take as much beer as you can fit in your car. Because the on-mountain supply runs dangerously low by the end of the weekend, you can finance your riding for the next season with some simple business skills.

more than a bunch of Yosemite Sam clones.

Alaskan Myth: Folksy *Northern Exposure* communities full of old men dating cheerleaders, longhaired poets, and dead bodies surfacing out of the glaciers from time to time.

Alaskan Reality: If that's what you want, you might be able to find it in Alaska, although *Northern Exposure* was shot just outside of Seattle. In reality, there's a tremendous growth of industry in the state, and Anchorage and Juneau are downright metropolitan. So much so that resource management is going to be a real issue in the coming years as environmentalists try to prevent the state from making the same mistakes that have been made, and continue to be made, in the lower forty-eight. We heard stories of rivers choked with king salmon, of valleys filled with animals that have never seen a human being, of brown bears peering into kitchen windows, of fishing in the summer until four in the morning.

The magic of Alaska lies in the fact that wild things still thrive there.

Maybe the myths about Alaska abound because of the sheer size of the place and the true magnificence of its terrain. The ancient Greeks came surprisingly close to describing what exists in the northern extremes when they wrote that beyond the frozen seas there was a country of good soil, blue skies, cool breezes, fruit trees, and the oldest race of human inhabitants on earth. The Greeks were wrong about the fruit trees. But in their concept of a paradise lying inside the confines of the frozen terrain, they were right on.

The first thing you should do when you arrive in Alaska is attempt to gain some insider's knowledge of the area, and the best way to accomplish this is to stop by the local board shop, which in Alaska means the Liska brothers' Boarderline shops: 5011 Arctic Boulevard in Anchorage, (907) 562-7972; on the Strand in Girdwood, (907) 783-2427; and 369 South Franklin in Juneau, (907) 463-3343.

Any way you can do it, go to Alaska. It will be a trip of a lifetime. We saw a moose chewing on a tree in someone's front yard, a bald eagle skimming over the flats near the shore—animals so tied up in the symbolism of America it makes you wonder why you've never seen one before. Just imagine what it's like when you're not leaning out the window of a Buick.

Alpenglow at Arctic Valley

P.O. Box 92121
Anchorage, AK 99509

Phone: (907) 428-1208
Snowphone: (907) 249-9292
Elevation: base, 2,900'; top, 4,200'; vertical, 1,300'
Lifts: 3 chairs, 1 T-bar
Terrain Variety: 35% advanced, 40% intermediate, 25% beginner

The Season and Hours

The mountain opens as soon as the snow allows, usually in mid- to late October, and stays open through April. Night boarding begins at 5:00 P.M. on chair 1 and the T-bar and continues until 9:00 P.M.

Lift Tickets

All day—Adult/Child/Senior: $22/$14/$14
Half day—Adult/Child/Senior: $15/$12/$12
Night—Adult/Child/Senior: $12/$10/$10

If you have a military ID card, you may board anytime for the low price of $12. To get a military ID, you'll have to let a militant group of scary men shave your head, scream at you, and make you do push-ups for several years. Think before you leap.

Specials

A three-day punch card is good for three nonconsecutive days during the season and costs $45. A nine-day punch card runs $135. A family of four can ski/board for the day for $65.

Logistics

From Anchorage, take the Glenn Highway to the Arctic Valley Road exit. It's a seven-mile climb to the area. Look for signs at the bottom for chain requirements. Park at the lodge on the Alpenglow side for food and phone access.

The Local Scene

Alpenglow at Arctic Valley is actually two resorts. The military owns the mountain and operates one lift. It leases the rest of the area to Alpenglow, which operates the other two lifts and the T-bar. As you face the mountain, Alpenglow is on the left side of the area. It's the closest resort to Anchorage that offers steep terrain, so you'll find the slopes packed with boarders—30–40 percent on most days. It's a local scene for the most part, with packs of grommets and future hotties tearing down the slopes.

Where to Stay

The area has no lodging, so you'll be bunking down in Anchorage. Call the **Chamber of Commerce** at (907) 272-2401 for information on the hotels in the area.

The Mountain

The mountain is treeless and mostly wind-groomed, and you can see the entire area from the parking lot. The powder, though, is heavenly when it falls (which is often). When you go up, you'll want to make a beeline for the Arctic Valley side, which features a terrain park and a nice line of hits. A good-sized cornice builds up near the top of the far left-hand side. The runs aren't named except for the chairs that serve them, but it's an easy mountain to navigate. Night boarding here is an adventure in T-bar riding. The one T-bar that services the top of the hill at night is jammed with boarders hopping through the line with both feet strapped in; it's harder to ride up than down.

Freeriders

The Alpenglow side offers longboarders the best terrain for making big turns through the steeps. The Back Bowl area features good accumulations of powder after a dump. Also check out the Chair 2, which contains the steeps on the mountain, and the High Traverse off Chair 2. If you get tired of turning, you can line up some hits at Arctic Valley that simulate the rock-garden experience.

Cruisers

The runs are short but the groomers hit the entire mountain at various intervals, except for the runs off chair 2. The mountain is wide open and steep, and on windblown days the hard boots are where it's at. Races are usually held between chair 1 and the Arctic Valley side.

Freestylers

Go to the Arctic Valley side. There's a terrain park with some nice tabletops, a spine, and some gap jumps. It's home to both slope-style and boarder-cross events from time to time. The Alpenglow side offers a half-pipe that was built to competition specifications. The only problem is they've built it on an eighteen-degree slope that just doesn't offer quite enough pitch to get you moving through it. As a result, it's largely ignored.

Grommets

The Learn-to-Snowboard package ($39) includes boots and board rental and a two-hour lesson. The snowboard staff is named William and offers lessons for riders of all abilities.

Nonbelievers

Because of its proximity to Anchorage, Alpenglow is a family destination where skiers, pinheads, and boarders live in harmony.

Alyeska Resort

P.O. Box 249
Girdwood, AK 99587

Phone: (907) 783-2222
Fax: (907) 783-2814
Snowphone: (907) SKI-SNOW
Elevation: base, 250'; top, 3,939'; vertical, 3,689'
Lifts: 7 lifts and a 60-person tram, covering 470 acres
Terrain Variety: 17% advanced, 71% intermediate, 12% beginner

The Season and Hours

The mountain opens on weekends in early November, then operates daily from mid-December through early May. Functional light on December 21 (winter solstice) lasts from 10:30 A.M. until 4:00 P.M. After that, you gain five minutes a day, so that by March your legs are gone long before the light. From mid-December through March, the slopes under the main quad are lit Thursdays through Saturdays until 9:30 P.M.

Lift Tickets

All day—Adult/Student/7–13, 60+/under 7: $29/$23/$17/$7
Half day—Adult/Student/7–13, 60+: $24/$21/$17
Half day/night—Adult/Student/7–13, 60+: $29/$23/$17
Night—Adult/Student/7–13, 60+: $14/$14/$12

ALYESKA

Mt. Alyeska
3,939'

Max's Mountain
3,302'

RUNS

1. Chilkoot Ridge
2. Trapline
3. Mighty-Mite
4. Lolo's
5. Mambo
6. Gearjammer
7. Main Street
8. The Weir
9. Ptarmigan Gully
10. High Traverse
11. Ego Flats
12. Waterfall
13. Max's
14. International
15. Klondike
16. Cabbage Patch
17. Lower Race Trail
18. Upper Sourdough
19. Lower Sourdough
19. Prince Run

SPIRIT QUAD

MIDWAY

CHAIR 4 QUAD

CHAIR 3

PONY

CHAIR 7

ALYESKA TRAMWAY

TANAKA

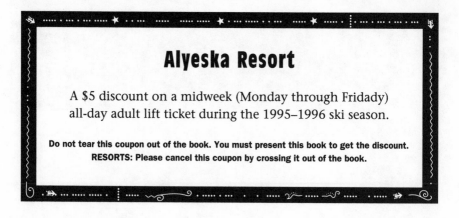

Alyeska Resort

A $5 discount on a midweek (Monday through Fridady) all-day adult lift ticket during the 1995–1996 ski season.

Do not tear this coupon out of the book. You must present this book to get the discount. RESORTS: Please cancel this coupon by crossing it out of the book.

Late night—Adult/Student/7–13, 60+: $8/$8/$8
Tram only—Adult/Student/under 7: $12/$10/$7

Specials

All-day lift tickets for a family of four (two adults, two children under age seventeen) cost $82. Instruction packages that include an all-mountain lift ticket and rentals are $55. Beginner-chair packages are $35. For information about private and group lessons and winter boarder camps, call the ski school at (907) 754-2280.

Logistics

From Anchorage International Airport, take Minnesota Drive to the Seward Highway. Go south for forty-five minutes and you're there. On the drive down, keep your eyes peeled for moose, sheep, and eagles. Park in the lower lots by the day lodge if you're staying in Anchorage. If your accommodations are in the Alyeska Prince, give the car keys to the valet and take the tram to check out the top of the mountain. Bring duct tape for your jaw because it will drop at the view going up.

The Local Scene

The Alyeska experience begins with the drive down the Seward Highway along the Turnagain Arm, where ice floes heave against each other on one side and on the other the mountains blast up into the sky. The road is a registered Scenic Highway and it's in-your-face gorgeous. You can spot the tourists because their cars are pulled over in the middle of avalanche areas (rule number 1: be a snowboarder, not a tourist). On the way down to Girdwood, stop by the **Birdhouse**, a roadhouse bar (next to the Texaco) about ten miles north of the resort.

There's no way to do it justice in words, so just go inside and soak up the atmosphere (bring a business card if you've got 'em).

The town of Girdwood is a little ski village, with its center at the Strand near the ski area's parking lot. Here you can fuel up on coffee and espresso drinks at the **Java Haus,** and the **Bake Shop** is a good place for lunch or après-boarding grinds ($5 buys all-you-can-eat chowder and bread on Fridays, and in the evening it's a good place for a slice and a beer). Also on the Strand is the **Boarderline Snowboard Shop,** (907) 783-2427, a full-service shop that offers boards, rentals, tunings, clothes, and whatever else you can imagine. The folks working there can also offer insight into some of the local backcountry spots, or direct you to the freshest snow on the mountain.

After a day of boarding, make sure you stop by the **Sitzmark Lounge** for nightly drinks specials, appetizers, Jaegermeister on tap, and live music. **Max's** is the other bar in town, where the Denali Cooks and Sporting Woodies (regular enough to be affectionately known as Band Number 1 and Band Number 2) supply the entertainment. If you're staying at the Alyeska Prince Hotel, the shuttle will provide transportation to and from the Sitz until midnight.

Where to Stay

If you don't feel like making the Anchorage commute, you'll want to stay at the **Alyeska Prince Hotel.** It's a brand-new 307-room chalet-style hotel. Every room throughout the seven stories has a view of some kind of amazing scenery. It's also one of the few hotels with a northern lights wake-up call, where the front desk buzzes your room when those funky green lights start swirling. Full snowboard rental, fitness center, whirlpool that fits you and your fifteen best friends, sauna, and six restaurants are among the features of the resort. If you get a chance, a dinner at the **Seven Glaciers Restaurant** is well worth it. Located at the top of the mountain (take the tram up), it offers a combination of stunning scenery and an incredible menu (we had venison and pheasant chased down with a nice merlot, followed by something that looked like art but tasted like dessert). The rooms start at about $150 for a double, which doesn't make the bum's guide, but compared with what other destination resorts charge, this is a real value. There can be no better spot than the Prince for honeymooning snowboarders. It's a terrific family destination as well, so if you still have parents with credit cards, tell them to get on the phone and book a room. Call (907) 783-2222 to get the current rates and specials.

If you plan to stay in Anchorage, phone the **Chamber of Commerce** at (907) 272-2401 for information on the hotels in the area.

The Mountain

The mountain is beautiful, and it's steep. Annual snowfall averages 556 inches, and the 470 skiable acres offer just about every type of terrain imaginable. The daytime temperature averages twenty-eight degrees Fahrenheit, a couple of degrees warmer than most Colorado resorts. The mild temperatures are the result of the mountain's proximity to the water and its base elevation of 250 feet (the lowest of any U.S. ski area). On a clear day there's a view of Denali, and the Chugach peaks and Kenai Mountains rising up across the Turnagain Arm capture the intense hues of the all-day morning light. It's a challenging mountain, and a few in-bounds hikes can lead you to some sick terrain. Glacier Bowl is home of the World Extreme preliminary trials.

Freeriders

If you're a freerider, you'll want to spend most of your time on the South Face, which offers the most challenging runs. The steeps and trees off LoLo's and Gearjammer will challenge every boarder. There are some big launching pads as well: Kitchen Table at the top of the South Face, Picnic Rock off LoLo's, and Eagle Rock coming off Main Street (this landing gets compacted pretty quickly, so have your buddy scout it for you). Even gnarlier stuff waits a hike away—take the high-speed Spirit Quad to the top, traverse along Silvertip, and unbuckle to hike up the ridge. Glacier Bowl offers the best pow on the mountain. Also, a long skate along the High Traverse will take you to Ptarmigan Gully and Max's—frequently closed because of avalanche danger, but another big open area that is heaven in good snow and worth the traverse.

Cruisers

The overall steepness of Alyeska make this a great cruiser hill. Almost every groomed run gives you the chance to groove some big turns. The best runs are in the central part of the mountain. Follow the downhill racecourse down Silvertip to Runaway, which funnels down to the Upper and Lower Race Trails. Another good route is Main Street to the Weir, which continues down through Ego Flats, Waterfall, Klondike, and Cabbage Patch. There are all sorts of rolls and bumps to keep the runs interesting. The South Face also provides some great terrain, with a few hits sprinkled off Mambo and Denali and kickers on the edges all the way down.

Freestylers

If you're a jibber, you might feel lost at Alyeska, which is mostly a freerider's mountain. You'll see snowboarders performing any number of tricks, but they do so mostly on natural terrain. If you're searching for a run where a few hits line up, take the Spirit Quad to the top of the mountain and come down Mighty Mite and Trapline. There's also a nice kicker that builds up along the sides of Weir and Ego Flats. There's no jib park at Alyeska, and we didn't hear any loud cries for one, either.

Grommets

Chairs 3 and 7 (the Pony lift) service a large beginners' area that has a good variety of learning and honing terrain. If you want to get your basics wired, take a lesson from one of Alyeska's snowboard instructors—they're good riders and good folks.

Nonbelievers

Even without a snowboard, you'll still have a great time at Alyeska. Alpine skiers know it as the place where Olympic star Tommy Moe honed his craft (ask a local to describe his top-to-bottom tucked run that included a hundred-foot flight over Waterfall; rumor has it Tommy got his pass yanked for life, then somehow got it back after Lillehammer). There are fifty kilometers of cross-country trails, and you can add ice fishing, dogsledding, ice skating, and snowmachining to the list of activities in the area.

Eaglecrest Ski Area

155 South Seward Street
Juneau, AK 99801

Phone: (907) 790-2000
Snowphone: (907) 586-5330
Elevation: base, 1,200'; top, 2,600'; vertical, 1,400'
Lifts: 3 (2 doubles, 1 surface lift)
Terrain Variety: 40% advanced, 40% intermediate, 20% beginner

The Season and Hours

The lifts start running in December and keep going until April. Chairs run from 9:00 A.M. until 3:30 P.M.

Lift Tickets

All day—Adult/Youth/Senior/Child: $24/$17/$17/$12
Half day—Adult/Youth/Senior/Child: $19/$12/$12/$12
Night—Adult/Youth/Senior/Child: $12/$8/$8/$8
Surface lift only: $7

Specials

Snowboard lesson-and-lift packages are available for $16 (with rentals, $41).

Logistics

Getting to Juneau is possibly the toughest logistically of all the snow-boarding areas in this book. Even though it's the state capital, the only way to get there is to fly or take a boat. Regular flights are available from Anchorage and Seattle on **Mark Air** and **Southwest.** Landing in Juneau is by all accounts (especially ours) the most harrowing, stomach-twisting experience you're likely to have in an airplane. It's like flying sideways into an icy shoe box. Assuming you arrive intact at the airport, you'll need to rent a car to drive into Juneau, over the bridge, and back around to the ski area. Alternatively, if you're staying at one of the Juneau hotels, you can catch the **Ski Bus** that runs on weekends and holidays only ($6 round-trip).

The Local Scene

Juneau's a beautiful little town with a picturesque harbor and a large working fleet of fishing boats. On the drive from the airport, we saw bald eagles circling over the water. It's not the kind of place you'll go to for a big ski getaway. But if you're looking for a total change of pace and scenery, it's a really cool alternative. Juneau's a locals' town if ever there was one. Few people who aren't on state business will find suffi-cient reason to ride the fright flight into the Juneau airport, and the cruise ships that visit in the summer are scarcer than narwhals during snowboarding season. That means the mountain is peopled by school-kids, mom, pop, and the occasional senator, but not many others. Be-cause most of the kids in town have never seen another snowboarding park, they have a refreshing make-it-up-as-you-go attitude. When we went to Juneau, we found about thirty after-school kids begging for more shovels. They were all working on building their own half-pipe.

Where to Stay

There are numerous hotels in Juneau, but you'll have to shop around to find the best deals, since senators on expense accounts don't go in for the cheap stuff. Call the **Juneau Convention and Visitors Bureau** at (907) 586-2201.

Tell Your Friends

We found a few bars worth visiting—try the **Alaskan** and **Lindy's** in old-town Juneau—but not much else in the way of hangouts. Beer prices are off the scale in this part of Alaska, so plan on doing most of your talking over a cold soda.

The Mountain

Eaglecrest isn't a huge mountain. On the other hand, given the fact that it has only two chairlifts and a rope tow, it's a lot bigger than you'd expect, and it has a big-mountain feel in terms of freeriding terrain. While the upper lift, Ptarmigan chair, services the whole top half of the mountain, much of Eaglecrest's best terrain is open only to those willing to take a short hike. Below Pittman's Ridge, steep chutes tumble down all along the terrain, especially in West Bowl and East Bowl, but both of these areas lie uphill from the top of the Ptarmigan chair.

West Bowl offers the best deep-powder boarding when you can get it. While East Bowl is also great in powder, it dumps you out onto the long semiflat Williwaw beginners' track.

A great tree glade begins at the top of Waterfall and drops you into a series of tight gullies along Waterfall and Bear Trap. This is where you'll find the best powder stashes on the mountain.

On the other side of the long Super G run that bisects the mountain, a series of really steep runs called Steep Chutes falls into some easy beginner runs. Beginners can take the East Bowl trail down to these easier areas.

Freeriders

The entire West Bowl and the tree glades below it, including Waterfall, Bear Trap, Raven, and Logjam, are classic freeriding areas. By searching around in this area, you'll find some good-sized cliff drops and other hits. The Waterfall chute is a really steep gully.

Cruisers

Because of Eaglecrest's single slow chair to the summit, Juneau is not an ideal place to score tens of thousands of vertical feet in a day. On the other hand, Super G lives up to its name, and Hillary's, Raven, and Logjam are all good cruising runs.

Freestylers

Eaglecrest's terrain park features rails, spines, quarter-pipes, and a couple of big hits, but the mountain is really a freerider's domain. An experimental half-pipe was emerging from the snows in the Spruce Chute area, so look for continuing improvements to the jibbing terrain.

Grommets

Eaglecrest has an excellent beginners' program, since a large part of its market is schoolkids. If you've already had lessons and just want to put in some time on the mountain, you can stick to the Hooter chair and ride down Ego, Soudow, and Sneaky. If you're after something bigger, ride the Ptarmigan chair to the summit and take the East Bowl track down to Williwaw, Otter Slide, and Mother Lode.

Nonbelievers

Eaglecrest has a scenic Nordic ski area, while downhill skiers will find the mountain a friendly, low-pressure place to hang out. Juneau is a million miles from Squaw Valley USA.

Hatcher Pass Glacier Snowcat

7001 East Tree Court
Anchorage, AK 99516

Phone: (907) 346-1276

The Season and Hours

The snowcat starts running in October and goes through May. You need to be at the Motherlode Lodge at 8:30 A.M. to sign in. You'll be hip-deep by 10:00 A.M., and you'll keep going as long as there's light and your legs will hold you up.

Cost

At $125 a day, with no limit on the amount of vertical ("we go until your legs burn and you're crying like a baby, or until you ask us to stop"), this is by far the best deal in backcountry boarding to be found anywhere. If you plan to stay a few days, the deal gets only better, with three days going for $325, and five days for $500. The snowcat carries a maximum of twelve clients and needs a minimum of six to go out. Call in advance to make your reservations.

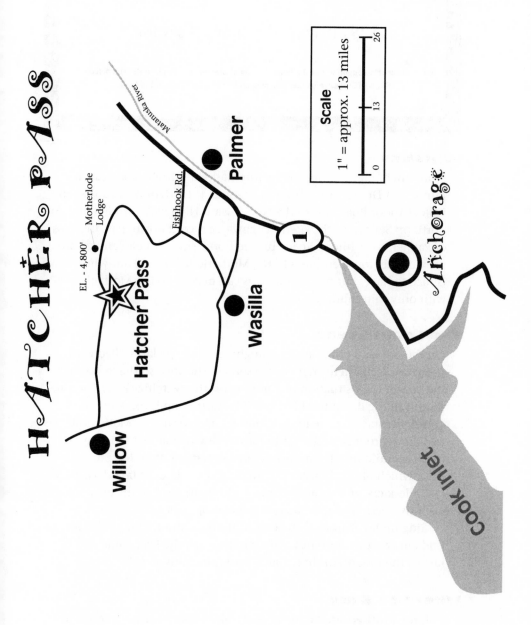

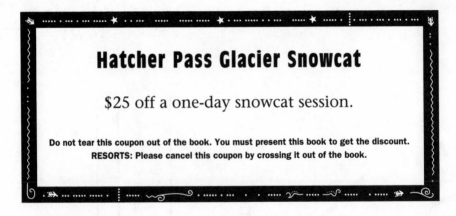

Logistics

From Anchorage airport, follow International Airport Road east to
Minnesota Drive. Turn left on Minnesota, then right on Tudor Road.
Follow Tudor Road east to the New Seward Highway. Turn left and go
north on Seward to the Glenn Highway. Proceed north, past the town
of Palmer, to Fishhook Road. Turn left on Fishhook Road and go ap-
proximately fourteen miles to the Motherlode Lodge. Four-wheel drive
is nice to have, but most rental cars can make it to the Motherlode
with only minimum slippage.

The Local Scene

On the drive up Fishhook, you might see some pickups filled with
snowboarders. There aren't any resorts in the area, so the locals make
the best of their situation by jumping off the switchback road at Mile
16 and riding down to Mile 12. A little farther up is the Motherlode
Lodge, the meeting site for the snowcat operation. The Motherlode has
two dining rooms, and a bar to hunker down at after a long day of riding. The building sits on the edge of the Hatcher Pass Recreational
Area, which offers thousands of undeveloped acres to boarders, Nordic
and teleskiers, and snowmachiners (although most of the area is under
exclusive permit to the Hatcher Snowcat operation).

Ring up Jay Bennet at the **Out of Bounds Shop**, (907) 745-0369, to
find out what conditions have been like. He's the lead guide and
knows the mountains in the area better than anyone else.

Where to Stay

Call the **Motherlode Lodge** at (907) 746-1464 to reserve a room. The
accommodations are unspectacular but the rates are good, and after a
day on the mountain and a celebratory libation, you might be better

off hanging out for the night. During your après-boarding stop at the bar, don't miss out on the Motherlode nachos—big as a moose—for $5. The **Hatcher Pass Bed and Breakfast**, (907) 745-4210, is another option on down the hill, and there are additional accommodations available in the nearby towns of Palmer and Wasilla.

Safety Talk

This is backcountry boarding, which means untracked snow. It also carries with it the risks of boarding an area that isn't avalanche-controlled, so everyone gets instruction on backcountry safety and carries a rescue beacon. The guides are backcountry experts, and as long as you go where they tell you to go, you'll be cruising through the fresh instead of swimming through a drift. They give you a whole lot of leeway with your line, so don't worry about missing out on the goods.

The Mountain

The guides will tell you that their virtue could be compromised in the pursuit of fresh snow. In an average day you rack up over sixteen thousand feet of vertical (the record day hovers around twenty-seven thousand feet), and the runs are two to three miles long and over two thousand vertical feet. The fifteen hundred acres of runs mean that on a typical day you don't cross your own tracks. Remember that the best deal is in the spring when the days are longest.

The terrain is steep and varied, with big bowls, wide-open slopes, and natural half-pipes. There are some big rocks to huck from, and endless wind lips to roller-coaster through. The area, which lies within the Talkeetna Mountains, gets four hundred to five hundred inches of snow a year. The guides know where to find the fresh (and where to avoid avalanches); they'll choose the runs based on snow conditions and the abilities of the group. If you are visiting Alaska and there's any way possible to get to Hatcher, go there. Do, do.

When you first step out of the snowcat's cab, you're surrounded by views of the Talkeetna and Chugach peaks. Warm up with a run down Fat Bob; then take turns going down Sunny Side (forty-six hundred feet) and the various chutes leading into Government Bowl. Lunch is provided, but bring something (nonalcoholic) to drink and stash it in the snowcat for between runs. You'll be working hard, and hydration's key.

Freeriders

Bring your powder board.

Cruisers

Bring your powder board.

Freestylers

Bring your powder board.

Grommets

While there are intermediate slopes for boarders with less experience, Hatcher Pass isn't the place to learn the basics. If you find yourself going slower than the group, don't sweat it. The snowcat will run the faster riders back to the top while you work your way down, so take your time and have fun.

Nonbelievers

All who ride at Hatcher Pass, regardless of what they have on their feet, are believers in something. Why else would they be there? Ullr loves those who love big snow.

Ullr, God of Snow

If you're ever wondering who to pray to when you're praying for snow, know that Alaskans pay homage to the Norse god of winter, Ullr (rhymes with cooler). At Alyeska they have Winterfest in Ullr's honor every January, and just about every snowboarder knows that the best way to get pow-pow is to down a couple of beers in his honor (if you are of legal age, this works quite well).

Ullr was the son of Sif and stepson of Thor. Ullr's prowess on snowshoes, ice skates, and telemark skis is key to his identity. Although the invention of the snowboard was to come a few thousand years later, it is generally agreed among scholars that Ullr would have been very much the hard-core boarder.

On occasion, the *Edda,* which tells the stories of the Norse gods, speaks of Ullr as the highest of the gods. Some stories point to him as the god of death; and he is also named as exercising the punishment of injustice. His snowshoes were thought to be enchanted: when he spoke magic runes over them, they changed into a ship or vessel that bore him over land and sea at will. And as snowshoes are shaped like a shield, Ullr was surnamed the shield-god and was invoked especially by people about to engage in a desperate fight. But above and beyond this, Ullr controls the fate of the snow, and for snowboarders there can be no higher god.

Ullr pretty much keeps to the frozen North or the tops of the Alps, where he built a summerhouse. As god of winter, Ullr controls the destiny of the snow. He is also responsible for the aurora borealis that flashes across the northern sky during the long nights. Ullr isn't a god who has ever been especially concerned with people, so how you pay tribute to him isn't all that important. Duct-tape effigies, sacrificed virgins, bonfires, loud music, a simple chant sustained for hours—take your pick. And when you wake up to a foot of fresh, ride hard to show you appreciate his efforts.

Hilltop Ski Area

7015 Abbott Road
Anchorage, AK 99516

Phone: (907) 346-1446
Snowphone: (907) 346-2167
Elevation: base, 2,500'; top, 2,800'; vertical, 300'
Lifts: 1 chair
Terrain Variety: 50% intermediate, 50% beginner

The Season and Hours

The lift begins running in mid-November and doesn't stop until April 15. During the week the mountain opens at 3:00 P.M. and stays lit until 10:00 P.M. On Friday the mountain opens at noon, and on weekends and holidays you can get a 9:00 A.M. start.

Lift Tickets

Weekend—Adult/Student/Child, Senior, Military: $18/$16/$7
Weekday—Adult/Student/Child, Senior, Military: $16/$14/$7

Specials

The Night Owl special (7:45 P.M.–10:00 P.M.) costs $10. Supposedly there's a group of ladies who have a regular night on the mountain followed by a big night on the town.

Logistics

Located in Anchorage, the area lies four miles east of the Seward Highway on Dimond Road.

Hilltop Ski Area

Free waxing of board with complete board tune-up.
Offer good entire season. Tune-up with waxing will require a scheduled appointment; forty-eight-hour turnaround.

Do not tear this coupon out of the book. You must present this book to get the discount.
RESORTS: Please cancel this coupon by crossing it out of the book.

The Local Scene

Hilltop is a beginners' mountain with a full range of lessons available and a very relaxed environment. It's the family destination for the Anchorage area, where many mothers drop off their micro-shredders for après-school activities. For those more practiced in the craft, Hilltop has a 120-foot-long, 60-foot-wide half-pipe that plays host to numerous contests throughout the year.

Where to Stay

When in Anchorage, stay in Anchorage. Call the **Chamber of Commerce** at (907) 272-2401 for lodging options.

Snowboarder Access Denied

The Carl Eid Ski Jumping Facility includes fifteen-, thirty-, and sixty-meter alpine kickers that are off-limits to snowboarders (everyone, really, who doesn't own a funky bodysuit and wide free-heel skis and a brain full of oatmeal). Either they're under orders from their insurer, or they just don't know snowboarders.

The Mountain

With only three hundred feet of vert on thirty-five acres, the mountain doesn't offer many big surprises. It's the only resort that stays lit seven nights a week, and if you're looking to fill a midweek longing for some easy cruising or pipe riding, it's the place to be.

Freeriders

Try to talk the staff into letting you practice for the Big Air contest at the ski-jumping facility.

Cruisers

Cruise the left side, then cruise the right side, then cruise the middle.

Freestylers

Session the half-pipe.

Grommets

Beginners' packages run $40 for board and boots, a two-hour lesson, and two hours of riding afterward. The lessons begin at 6:00 P.M. on Mondays and Fridays, 5:00 P.M. on Saturdays.

Nonbelievers

Everyone, everyone.

Chapter 2

When we consulted our trusty
Ski Areas map before beginning our roadtrip, we saw that British
Columbia is swarming with resorts all across the border—from
the Coast Range heading east into the Coast Mountains, the North
Cascades, the Monashees, the Cariboo and Selkirk ranges, the
Purcells, the MacDonald Range, and finally the Rockies crossing
into Alberta. Enough places that we could have spent the whole
season in British Columbia alone. To give you a better idea: we met
a snowboarder who spent an entire season at Whistler-Blackcomb.
He told us that when he left he still hadn't done all the runs.

The snowboarding in western British Columbia occurs mostly in
the Coast Mountains that extend north from Vancouver through
Alaska. Mt. Waddington ranks as the highest peak, at 13,260 feet,
and is covered by the Franklin Glacier. The summits in this range
rarely exceed 10,000 feet, but because of the numerous glaciers and
annual snowfall of about thirty feet a year, the backcountry has a
legendary status.

From Vancouver Island going east, snowboarding is rapidly emerging as the sport of choice for most people under thirty. And because of the long season (over two hundred days), an increasing number of longtime skiers are learning to snowboard for the powder and slush days.

The Coast Range and Coast Mountains receive the mild weather patterns brought down by the warm Japanese current. This results in a variety of conditions throughout the year, from dry powder to wet oatmeal. And because these mountains are near the ocean, inversions (the top of the mountain being warmer than the bottom) are common.

There are numerous glaciers through these mountains (in which the Yeti is reported to live), so technically, there's "snow" all year round. Several good snowboarding hills can be found practically within walking distance of downtown Vancouver, but like most

Units of Measure, Money, Taxes

When you go big, it does you little good to try to explain it in feet. Fifty feet of air means nothing to a Canadian, and saying you got fifteen meters sounds small to an American. Much like a surfer's tendency to describe waves as one, two, three people tall, you need to find the appropriate symbolic representation for your air. House air, school bus air—when you use descriptions of commonly known objects to qualify your clearance, you'll have better luck communicating.

It may seem like everything is more expensive in Canada. An economist might argue that given the exchange rate and the U.S. dollar's strength in Canada, things are relatively less expensive, but it's tough to think of a twelve-pack of beer for $13 as a good deal. Gas and milk come in liters, you weigh out your produce in kilos, and when you ask how many miles it is to someplace, you'll get a lot of shrugs.

When you pull out your wallet, remember that the Canadian government imposes a *Goods and Services Tax (GST)* on all purchases. It's roughly 7 percent on top of local sales taxes. The trick here is to save all your receipts. Then, on your way back, stop at a Canadian duty-free store and fill out your Visitor Refund Application for Goods and Services Tax and Provincial Sales Tax (form GST 327). Basically, this will cover lodging and goods (clothing, equipment) that you paid for in Canada. They will give you a cash refund and set you loose among the cheap smokes and whiskey, perfume and irresistible Lladros—those porcelain figures that your grandmother keeps near the couch you can't sit on. If you can escape the duty-free store without spending all your refund, you'll find that going on vacation is expensive, but not more so than in the States.

You'll probably get better exchange rates if you trade in your U.S. dollars for Canadian ones, although almost every establishment accepts U.S. dollars and will calculate your exchange rate at the register.

tourists who bother to travel all this way, we made a beeline for Whistler-Blackcomb, by all accounts the largest boardable duo of adjacent mountains in North America.

Backcountry Opportunities

British Columbia is perhaps most famous for its heli operations. If you're single, it's a good way to meet your future mate, as evidenced by Christie Brinkley's helicopter crash and subsequent marriage to the guy she went down with. If you don't believe in love at first crash, then it's also the way to get into some prime (though pricey) fresh. Here are a few heli operations near the Whistler area:

Whistler Heli-Skiing, (604) 932-4105, #3-4241 Village Stroll, Box 368, Whistler, B.C., V0N 1B0.

Mountain Heli Sports, (604) 932-2070, Box 460, Whistler, B.C., V0N 1B0.

Tyax Heli-Skiing, (604) 932-7007, (800) 663-8126 (U.S. toll-free), P.O. Box 849, Whistler, B.C., V0N 1B0.

Black Tusk Helicopter Inc., (604) 898-4800, P.O. Box 1469, Squamish, B.C., V0N 3G0 (located between Whistler and Vancouver).

Call the operations for current rates. In general, a day of heli board-ing costs around $350 (Cdn.) for three runs, with additional runs cost-ing extra. Each outfit also offers lodging packages aimed at the luxury-class skier. If you need to ask how much it costs, it's probably too much.

Blackcomb Mountain

4545 Blackcomb Way
Whistler, British Columbia
Canada V0N 1B4

Phone: (604) 932-3141 or (604) 687-1032 (toll-free from Vancouver)
Fax: (604) 938-7527
Snowphone: (604) 687-7507 (Vancouver); (604) 932-4122 (Whistler)
Elevation: base, 2,214'; top, 7,494'; vertical, 5,280'
Lifts: 8-person gondola, 9 chairs (6 detachable quads), 2 T-bars, rope tow, covering 2,240 acres
Terrain Variety: 25% advanced, 55% intermediate, 20% beginner

The Season and Hours

The season begins at the end of November and runs through the last week of May. Midweek the lifts open at 9:00 A.M., and on

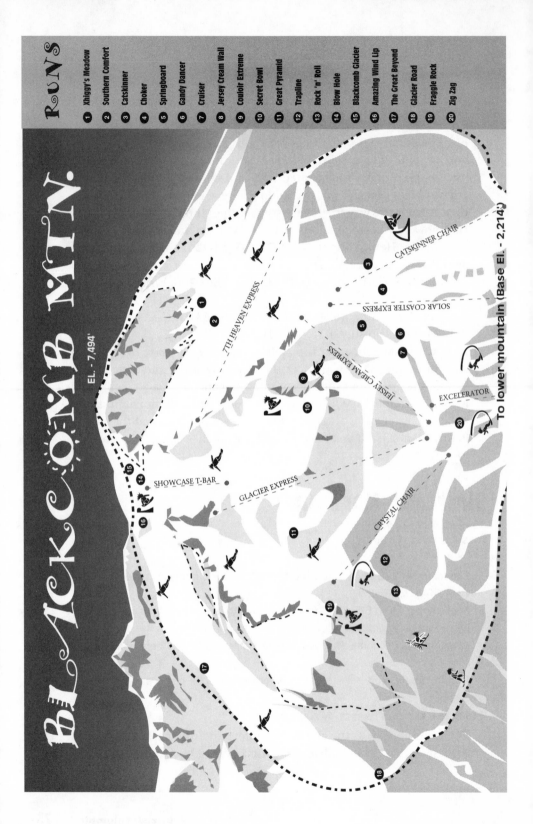

BLACKCOMB MTN.

El. - 7,494'

RUNS

1. Xhiggy's Meadow
2. Southern Comfort
3. Catskinner
4. Choker
5. Springboard
6. Gandy Dancer
7. Cruiser
8. Jersey Cream Wall
9. Couloir Extreme
10. Secret Bowl
11. Great Pyramid
12. Trapline
13. Rock 'n' Roll
14. Blow Hole
15. Blackcomb Glacier
16. Amazing Wind Lip
17. The Great Beyond
18. Glacier Road
19. Fraggle Rock
20. Zig Zag

CATSKINNER CHAIR

SOLAR COASTER EXPRESS

7TH HEAVEN EXPRESS

JERSEY CREAM EXPRESS

EXCELERATOR

SHOWCASE T-BAR

GLACIER EXPRESS

CRYSTAL CHAIR

To lower mountain (Base El. - 2,214')

weekends you can start your day at 8:30. All lifts shut down at 3:00 P.M., so be up top by then. Summer boarding on Horstman Glacier runs from June through August, and they build a half-pipe or two whenever conditions permit. The Magic and Wizard chairs are open for night boarding every Wednesday and Saturday from 5:00 to 9:00 P.M.

Lift Tickets

Every day—Adult/Youth/Senior/Child: $46/$36/$30/$20 (Cdn.)

Specials

Multiday discounts are available. Also, stop by Save-on-Foods and ask for a discount coupon.

Logistics, the Local Scene, Where to Stay

See the Whistler Village sidebar on page 34.

The Mountain

Blackcomb has the goods when it comes to terrain, and it has created a snowboard-friendly environment amid the largest ski enclave in North America. The mountain itself is huge, with big potential for fun. From top to bottom there's a mile of vertical. Blackcomb boasts a seven-mile-long run (but it's mostly a big, long traverse that's not much fun for boarders).

The environment at this mondo international tourist destination is very warm when it comes to snowboarders. There's only one foot-out traverse (coming out of the Great Beyond), and Blackcomb has recently instituted a half-pipe series, along with boarder-cross and big-air events. At the Kokanee Snowboard Park you can race your buds at the Kokanee Kross Trainer boarder-cross run. And yes, there are tunes. The mountain recently became one of the few owners of a Pipe Dragon, so the pipes are always in cryp shape.

The Blackcomb Snowboard Club is for the hard-core competitor looking to take on the world. It invites riders in both racing and freestyle disciplines. Call (604) 932-6226. The Blackcomb Snowboard Task Force meets with boarders of all ages to solicit input for its future snowboarding direction.

Freeriders

Blackcomb is to freeriders what mud is to pigs. There are so many cliffs, rock gardens, glades, chutes, bowls, and lips that even the locals have a long list of lines they still haven't taken. But here are a few spots to think about. At the top of the Great Beyond (the backside of

What Conflict?

The skier–snowboarder conflict gets a lot of press, more in fact than it deserves. Maybe it's different in other parts of the world, but on the West Coast we've found very few signs of animosity between skiers and snowboarders. Five years ago when we were first learning, it was the skiers who were always asking questions like, "Is it hard? Does it hurt?" Things you hear most often in bed. Now that the sport's been around for a while and is growing faster than manufacturers can make boards, the skiers don't ask as many questions. Most of them have tried snowboarding. At Blackcomb Mountain, we ran into an old Canuck who said he skis about 160 days a year. But he boards about 25, "on powder days and when it's slushy. The board works better in those conditions." If a salty Canadian skier can embrace snowboarding, if only for utilitarian reasons, why can't the old-fart contingents at Alpine Meadows and Park City get a clue?

A few "responsible" media providers (Associated Press, *Newsweek*) have run stories that seem bent on fanning the flames of the assumed controversy. It's like skiers and snowboarders are headed for a showdown. There are two problems with this theory: (1) the snowboarders don't know they're being called out and don't really care, and (2) if it came down to fisticuffs, the snowboarders would be able to stick and move much better in their softer boots. Right now, it's come down to economics, and only a handful of mountains across the nation are able to keep snowboarders out and still sell enough tickets to turn a profit. Some mountains have designated skiers-only runs, but a far greater number have created snowboard-only terrain parks.

On the mountain, there are times when a skier will get in your face because he thinks you're not riding responsibly. For example, when we were at Mammoth, a skier came up to us and said we had cut him off. We patiently explained that because of their stance, snowboarders have a blind spot when making a heelside turn. The skier was kind of confused by our ability to both snowboard and articulate field-of-vision laws; he mumbled something like, "Well, don't do it again," and then shuffled off to the lift line.

Boarders need to remember that skiers were here first and that some of them are having a hard time understanding snowboarders. If a skier starts vibing you, try to send out tremendous waves of love toward him or her, say *Yes sir* and *No ma'am*, and nod your head a lot. If he or she starts lecturing you, ask the skier to buy you a beer at the end of the day when you can talk to your heart's content. Whatever you do, don't escalate the conflict. There's nothing to be gained by arguing with a hostile skier, and chances are you'll lose a run or two and get bummed out from the experience. A simple rule for riding and living: take the high road.

Blackcomb Glacier) lies the famous, insane, ski-jump-style Wind Lip next to the Blow Hole run. You have to hike the slope above it, and then hope the G's on the long transition don't crumple you before you launch. According to an eyewitness at a big-air contest, one rider flew off the lip, up into the fog, and over the judges' heads, and then exploded into the powder near the three-hundred-foot mark to win the contest. Sick. If the Wind Lip isn't going off due to weather conditions, take a high traverse on the backside to find the best snow. And if you're up for a hike, there are numerous chutes coming down off the Spearhead, including Corona and You Sue Me (observe all closed signs and play by the rules or you'll die—guaranteed). The only drawback to the Great Beyond is that you might have to unbuckle to get out of the valley unless you stay up high. Once you reach Blackcomb Road, just keep your speed up and you should be able to make it back to the Excelerator chair with no worries.

Couloir Extreme and Big Bang are two more expert routes on the main face. The Seventh Heaven area is filled with wind lips, gullies, and little bowls that make it a natural playground. If you're in search of snow a couple of days after a dump, check out the area near Fraggle Rock, just below the Crystal hut. There are also some nice boulder gardens near the Crystal chair.

Cruisers

Cruisers will have no trouble finding some of the best fall-line runs on the planet. The Solar Coaster Express is your best bet, and you can really open it up on the Cruiser and Springboard trails. Gandy Dancer and Choker have a nice pitch and plenty of room. Off the Crystal chair, Ridgerunner and Rock 'n' Roll are good speed runs. Blackcomb has miles of groomed trails, so check with the lifties to find out what's hot.

Freestylers

Go to the Catskinner chair. On the ride up you'll see the Kokanee Snowboard Park. A half-pipe leads into gap jumps, fun boxes, table-tops, and quarter-pipes. Right next to the park is the boarder-cross course, a great place to practice banked turns. There's another half-pipe located just above the Catskinner chair, so you may want to ride the Solar Coaster Express (faster, too) in order to maximize your session time. Hits are all over the mountain, but riders tend to set up good lines on Honeycomb off the Cruiser trail.

Grommets

A two-hour lesson, lift, and beginners' chair package goes for $62. Lesson packages take you up through the skill sets, and the snowboarding instructors are numerous and friendly. Once you're linking turns, you'll want to hang out on the Wizard chair, and then move to the Solar Coaster and Excelerator for a little more pitch.

Mt. Washington Resort

Box 3069
Courtenay, British Columbia
Canada V9N 5N3

Phone: (604) 338-1386
Fax: (604) 338-7295
Snowphone: (604) 657-2734 (Vancouver); (604) 756-5731 (Nanaimo)
Elevation: base, 3,600'; top, 5,200'; vertical, 1,600'
Lifts: 4 doubles, one quad, 2 surface
Terrain Variety: 37% advanced, 41% intermediate, 22% beginner

The Season and Hours

The resort opens after Thanksgiving and operates through mid-April, from 8:30 A.M. until 4:00 P.M.

Lift Tickets

All day—Adult/13–18/7–12/3–6/65+: $34/$26.50/$19/Free/$21.50 (Cdn.)
Half day—Adult/13–18/7–12/3–6/65+: $22/$18/$12.50/Free/$15 (Cdn.)

Specials

Group rates and multiday rates are available. Note that a small ($0.50–$1.00) road-improvement tax is tacked on to all lift-ticket prices.

Logistics

From the mainland take Highway 17 to the Tsawwassen ferry terminal, south of Vancouver ([604] 685-1021). Ride the ferry to Nanaimo (about two hours, with ferries leaving every two to three hours during the day). From Nanaimo, proceed north on Highway 19 to the town of Courtenay, through fast-food-and-billboard tourist blight that eventually gives way to scenic forest and ocean views. Find the turnoff to Ski Areas and carefully follow the signs to Mt. Washington. Driving on frozen mud is an experience no one should miss, but the permafrost road to Mt. Washington should be completely paved over by the time you read this. In the event that construction is behind schedule, use caution when driving. On both the drive in and the drive out, we found cars crumpled in ditches next to the road.

The Local Scene

Mt. Washington's claim to fame is that it's the busiest mountain in western British Columbia that isn't Whistler or Blackcomb. On its most crowded day last year, Mt. Washington had more than nine

MT. WASHINGTON

EL. 5,200'

Base Elevation - 3,600'

SUNRISE QUAD

WHISKEY JACK CHAIR

BLUE CHAIR

HANDLE TOW

DISCOVERY LIFT

GREEN CHAIR

RED CHAIR

RUNS

1. Powder Face
2. Boundary
3. Far Out
4. Raven
5. Westerly
6. Tyee
7. Oh, Henry!
8. Whiskey Jack
9. Coaster
10. Lynton's Loop
11. The Gully
12. Invitation
13. Schum's Delight
14. Fletcher's Challenge
15. Fantastic
16. Rainbow
17. Freeway
18. Easy Rider
19. Jack's Trail
20. Green Acres

thousand visitors, while Whistler on its busiest day boasted just over ten thousand. So why is it that unless you're from the immediate neighborhood, you've probably never heard of Mt. Washington? Partly, it's a matter of getting there: Mt. Washington is near the center of Vancouver Island, the offshore landmass across from the city of Vancouver, and to get there, you have to catch a ferry from the mainland. These big boats run regularly from Tsawwassen, just south of Vancouver, to the island town of Nanaimo, and rides cost about $20 per car, plus $6.50 per person, each way (again, keep in mind the exchange rate). The other reason Mt. Washington's such a secret on the mainland is that it's visited almost exclusively by Vancouver Island's 750,000 permanent residents. People from the mainland are much closer to Whistler-Blackcomb and smaller local hills, so they have little reason to ride a boat to the island unless they're searching for a getaway.

Where to Stay

There are more than two thousand privately owned beds in the immediate Mt. Washington area and most of them are for rent some of the time. **Mt. Washington Chalets** handles condos and cabins; phone: (604) 658-5533; fax: (604) 658-0087. **Mile High Accommodations** can also arrange lodging; phone: (800) 699-6499; fax: (604) 334-4069. There is an RV park on site if you happen to have an Airstream in tow.

If you're visiting midweek and hope to find some nightlife, the best bet is to stay in Courtenay, about twelve miles from the mountain. A motel called the **Washington Inn** ([604] 338-5441) has a nightclub on one end dubbed the **Loft**, where local boarders hang out after a day on the mountain, and a restaurant called the **Mex**, where you can get some grub. The Mt. Washington Resort can provide you with information about other hotels in Courtenay.

On weekend nights, the **Whiskey Jack Saloon** at the main lodge is jam-packed with good-looking, hard-partying Canucks and often features a live band. If you're looking for fine food during your stay, the cafeteria-by-day becomes a nice sit-down restaurant at night, with tablecloths, candles, and good, reasonably priced food.

The Mountain

Despite the logistics of getting there, Mt. Washington is well worth a visit, and it's an extremely popular spot for boarders. For starters, the resort has fourteen snowboard instructors and more than 170 rental boards, a half-pipe and snowboard park, and—the clincher—well over five hundred centimeters (two hundred inches) of snow each season.

The snow is an anomaly for the island; when you drive up the dirt road to the resort, you move from balmy green pastures and forests to huge mounds of white stuff in a matter of minutes. Mt. Washington is one tip of a snowbound triangle whose base is a wide ridge of glaciers and a huge valley checked with clear-cuts. The snow on the mountain often lasts through July, although the resort is typically open only through mid-April.

While Mt. Washington isn't a big hill, it has plenty of big-hill features, including a cornice and big steeps in the West Bowl, lots of silky-smooth groomed runs for cruising, several big bump fields such as O'Henry! into which unsuspecting boarders may disappear between head-high moguls, a few tree glades, and lots and lots of kickers and hits all over. We found many new-schoolers sticking 360s and other tricks in the park, but locals say there are plenty of die-hard freeriders and even one or two septuagenarian boarders on the scene. One thing about Mt. Washington that's different from other mountains is the laid-back approach to the lifts. None of them is of the high-speed detachable variety, so expect long lines on busy weekends. On the other hand, midweek riders can usually cruise right onto the chairs.

Freeriders

On fresh-snow days, freeriders will head for the western end of the area and hang out on the aptly named Powder Face. Beyond this, Far Out and Raven are big steep runs, but you'll have to hold your speed at the bottom to make it back around to the base of the Red chair (from there, you cruise over to the Blue chair for the ride to the summit). When the snow's been settling for a few days, the tree glade between Schum's Delight and Fletcher's Challenge (off the Sunrise quad) is good, and it leads into lots of quarter-pipe banks and hits.

Cruisers

Good groomed trails are everywhere on Mt. Washington, but Fletcher's Challenge (Sunrise quad) and Lynton's Loop and Coaster (Blue chair) are classics, depending on how fast you like them.

Freestylers

Mt. Washington has a big, well-designed terrain park. However, while we're normally happy to share the hill with skiers, Washington's all-comer policy regarding the terrain garden is a bit dicey. The skiers tend to take long, straight lines through the park, getting big speed and huge, out-of-control air off the hits. It's not a very compatible style with the snowboarder's midspeed, zigzag approach to a hit garden. Nevertheless, it's a great park, with berms, wedges, tabletops, gaps, and other goods.

Grommets

Mt. Washington's lessons hang out around the Green chair and the two surface tows at the base of the mountain, far from high-speed dangers. There's a tight-knit group of snowboard instructors here and they seem really friendly.

Nonbelievers

In addition to excellent skiing, Mt. Washington Resort offers a complete Nordic facility, with lessons and equipment rentals. It's located near the Alpine base lodge.

Whistler Mountain

4010 Whistler Way
Whistler, British Columbia
Canada V0N 1B4

Phone: (604) 932-3928
Fax: (604) 932-7231
Snowphone: (604) 932-4191
Elevation: base, 2,140'; top, 7,160'; vertical, 5,020'
Lifts: 10-person gondola, 9 chairs (4 detachable quads), T-bar, and 2 rope tows
Terrain Variety: 25% advanced, 55% intermediate, 20% beginner

The Season and Hours

The mountain opens the third week of November and operates through April 23. Midweek the lifts open at 9:00 A.M., and on weekends you can start your day at 8:30, which is good because the lifts close each day at 3:00 P.M.

Lift Tickets

Every day—Adult/Youth/Senior/Child: $46/$36/$30/$20 (Cdn.)

Specials

Multiday discounts are available. Also, stop by Save-on-Foods and ask for a discount coupon.

Logistics, the Local Scene, Where to Stay

See the Whistler Village sidebar on page 34.

WHISTLER MTN.
EL. - 7,160'

Base Elevation - 2,140'

PEAK CHAIR

T-BAR

HARMONY EXPRESS

REDLINE EXPRESS

GREEN EXPRESS

BLACK CHAIR

UPPER GONDOLA

ORANGE CHAIR

QUICKSILVER EXPRESS

Whistler Village

To say that Whistler-Blackcomb is the largest combined ski resort in North America hardly begins to describe the scene there. It's really an entire, highly planned village that exists in support of the two mountains. Tour buses, trains, helicopters, limousines, and a beautiful highway deliver tourists from all over the world. Since no one wants to choose between Blackcomb and Whistler, a lift ticket at one mountain is honored on both—particularly nice if you're staying for several days and purchase a multi-day ticket. Not that you'll get bored with either mountain on a typical vacation: they're both so big that a week is probably enough time to ride all the lifts . . . once. After you get to the village, there aren't many logistics to contend with, since nearly everything, including the base of both mountains, is within easy walking distance. For things that aren't, such as the west side of Whistler Mountain, there's a bus that runs up and down the length of the town (for a couple of bucks).

Logistics

From Vancouver, take Highway 99, the Sea to Sky Highway, seventy-five miles north right to the doorstep. It's a winding, two-lane road with the occasional passing lane, so be prepared for some excitement if it's snowing. This is a beautiful drive through the fjordlike Squamish, past a towering Yosemite-style granite dome called the Sleeping Chief, and on through a rugged alpine pass. Near Squamish, we crossed a river festooned with bald eagles (the 1994 census reported about twenty-nine hundred of them), so keep an eye out. British Columbia Railway offers daily service from North Vancouver on the most scenic routes in Canada and free shuttle service to the mountain. Call (604) 984-2546 for rates and schedules. From Seattle, you can ride the bus up. Call Ski Express at (800) 665-2122.

The Local Scene

Whistler Valley is home to Whistler and Blackcomb mountains, Whistler Village, and a lot of transients looking for powder. It's a sea of international humanity, but if you can navigate your way through the labyrinth, there are a few places you should check out. Showcase Snowboard Shop and Showcase II carry a good selection of boards and clothing. Also stop by Westbeach Snowboard Shop for the latest in snowboard and skateboard gear.

There's a booming nightlife in the Village if you're old enough to drink. This is one of the biggest destination ski resorts anywhere, and it's particularly popular with Japanese travelers.

Our favorite nightspot was Tommy Africa's, a basement nightclub with booming tunes, snowboarding videos on a big screen, a crowd of funky young boarder types rocking on the dance floor, and lots of, well, action. There's no sign out front, so look for the zebra-striped doors or ask someone to point you in the right direction and listen for the beat. Mondays are seventies-music nights and you don't want to miss out on the new-school disco moves. Another nightspot is The Boot (Das Boot), a bar filled with picnic tables and live music, usually of the reggae or progressive varieties. It's located two minutes north of the Village by car. Hitchers have a good chance of making it there, but getting home is another story.

There are a lot of places you probably don't want to go, but because everything's so close, it's easy to rule out the duds. If you enjoy hanging out with mature vacationers, you may like half the bars in town. A typical example is one of the main nightspots, the Longhorn Pub, located a few feet from the main Whistler gondola. It's usually populated by an older, mellower crowd that has "rich tourists" written all over it.

One indicator of an establishment's merit can be found on its TVs—if a snowboard video is playing, there's a chance you're in the right place; not a sure thing these days, but at least there's a chance.

The main part of Whistler Village is a pedestrian-only, brick-paved aggregate of hotels, shops, restaurants, bars, and offices. Although it's called Whistler Village, the main people-mover gondolas for both Whistler and Blackcomb stop within a hundred yards of each other. There are many things to buy if you have money, many places to eat and drink if you have the appetite, and every place except the liquor store accepts credit cards. Below is a listing of a few of the services you can find in Whistler Village:

Aerobics classes, animal shelter, baby-sitting, banks, barbershop, billiards, bookstore, church services, day care, dentist, dry cleaners, fire department, florists, galleries, grocery stores, gym, hair salons, helicopter rides, ice-skating rink, indoor tennis, jewelers, karaoke, legal services, lingerie, massage, medical clinic, movie theater, museum, optical services, paragliding, pharmacies, photo finishing, physiotherapy, pizza delivery, police, pools, post office, printing and publishing, public library, real estate agents, rental cars, snowmobile rental, snowshoes, video rentals.

Where to Stay

You can choose among sixty-five resorts that offer rooms, condos, and bed-and-breakfast. Call (800) 944-7853. Let them know what you want and what you don't want. If you're looking to rent a cabin, refer to the list of property-management companies below. If you're one of those people who know how to plan ahead, you might find some lodging–lift ticket deals in the early and late season.

A good example of a "typical" lodge is the Tantalus. The room features separate bedrooms, kitchen, cable TV, and it's located an easy walk from the slopes.

Bargain hunters may want to give the Shoestring Lodge a call at (604) 932-3338. It's a dormitory setting (next to The Boot) that goes for about $20 a night. In general, lodging averages about $100 (Canadian) for a room and goes up or down depending on the day of the week, time of year, and amenities.

If you're looking into renting a house or cabin for your stay, here's a list of local property-management companies (area code is 604 unless otherwise indicated):

Alpine Vacation Accommodations, 938-0707

Blackcomb Hotels and Resorts, (800) 777-0185

Crown Resort Accommodations, (800) 565-1444

Four Season Vacation Rentals, 932-3252

M & H Enterprises, 932-1169

Mountain Resort Accommodations, 938-3369

Northern Comfort Accommodations, 932-5403

Rainbow Retreats, 932-2343

Vance Management, 947-0795

Whiski Jack Resorts, Ltd., (800) 944-7545

Whistler Chalets and Accommodations, (800) 663-7711

Whistler Exclusive Property Management, 932-5353

(continued on next page)

Whistler Sportpack International, 938-1184

Wildflower Exclusive Accommodations, 932-4113

Summer at Blackcomb

Horstman Glacier at Blackcomb Mountain provides the opportunity for a full summer of boarding. If you're looking for some form of summer school, call up the camps listed below to get information on which one is right for you.

Carrbassett Valley Academy Summer Racing Camp, Blackcomb Mountain, Road No. 1, Box 2240, Kingfield, ME 04947. Phone: (207) 237-2250; fax: (207) 237-2213. Race-specific training with some freeriding; geared for the intermediate to seriously competitive snowboard racer.

Craig Kelly's World Snowboard Camp, Blackcomb Mountain, P.O. Box 5090, Glacier, WA 98244. Phone or fax: (360) 599-1258. Half-pipe, park, extreme steeps, backcountry crevasse exploring, freeriding, carving, and trick instruction, plus the usual variety of off-snow activities, including skateboard, paintball, and mountain biking.

The Snowboard Shop Camp of Champions, Whistler, British Columbia, Canada VON 1B4. Phone: (604) 932-4440; fax: (604) 938-1300. Half-pipe, park, freeriding and carving instruction, plus off-snow activities to carry you through the day.

Do People Who Don't Snowboard Have a Good Time Here?

Snowboarders used to being the fastest thing on the mountain should prepare themselves for a gaggle of Canucks who've been skiing since they could walk. There are all sorts of sick lines made by the biped skiers, and there's nothing to do but respect them. Everyone shares the mountain here, but there's plenty of it to go around. And if for some reason you don't want to go on the mountain at all, there's more to do in Whistler Village than in most people's hometowns, so go nuts.

⇡ ⇣ ⇡

Tell Your Friends

If it's been snowing, a great deal is the **Fresh Tracks**, an all-you-can-eat breakfast smorgasbord at midmountain. Bring your backpack if you want to save on lunch. While you're eating, you'll be the first to hear when the Ski Patrol has finished its sweep. Being halfway up, you're poised for freshie, so pick a good run and rip it up.

The Mountain

Whistler means big faces and wide-open bowls. On powder days there's nothing like getting fresh tracks down any one of the seven vast expanses of snow. There are cornices and wind lips and all sorts of big rocks to fly off. After a few days, though, the skiers tend to bump out the big bowls, and then the adventure begins. With 3,657 rideable acres, it's the largest area in North America, and there are plenty of goods if you know how to find them. The problem is, you'd need a year to properly explore the mountain, so unless you have the time you'll have to content yourself with the highlights.

There are a couple of drawbacks to boarding at Whistler, one being the many foot-out traverses along the top ridge. If you take Highway 86 or the Burnt Stew Trail, expect to do some unbuckling and walking. Also, stay high when you're exiting the bowls because many of them feed into brutally flat cat tracks. And never get on the gondola before 10:30 A.M. If you follow these suggestions, you should have no trouble navigating the mountain.

That said, Whistler is the truth when it comes to natural terrain. If you can ride there, you can ride anywhere.

Freeriders

What makes Whistler great is its bowl riding, which in pow is incomparable. Stick to the central bowls after a dump, and then fan out to Symphony Bowl and Bagel Bowl in the following days. There are any number of sick steeps and chutes, such as the Couloir and the Cirque in Glacier Bowl. The snow stays nice beneath the mid-unload off the Peak chair, and there are some nice rock bands with good steep landings. Every bowl has a cornice—some are way too scary even to look at, others are avalanches waiting to happen (tragically, one collapsed under someone while we were there), and still others are great big launching pads that will give you all the air you can handle. You'll find good glades to the right coming down Bear Paw, and Whistler Bowl offers a series of steeps that are a blast before they get bumped out. As you know, when the snow is good, any mountain will be fun. On these days, though, Whistler becomes a place people write long poems about.

Cruisers

The center nose is where cruisers want to be. The Dave Murray Downhill offers a screamer of a run. Franz's is the favorite with the alpine riders—as much corduroy as your legs can take, and two express chairs (Quicksilver and Redline) to get you back up in a rush. When the steep stuff up top gets bumped out, you'll find some good runs off Harmony Ridge. After you've checked out these runs, ask a liftie for the groomers' special-of-the-day, which depending on the sun and the conditions could be found anywhere on the mountain.

Freestylers

The Peel runs—Orange Peel and Banana Peel—are a great place to work your Emma Peel if you've got one, but there are all sorts of kickers off Franz's and the Dave Murray Downhill, and down through Goats Gully. You'll want to work the runs beneath the Redline Express to get started, and then branch out toward the Green chair and Black chair to find the hit lines.

Grommets

A two-hour lesson, lift, and beginners' chair package goes for $68. There's also a two-day Oxygen Adult Snowboard Camp for the older grommets. The Green chair services a good number of beginner runs, along with the Redline for a little more pitch. Stay away from the top of the mountain until you can link turns on intermediate pitches; otherwise, you'll spend your time sideslipping or riding a gondola down.

Chapter 3

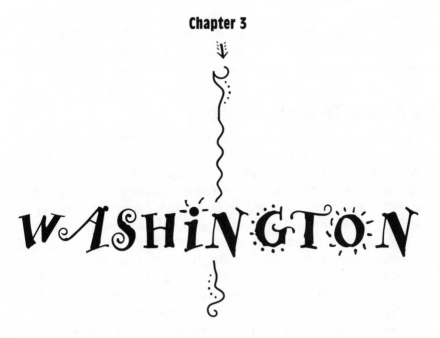

WASHINGTON

When it rains, it snows. Sometimes both at the same time. The same Pacific storms that rain on Seattle account for hundreds of inches of snow in the Cascades. Mt. Baker receives an annual snowfall of about 750 inches. Stevens Pass gets over 400 inches. Every year there's a storm that dumps four to five feet of snow in one day.

Before you rent the U-Haul, remember that when the snow comes down it's often a wet stuff resembling oatmeal. At least once a season, a monsoon moves through the state, dumping rain from base to summit. Then temperatures drop, freezing the snowpack harder than an old futon.

Snowboarders hate to be told how to dress, but just remember that if you wear your baggy pants that hang down around your hips, chances are your plumber's crevasse will get packed with snow. You're going to get wet snowboarding in Washington, even when you do take all the proper precautions. There's not much you can do about it when it's thirty-two degrees out and snowing.

Gortex, Entrant GII, or a Costco rain suit offer fabrics that will increase your comfort level. At least one spare pair of goggles is a

necessity. Dressing for the temperature is also important: the temperatures rarely drop below the low twenties, so don't layer on the polypro
unless you need it. A hood, powder skirt, and cuff seals are also good
ideas. You'll notice that in Washington, function wins out over fashion for the majority of the season.

Washington is the largest night-skiing region in the country. Make
sure to check on whether a resort offers night-boarding opportunities.
Again, we're not telling you how to dress, but we will mention that it
gets butt cold forty feet above the ground at 9:00 P.M.

Backcountry Opportunities

One aspect of boarding that characterizes Washington is the out-of-
bounds hike. Although this is illegal in California, many resorts in
Washington maintain gate access to the adjacent backcountry. The
Shuksan Arm of Mt. Baker, the Great Scott backcountry off Alpental,
and Crystal Mountain's North and South backcountries are a few ex-
amples. These areas are unpatrolled, and no avalanche control takes
place. There are unmarked cliffs, lines that will take you to flat meadows that require a few hours of hiking to the road, and many un-
named obstacles to discover. The rules here are simple—know a thing
or two about snow stability, bring a friend (someone to tell your family that you died well), and have a clue as to where you're going.

Here's something that almost happened: midway down our descent
of the Shuksan Arm, we saw a gully that was full of untracked powder.
As we headed for it, our friend told us there was probably a reason no
one had taken the freshies. We took another line down, but at the bottom we sighted the gully, and a forty-foot waterfall we would have
been required to drop in order to make it down.

All this talk sounds schoolmarmish, and maybe it is, but if snowboarders are going to reproduce and multiply and eventually take over
the world, we've got to keep the lemming acts down to a minimum.

All this said, if you're serious about discovering the best of Washington, you've got to be prepared to unbuckle and hike. There's almost
always a kick trail going up, and if the gate is open and you're comfortable riding the steeps, you've got no excuse to let everyone else get
the powder turns.

If you have a lot of money, your other option is to do some heli
boarding. **North Cascade Heli-Skiing**, (800) 494-HELI, is Washington's only heli operation. It runs out of Winthrop, in the north-central
part of the state, and offers one-day and three-day packages ($420 and
$1,500, respectively). When the weather doesn't allow the bird in the
air, they also operate a snowcat. Eighty designated runs over their
300,000-acre permit in the Okanogan National Forest ensure that you

won't see another track or another person during your session. The runs range from fifteen hundred to four thousand vertical feet, with a guarantee of ten thousand vertical feet a day. If you've got money you don't know where to burn, the heli will do it with style.

Alpental, Snoqualmie, Ski Acres, Hyak

7900 Southeast Twenty-eighth Street, Suite 200
Mercer Island, WA 98040

Phone: (206) 434-7669
Fax: (206) 232-1721
Snowphone: (206) 236-1600
Elevation: base, 3,200'; top, 5,400'; vertical, 2,200'
Lifts: 23 chairs covering 1,916 acres
Terrain Variety: 37% advanced, 43% intermediate, 20% beginner

The Season and Hours

The lifts open at 9:30 A.M. on weekdays and 9:00 A.M. on weekends; they run until 10:30 P.M. with the help of artificial light. The Snoqualmie Pass has the largest night operation in the world, with 909 acres of lit terrain. The mountain opens in late November and operates through mid-April, but the four areas keep their own schedules. Alpental and Snoqualmie are closed on Mondays, Ski Acres is closed on Tuesdays, and Hyak operates only on weekends.

Lift Tickets

Monday, Tuesday: $14
Wednesday, Thursday: $16
Friday: $18
Weekend, holiday: $27
Night: Sunday–Tuesday, $14; Wednesday, Thursday, $16; weekend, holiday, $18

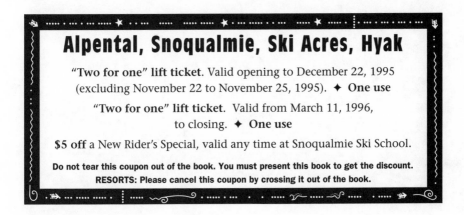

ALPENTAL

EL. - 5,400'

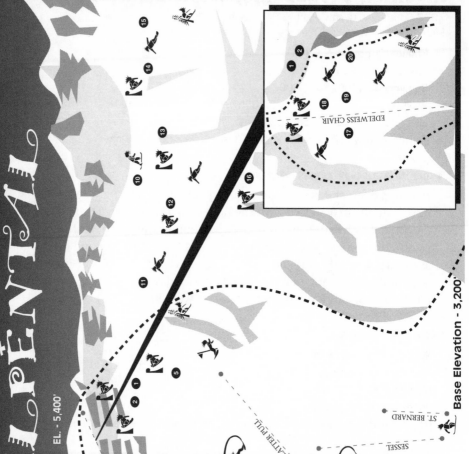

RUNS

1. Upper International
2. Adrenaline
3. Cat Track
4. Meister
5. Snake Dance
6. Red Robin
7. Debbie's Gold
8. Eisfallen
9. Dom
10. Great Scott Traverse
11. Sharon Bowl
12. March's Couloir
13. Martini Bowl
14. Stokes Bowl
15. Draft Dodger Ridge
16. The Bluffs
17. Edelweiss Bowl
18. Schluct
19. Rollen
20. The Fan

EDELWEISS CHAIR

PLATTER PULL

DEBBIE'S GOLD

ST. BERNARD

SESSEL

EDELWEISS CHAIR

Base Elevation - 3,200'

Specials

If you want to ride from opening to closing, it only costs you $2 more. Saturday nights are family nights, when children age seventeen and under ride for half price when accompanied by a paying adult.

Logistics

Located forty-three miles east of the I-405/I-90 junction, the mountain can be reached from Seattle in less than an hour (assuming no bad traffic, big rain, or falling snow). Take I-90 east to exit 52 for Alpental and Snoqualmie, exit 53 for Ski Acres, and exit 54 for Hyak.

The Local Scene

Skiing at Snoqualmie Pass ("the Pass") began during World War II when Mt. Baker and Mt. Rainier were closed to the public so the Tenth Mountain Division could train. The skiers in the Northwest resorted to the Pass, which installed numerous rope tows to meet the instant demand for mountain access. Later, when the rope-ops realized that the days were disappearing without their getting on the mountain, they installed old gas station lights on the poles and trees, and night skiing came into being.

Now, the Pass, as the closest area to Seattle, has become a popular place to go after school or work during the week for night boarding. In fact, more people come out at night than during the day. The Jellystone Board Park is fully lit, and gates are set up in the evenings if you want to hone your alpinist abilities. On the weekends, the greater Seattle area descends on the mountain. There are ways to avoid the crowds, though, so read on.

The **Summit Lodge** has a board shop, but for more variety check out the **Urban Circus** in Issaquah or the **West Beach** and **Boarderline** shops in Bellevue.

Where to Stay

Because of the Pass's proximity to Seattle, lodging is somewhat scarce at the mountain. The **Summit Inn** provides the majority of beds, with eighty rooms, Jacuzzi, sauna, restaurant, and free cable (free!). Call (206) 434-6300 for reservations. The main phone number, (206) 434-7669, will get you in touch with a number of condominiums at the base of each mountain. **Wardholm West**, a bed-and-breakfast off exit 53, is a lodge-style inn with separate cabins as well. They say they're the best-kept secret at the Pass, and they don't have a phone listing, so I guess they might stay that way.

The Mountain

The Pass actually includes four peaks, each one being a separate ski area. As generalizations go, Alpental is steep and offers the best extreme boarding; Snoqualmie is for the cruiser and NASTAR racer; Ski Acres is a mix of short steeps, rock drops, and flat spots; and Hyak is hard to get to. This saves Hyak from the crowds on the weekends, and a trip there gives you the opportunity to catch a ride with Frank, the legendary bus driver.

Because the Pass chairs cover so much area, you won't have a hard time getting off the beaten track. And when it's open, there's some amazing backcountry off the Alpental side.

Freeriders

If you like the steeps, you'll be blown away by Alpental. Coming down off the Edelweiss chair, you'll have the opportunity for some sick descents through Upper Internationale and Adrenaline, the chutes beneath the chair. Most of the cliff area is closed, and unless you like rock enemas, it's best to heed the warnings. On the backside of the chair is the Edelweiss Chair area, which offers some equally challenging though less rocky lines down.

While the expert boarders will want to spend the majority of their time at Alpental, Ski Acres also offers some nice steeps up top and some rock jumps to the left of the Bonanza Face run. Be warned, though, that the runs feed into a big flat zone where you'll be driving Miss Daisy in order to reach the lift.

For trees and hidden powder caches, keep moving over toward Hyak. There are hits sprinkled through the trees everywhere. As you keep heading to the skiers' right toward the boundary, you'll encounter more cliffs and your best chance for good snow in the trees next to the chair.

For the best riding, though, you need to get an Edelweiss Backcountry pass, which entails some strange decision-making process by the Ski Patrol as to your backcountry abilities. If the backcountry's open, go to the Ski Patrol at the top of chair 17. They'll probably sign you up for one of their tours, which is a good idea given the numerous cliffs and omnipresent avalanche danger. Once you're in with the Ski Patrol, you've got nothing but goods in store for you. One spot we heard about was the Devil Pit, a now-discovered quarter-pipe that has a deep hole full of rocks you have to clear for reentry. After this, you continue down through a gigantic natural half-pipe. Big powder bowls spread out along the Great Scott Traverse offer you any number of lines to take down. There's no substitute for local knowledge, so when you're visiting see if you can hook up with a group of riders who can show you the secret spots.

Cruisers

The presence of NASTAR racing at Snoqualmie also means immaculate grooming and fall-line pitches coming down the main face. Hard-boot riders will have a great time laying out turns on any of the Snoqualmie runs, and this is by far your best bet. Ski Acres tends to get bumped out, especially in the steep upper parts of the mountain, and the bottom third gets flat, so unless you're following a groomer you may have to do some searching for a good cruiser. The run beneath the Grayson chair at Hyak is wide open and comes down the fall line, and the designated runs on this side of the mountain are all groomed for some easy turning runs. Alpental's main face also offers some challenging alpine riding, but unless you're up for a variety of terrains, you may spend more time on the cat track than anywhere else.

Freestylers

Jellystone Board Park, serviced by the 360 Bowl chair, offers some good hits and spines, and a mailbox. It's lit at night, so if you're cursed with a day job and are in need of a midweek session, this is the place to come. On weekends, you'll find the majority of riders over at Hyak. About every three or four feet through the trees you can find a hit, especially to the skiers' left, beyond the nonoperating double chair. A half-pipe at the top of Blowdown makes Hyak the perfect weekend getaway for snowboarders at the Pass.

Grommets

The New Snowboarder package runs $35 at midweek and $40 on weekends and holidays. At the bottom of each mountain, you'll be able to find a good variety of beginner runs. The Gallery and Holiday chairs at Ski Acres and Julie's chair at Snoqualmie are your best bets for wide-open turning with enough pitch to keep you moving.

Nonbelievers

The Pass has a long tradition in skiing, with NASTAR racing Tuesday through Sunday nights. Cross-country skiing and tubing round out the snow opportunities. The area is a family and locals' destination, and just about everyone in the Northwest says he or she learned to ski at Snoqualmie. It's true. Everyone says that.

Crystal Mountain Resort

1 Crystal Mountain Boulevard
Crystal Mountain, WA 98022

Phone: (360) 663-2265
Fax: (360) 663-0148
Snowphone: (360) 634-3771 (Seattle); (360) 922-1832 (Tacoma)
Elevation: base, 4,130'; top, 7,002'; vertical, 2,872'
Lifts: 10 chairs (2 detachable quads) and 1 rope tow
Terrain Variety: 30% advanced, 57% intermediate, 13% beginner

The Season and Hours

The mountain typically opens around Halloween and operates through early April. Lifts open at 9:00 A.M. on weekdays and 8:30 A.M. on weekends and close every day at 4:30 P.M. From mid-December through late March, night operations begin at 4:00 P.M. and last through 10:00 P.M. on Fridays, Saturdays, Sundays, and holidays.

Lift Tickets

Monday, Tuesday—$16
Wednesday–Friday—Adult/Teen: $20
Weekend, holiday—Adult/Teen/Senior/Youth (7–11): $32/$27/$27/$20
Night—$16

Specials

From March 1 through the season's end, the Afternoon Delight special offers lift tickets for $16, good from noon to 8:00 P.M. on Wednesdays and Thursdays. Midweek lodging-and-lift packages start at $49 per person per night. You have to stay at least two nights. Call (206) 663-2558.

Crystal Mountain Resort

Thirty percent off lodging in the Village Inn. Offer good Monday through Thursday, non-holiday, based on two-night minimum and double occupancy. ✦ Includes 50 percent off one lift ticket with lodging.

Do not tear this coupon out of the book. You must present this book to get the discount.
RESORTS: Please cancel this coupon by crossing it out of the book.

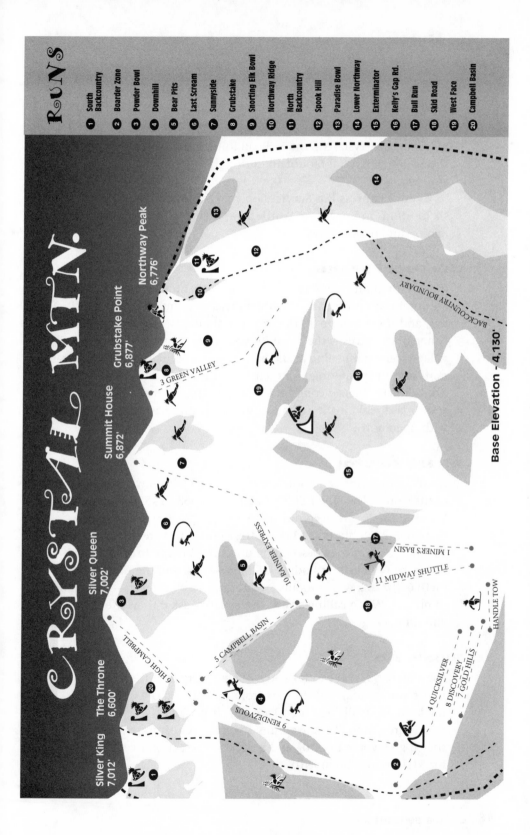

CRYSTAL MTN.

Silver King
7,012'

The Throne
6,600'

Silver Queen
7,002'

Summit House
6,872'

Grubstake Point
6,877'

Northway Peak
6,776'

Base Elevation - 4,130'

BACKCOUNTRY BOUNDARY

3 GREEN VALLEY

10 RAINIER EXPRESS

9 HIGH CAMPBELL

5 CAMPBELL BASIN

9 RENDEZVOUS

1 MINER'S BASIN

11 MIDWAY SHUTTLE

4 QUICKSILVER

8 DISCOVERY

7 GOLD HILLS

HANDLE TOW

RUNS

1. South Backcountry
2. Boarder Zone
3. Powder Bowl
4. Downhill
5. Bear Pits
6. Last Scream
7. Sunnyside
8. Grubstake
9. Snorting Elk Bowl
10. Northway Ridge
11. North Backcountry
12. Spook Hill
13. Paradise Bowl
14. Lower Northway
15. Exterminator
16. Kelly's Gap Rd.
17. Bull Run
18. Skid Road
19. West Face
20. Campbell Basin

Logistics

Crystal Mountain is located seventy-six miles from Seattle, in the Mt. Baker–Snoqualmie National Forest on the northeast boundary of Mt. Rainier National Park. From Seattle, take I-5 south to exit 142A to Auburn; follow Highway 164 to Enumclaw and Highway 410 east for thirty-three miles before entering Mt. Rainier National Park. Go six miles up the Crystal Mountain Road to the resort. Highway 410 is closed east of Crystal Mountain during the winter, so you can't loop around.

Crystal Express Bus Services operate Friday through Monday from six locations in the greater Seattle area. Call (206) 626-5208 for information and reservations.

The Local Scene

If a "destination resort" can be found in Washington, it's Crystal Mountain. It's nicer than the other areas in terms of lifts and facilities, and if you're into all the extras (restaurants, day care, on-site condos), then this is the place for you. They've got their own little village scene happening at the base of the mountain, with five restaurants and four watering holes (check out the **Pub** and the **Snorting Elk Cellar**). When it comes to snowboarding, Crystal has built a snowboard park, instituted a contest series, and basically greets riders with open arms.

Where to Stay

A variety of condos and hotels may be found within walking distance of the slopes. The **Silver Skis Chalet**, (360) 663-0145, has rooms starting at $118 a night sleeping one to four people. **Crystal Chalets**, (360) 663-2558, starts at $110 for the same. There are three hotels, listed here in order of descending price: the **Village Inn**, (360) 663-2558; the **Quicksilver Lodge**, (360) 663-2558; and the **Alpine Inn**, (360) 663-2262, where rooms are categorized by showers—hall, shared, or private. When calling any of these places, ask if they offer lodging-and-lift packages.

Bum's Tip

For a mere $3, you can take advantage of Crystal's hot tub, fitness room, sauna, and showers from 2:00 to 10:00 P.M. RV power hookups are available for $10 a night. If you're driving back to the Seattle area, stop at the **Natches Tavern** in Greenwater, where they'll give you a hot dog and a stick to roast it on over their fire for $1.50 (chips included).

The Mountain

With over twenty-three hundred acres that include two backcountry sections, Crystal offers every type of terrain you need to have a good session. Glades, chutes, big bowls, a snowboard park, hits sprinkled on the sides of runs, and insomniac groomers make this an all-style destination. The one drawback is that the run architecture favors skiers, and on the bottom half of the mountain you'll find yourself traversing a lot to get back to the lifts. Your best bet is to stay on the upper half—that's where the majority of the terrain lies, and your calves will thank you. On a clear day you'll get a great view of Mt. Rainier from the Summit House, so if you're a documenter of your life, be sure to bring a camera.

Freeriders

If it's open, make for the South Backcountry and don't come back until the end of the day. Going down into Avalanche Basin off the Throne, the chutes rage, as do the trees coming down toward the top of chair 4. A short hike will get you to Silver Basin, where you can find freshie many days after the last dump. Likewise, the North Backcountry offers lots of terrain to explore and the opportunity to find plenty of goods, but you have to take a bus back to the main lodge after your run, so you might want to save this one for the end of the day.

When the backcountry is closed (which is often, because of avalanche danger), make your way up to Silver Queen Peak off chair 6. There are good lines coming down into Powder Bowl, and some good rock bands, launches, and steeps. Snorting Elk Bowl is another favorite you can get to by traversing around the back of chair 10. Once you clear the nice steep trees there, you need to keep your speed up and cut hard to the left to make it back to the chair. And a day isn't complete without a visit to the Bear Pits, a series of tight gullies coming down through the trees beneath Powder Bowl.

Cruisers

Crystal offers terrific groomed runs, and you'll find a wealth of corduroy coming off chair 9. MacGoo's, CMAC, and Downhill are the best runs to lay out some big turns. Once you've sessioned there for a while, take a look at the Northway Ridge run, along with Sunnyside to Iceberg Gulch to Deer Fly. Your best bet is to check with the lift-ops to find out where the groomers have been most recently.

Freestylers

The terrain park off chair 4 lies right in the middle of the beginners' meadow, so be prepared for a number of human pylons positioned along the run that gets you back to the lift. There are a series of table-tops and gaps, a spine, two rails, and a couple of opportunities to go big. The half-pipe is of the smaller sort, only three to four feet deep, but they keep it in good shape when it's not buried in snow. Just below the snowboard park, on Quicksilver and Boondoggle, a few hits are usually set up, as well as a wide-open run for practicing your flat-land maneuvers. On the main mountain, the hit runs change during the season based on snow, but the cat-track jumps below chair 3 are always a favorite (as long as you take all necessary safety precautions), as are the sidewalls of those long traverses coming down from the upper mountain—Kelly's Gap Road, Skid Road, and Right Angle.

Grommets

Crystal's beginners' meadow off chair 4 is where you can learn to ride in full view of the snowboard park. You can see your future in the riders that cruise by you in a nose blunt on their way back to the chair. Lift/lesson/rental packages go for $49 midweek, $59 on weekends.

Nonbelievers

Crystal was built for skiers, as well as for the family getaway, and the terrain actually favors the biped (not that boarders can't rip it up as well).

Mission Ridge

P.O. Box 1668
Wenatchee, WA 98807-1668

Phone: (509) 663-7631
Fax: (509) 663-1838
Snowphone: (800) 374-1693
Elevation: base, 4,570'; top, 6,770'; vertical, 2,200'
Lifts: 4 doubles, 2 surface
Terrain Variety: 30% advanced, 60% intermediate, 10% beginner

The Season and Hours

Late November to mid-April. Weekend and holiday hours are 8:30 A.M.–4:00 P.M.; midweek hours are 9:00 A.M.–4:00 P.M.

Lift Tickets

Weekend, holiday—Adult/Student, Senior/Youth (7–15): $28/$20/$15
Weekday—Adult/Student, Senior/Youth: $15/$15/$15
Night—Adult/Student, Senior/Youth: $8/$8/$8

MISSION RIDGE

EL. 6,770'

Base Elevation - 4,570'

CHAIR 1
CHAIR 2
CHAIR 3
CHAIR 4
ROPE TOW
ROPE TOW

RUNS

1. Outback
2. Bowl Four
3. Microwave
4. Windy Ridge
5. Bomber Cliffs
6. Bomber Bowl
7. Castle Peak
8. Central Park
9. Midway
10. Chak Chak
11. Sittum
12. Skookum
13. Wa Wa
14. Maggie
15. Tyee
16. Tumwater
17. Lip Lip Face
18. Sunspot
19. Chutes Ka-wham
20. Mimi

Specials

Discounts are available for multiday tickets. Night skiing is free with an all-day ticket (call ahead to confirm night-skiing dates). Early- and late-season lift tickets (November to mid-December; mid-March to end of season) are $15 for all ages, with additional discounts for multiday tickets. All-day beginners' chair 1 lift tickets are $12. Children age six and under ride free, and all beginning boarders/skiers can ride the Pika Peak rope tow for free. Ride up to seventy-five minutes and return your ticket for a "ski check" if conditions are crud.

Logistics

Mission Ridge is about 138 miles from Seattle, depending on which part you're coming from. From Seattle, take Highway 2 east to Wenatchee and follow the signs to Mission Ridge. From Tacoma, take I-90 east to Cle Elum/Wenatchee Highway (Highway 970—exit 85) toward Wenatchee. Take Highway 97 north to Wenatchee, then Highway 2 east and follow the signs to Mission Ridge.

Amtrak services Wenatchee daily from east and west. Call (800) 872-7245 for information. A free SkiLink shuttle bus runs through Wenatchee and makes several stops on its way to the mountain (numerous times daily) during the regular season. Call (800) 851-LINK or (509) 662-1155 for a schedule.

The Local Scene

Mission Ridge is too far from everything to be anything other than a locals' scene, but the locals know some things that many riders from western Washington and northern Oregon don't. That is that Mission Ridge, being far inland on the edge of the desert, gets some of the coldest, driest snow of any mountain on the "West Coast." A dedicated crowd of school-aged riders, along with an unusually high number of alpine cruisers, makes up Mission Ridge's hard core.

The mountain is aggressively pursuing the vacation skier/boarder market. As a result, there is good transportation to and from the mountain, as well as great lodging-and-lift packages with the hotels in Wenatchee. The current dearth of cheap condo rentals in the area may account for the smallish crowds.

Board shops have started springing up in nearby towns. For clothing or equipment needs, make a point of stopping by **Wango Tango** and **Arlberg Sports** in Wenatchee and **Jailhouse Snowboard Shop** in East Wenatchee. For cheap eats and après-board, check out **McGlinn's Ale House**, (509) 663-9073.

Where to Stay

Lots of lodging choices are available in Wenatchee, and many hotels offer multiday lodging-and-lift packages that truly are a good deal. Call (509) 548-5807 for more information. Condo-style lodging is available in the Lake Chelan area; phone (800) 4-CHELAN.

Tell Your Friends

Mission Ridge's most distinctive feature is a series of big rock couloirs, called Bomber Cliffs, that drop into a wide-open face named Bomber Bowl. Boarders blast down the hairy but rideable chutes, as well as get fat air off the cat track and the lips below Ka-Wham into the bowl below.

Any ski hill looking to promote an aggro image could have concocted these names, but Mission Ridge is actually paying its respects to a real World War II airplane—one that some say is now dropping a peace payload on its resting place. On September 30, 1944, a B-24 Liberator bomber on a training mission augured into the mountain, killing all seven crew members. For many years, the twisted wreckage rested in Bomber Bowl, except for a salvaged wing that someone mounted on the day lodge wall. Then in 1992, a group of Boy Scouts took the wing from the lodge and placed it on a memorial platform near the crash site. According to locals, within an hour of the memorial being erected, a seven-year drought was broken by a record snowfall—the start of a trend that has continued ever since.

The Mountain

Mission Ridge receives less snow than many of the mountains farther west, a fact that the ski area's managers readily admit. However, they caution boarders against jumping to conclusions: Mission Ridge also gets much less rain than other Washington mountains, and the snow here, they argue, tends to be much colder and drier than at places like Crystal and Stevens. Because of this disparity, Mission prefers to report its "surface conditions" rather than its snow depth.

We think this is a fair approach. After all, it's far too common for West Coast boarders to be riding on a twenty-foot base with the consistency of concrete. If powder is your mantra, Mission Ridge can be the best bet in the West.

Mission has a U-shaped ridgeline dropping into a central valley area. Extensive grooming takes place primarily down the central funnel of the valley, while the ridges, accessible by hiking or traversing from any of the three main lifts, provide big, steep drops and chutes. There are numerous opportunities for in-bounds backcountry riding here, particularly along the high north-facing ridges known as Windy, Microwave, Bowl Four, and Outback. These areas are primarily reached by traversing/hiking from the top of chair 2. The Ski Patrol at the top of any of the upper lifts will fill you in on prevailing avalanche conditions and closures, as well as possibly pointing you to some freshie.

Don't Miss

The second weekend of March features a race called the Skookum Cooker. It's a banked-slalom gate race that features some high-speed action, big air, and challenging terrain. The course is due to become a

Clear-cuts

A long drive through Washington or Oregon will take you past some of the most beautiful forests in the world. Then you'll turn a bend and want to get carsick when you witness some of the ugliest swaths of clear-cuts. While riding a snowboard is and should be a nonpolitical activity, here are a few facts about clear-cutting that might inspire some action.

1. Timber companies don't have to clear-cut. It has been proved that timber companies can selectively log and still make a profit. It's just that they choose to make an even bigger profit, which, in the short term, will boost their stock's value and make shareholders happy.

2. The largest percentage of trees comes from National Forest lands. That's right, the lands owned by Bob and Betty Snowboarder, along with the rest of the American public. The Forest Service has been in bed with the timber industry for a long time now, and its stock argument is that jobs depend on logging, and jobs serve the nation better than trees.

   It's a shortsighted policy, and one that will bite us in the butt in a very short time. Right now the Forest Service builds the roads for the timber companies and then sells the rights for harvesting trees at less than market value. But this saves jobs. The timber companies clear-cut the trees (the most efficient way to harvest them), then wind up selling a good portion to the Japanese, who in turn sell them back to us in the form of finished goods (thereby creating a relationship in which the United States becomes a colony of Japan when it comes to wood).

3. Replanting doesn't work. Sometimes you'll see a sign proudly proclaiming that an area has been replanted. The problem is, replanting a hillside of Douglas firs does nothing to simulate the vegetative diversity that existed before the clear-cut. For example, the deer depend on the low-hanging branches of hemlock and cypress for shelter. When these trees are cut and replaced by firs with higher branch systems, the deer will move out. As a result, they'll crowd into areas with existing deer and create a competition for food that will weaken the entire herd. And it goes on down the line. We need biodiversity to maintain healthy ecosystems. Clear-cutting destroys an area's biodiversity.

4. What a timber company does on its own land affects other areas. The erosion created by a clear-cut will be felt

classic in a few years—if you enter the race now, you can say you were there in the old days.

Freeriders

In general, any of the three upper-mountain lifts will get you into the goods as soon as you leave the cat tracks. In particular, there's a big, wide tree glade below Windy Ridge, and all kinds of hits, drops, and chutes below the Microwave station between chairs 3 and 4. You can link these areas with Castle Peak or the glade below Chak Chak—both off chair 4—for a top-to-bottom all-terrain party.

in all the streams that run through that area. As soil is washed into the streams, the spawning grounds for trout and salmon are compromised. A clear-cut will affect streams and rivers thirty miles away. A series of clear-cuts can eliminate the vast majority of life in a waterway.

Here's what you can do:

1. Write to your representatives and senators. If you see clear-cuts on National Forest land, write to them and tell them you oppose that type of logging.

Your Senator / Your Representative
U.S. Senate / U.S. House
Washington, DC 20510 /
Washington, DC 20515

Ask for a reply to all your letters. When writing to a member of Congress, ask that your letter be entered as part of the *public record.* There are usually several pieces of legislation involving resources management in committee at any given time, so ask your senator or representative what's out there, and how he or she will vote on it.

2. Write to the Department of Agriculture, which oversees the Forest Service:

Jim Lyon
Department of Agriculture
Fourteenth Street and Independence
Washington, DC 20250

3. Write to the Forest Service and let them know what's on your mind:

Jack Ward Thomas
U.S. Forest Service
Box 96090
Washington, DC 20090

4. Write to the timber companies, telling them what you think of their logging practices. Remember, they listen to their stockholders, but they should be listening to their consumers. Hold them responsible to the people who buy their products.

None of this is the loggers' faults—they're just working for a living. The Japanese are just doing what Americans would do given the opportunity. The problem lies in how our elected officials and governmental agencies have been managing resources. They're having a hard time unmucking themselves from all the dollars that the timber industry sends to Washington. Start by writing a letter, and then another, and another. It's a lot better than complaining to the other people in the car.

⇑ ⇓ ⇑

Cruisers

Mission Ridge actively grooms the mountain's thirty-three designated runs, and there's a very active group of alpine riders here. In fact, many of the instructors ride hard boots and asymmetrical boards. There's a small but active racing team as well.

Freestylers

Mission Ridge has a half-pipe terrain park with its own rope tow off the top of chair 1. Bring your heavy leather work gloves if you plan to spend your day in the park.

Grommets

The Snowboard Ridge Riders is a six-week lesson program for riders of any skill level; prices vary depending on whether you need rentals and such. Mission Ridge has a fair amount of beginners' terrain, much of it serviced by chair 1 and a beginners' rope tow near the base lodge. There is an enthusiastic core of instructors (who seem to be considerably older than the average) ready to prep you for a lifetime of bombing.

Nonbelievers

Skiers will find every type of terrain at Mission Ridge, including well-groomed trails with good snowmaking coverage. The resort has a complete child-care and kid's lesson program, and the mountain still has that down-home family feel to it, at least for now.

Mt. Baker

1017 Iowa Street
Bellingham, WA 98226

Phone: (360) 734-6771
Fax: (360) 734-5332
Snowphone: (206) 634-0200
Elevation: base, 3,500'; top, 5,000'; vertical, 1,500'
Lifts: 8 chairs (2 quads, 6 doubles), 1 rope tow
Terrain Variety: 28% advanced, 42% intermediate, 30% beginner

The Season and Hours

The mountain opens on November 5, if conditions are favorable, and stays open through the end of April. During the week, lifts run from 9:00 A.M. to 3:30 P.M. They open at 8:30 A.M. on weekends.

MT. BAKER

Shuksan Arm
5,540'

Panorama Dome
5,000'

Base Elevation - 3,500'

RUNS

1. Daytona
2. Oh Zone
3. Hemispheres
4. Half-Pipe
5. Nose Dive
6. Sam's Ridge
7. Gables
8. Razorhone Canyon
9. Entrance
10. North Face
11. The Chute
12. Pan Face
13. Blueberry
14. Holiday
15. 7 Hills
16. Sneaky Pete
17. Easy Money
18. Espresso
19. Border
20. Gold Mine

CHAIR 1
CHAIR 2
R-1
CHAIR 3
CHAIR 6
CHAIR 4
CHAIR 5
CHAIR 7
CHAIR 8

Lift Tickets

Weekend—Adult/Senior/Youth: $27.50/$20/$20
Weekday—Adult/Senior/Youth: $18/$13/$13

Specials

If you're over age seventy or under age seven, you ride for free.

Logistics

Mt. Baker is a two-and-a-half- to three-hour drive from the Seattle area. Take I-5 north to Bellingham, then Highway 542 through the town of Glacier and up to the mountain. A quicker way when there's traffic is to take I-20 east, then Highway 9 north to Highway 542.

The Local Scene

While it has yet to be proved, it's quite likely that Glacier is the center of the universe. Every rider needs to pass through here at some point. Just don't stay—there are only so many dishwashing jobs in town and there's a line to get them.

A mandatory stop is the **Mt. Baker Snowboard Shop** to check in with George Dobis and his daughter, Marcella (a former world-champ rider who runs the store). To call George an ornery cur would be an understatement: with his wicked, gold-toothed smile and Czech accent, he's a natural for a pirate (actually, gold prospecting, shooting holes in steel armor, and drinking Coors in the back room with the likes of Craig and Tex are some of his favorite pastimes). But George is a big-hearted dude and sort of a big brother to the young riders who migrate here. He has been known to loan avalanche Pieps to backcountry boarders or stay up late into the night honing some racer's edges.

The town of Glacier is small, quiet (except during the Legendary Banked Slalom), and devoid of cops and churches (except during the Legendary Banked Slalom, when the sheriffs show up like yellow jackets swarming a watermelon). **Grahams Pub**, across the street from the snowboard shop, offers good burgers and beer, and **Milano's**, kitty-corner from there, is the locals' choice for killer Italian food. Up the road a couple of miles, the **Chandelier** has huge burgers and a bar that gets hopping on weekends (but take our advice and don't order the pizza).

Mt. Baker is the home of the Mt. Baker Hardcore, a group of riders who pioneered the sport in the Northwest. It's not a club you can sign up for, but the riders are characterized by the fat airs and sick lines they draw and their willingness to ride in any weather—rain, sleet, snow, even sunshine. The spirit they've fostered has passed on to the following waves of riders, and the result is a mountain filled with rip-pers going for it all. There's no board park or half-pipe at Mt. Baker, and if you're dreaming about going pro you'd be better off in South-ern California near the photographers who can get you exposure. The nice thing about the local scene at Baker is that hiking's encouraged, and self-promotion is not. Carter Turk sums up the feel best with the inscription on his photo in the Mt. Baker Snowboard Shop: "Ride alone."

Where to Stay

Glacier Creek Motel and Cabins, (360) 599-2991, is your best bet for reasonable lodging. Groups looking for cabin rentals should call **Mt. Baker Lodging** at (360) 599-2453. Other options are **Butterfly Mead-ows,** (360) 599-2312; **Country Hill B&B,** (360) 599-2047; **Mt. Baker Chalet,** (360) 599-2405; **Snowline Inn,** (800) 228-0119; **Thurston House B&B,** (360) 599-2261; and **Yodeler Inn B&B,** (800) 642-9033.

The Mountain

It has been called Mecca, and if you snowboard you know about Mt. Baker even if you haven't been there. It's world-famous for its natural terrain, and for its riders who have come into international promi-nence. There are chutes, steeps, and deep glades. Big bowls abound off the Hemispheres. The Razorhone Canyon is a natural terrain park, and even more fun can be had with a hike up the Shuksan Arm.

Mt. Baker is also renowned for the Legendary Banked Slalom, a gate race through Mt. Baker's natural half-pipe that attracts a world-class group of pros. This is in spite of (or possibly because of) the event's funky laid-back homegrown style.

We don't see this style changing, even though the resort is. The most recent addition is the **White Salmon Day Lodge.** Constructed out of native timbers and rock, it maintains the homey environment, and you can still get a big coffee and a muffin for about $2, with the choice of paying in U.S. or Canuck currency. It still snows more here than at almost any other resort in the United States, and it rains a few days as well. The snow is usually wet and heavy, and come to think of it, the chairs are slow and you really should stay closer to home. Leave the mountain to the fools who already ride there.

Freeriders

Mt. Baker is where the term *freeriding* came into its own, and the ter-rain is unbeatable when it comes to variety. The classics list includes Razorhone Canyon, a natural box canyon that sluices you down to

The Legendary Banked Slalom

For those of you who question whether snowboarding and racing should be mentioned in the same breath, a good argument for their nexus occurs every January at Mt. Baker, Washington. The Legendary Banked Slalom, a gate race held in the natural half-pipe off chair 5, attracts some of the world's best riders. It's the oldest event in the sport, and a partial list of winners—Tom Sims, Shaun Palmer, Craig Kelly, Amy Howatt, Marcella Dobis, Rob Morrow, Karleen Jeffery, Terje Haakanson—is a veritable who's who of snowboarding.

What contributes to the race's "legendary" status is the laid-back atmosphere that makes it a celebration of snowboarding rather than a teeth-gnashing competition. In 1995, the organizers missed one of their fingers or toes and promoted the Tenth Annual race when it was actually the eleventh year of the event. And it's not rare that a contestant "misses" his run when the mountain is going off.

When they do race, surviving the course is a victory in itself. The gates twist down a Rubenesque gully that resembles a luge run. By using the banks, a rider can pump speed through the turns, although most contestants are looking for places to scrub. The lines get rutted and icy, and the final section, composed of tight turns and a head-high drop, is known as the Toilet Bowl. There's a lot of butt-checking and sketching out, and the occasional starfish tumble, but there's no doubt that the course brings out the best in riders. In 1994, Craig Kelly fell during

the bottom between hundred-foot walls. In the canyon, the walls are geared for high-speed tears and loops, and the numerous hits make this a natural playground. In fresh snow, chair 1 goes off, as well as the steeps coming down chair 5. Of course, some of the best terrain you'll find is a hike away, through the gate at the top of chair 8. When it's open (which it isn't at times of extreme avalanche danger), you can hike up the Hemispheres (so named for its resemblance to a human brain) and ride back down to chair 8, or ride down to the funnel that brings you out at chair 5 (if you miss this funnel, you'll end up atop the cliff band—high, high above Razorhone Canyon—and you'll have to traverse over). The biggest out-of-bounds thrill is to hike up the Hemispheres and out along the spectacular Shuksan Arm. This sets you up for steep powder runs with wind lips and jumps all the way down. Don't go alone if you don't know the area: you'll encounter hazardous cliffs and waterfalls if you choose the wrong line. Scout the area from chair 8, and have someone guide you if it's your first time out. Also, as with any backcountry boarding, be alert to dangerous situations and be religiously respectful of Ski Patrol closures and warnings. We saw several big slides come down the Arm when we were at Baker and we'd hate to be under one of them.

his final run, but got up and finished the course to post the winning time. In the 1995 event, Terje posted a 1:09 on day one, with the next fastest time being a 1:14. On Saturday Terje rode fakie and posted a 1:14. On day three, the race turned hard-core when a monsoon dumped enough rain to form boot-deep puddles in the lift lines. The heats went on, and Terje won. So far, no hard-boot rider has taken first place in the Banked Slalom. Not to say that they won't, but the course creates mistakes, and hard boots make recovery more difficult.

Also contributing to the race's "legendary" status are the more than two hundred amateurs who sign up. In all reality, the contest is more a sideshow to a weekend of freeriding. When the gate to the Hemispheres is open, the Shuksan Arm becomes the most popular run. And when the sun goes down, you'll find most of the racers in Glacier attending strategy meetings, maybe listening to loud music or a band, possibly consuming high-energy drinks that make them appear very happy. It's highly recommended to carry a form of ID after dark, even if you're of age, because while Glacier doesn't employ any police officers, the state troopers seem to find their way to these gatherings.

The Banked Slalom has become a cult classic among riders in Oregon, Washington, and British Columbia. As a result, if you don't get your entry form in early, you'll be stuck on a long waiting list with little chance of getting a free T-shirt, not to mention the gilded duct-tape-roll trophy for winners. So sometime in December, call Mt. Baker's office at (360) 734-6771 and ask for the form.

⚑ ⚓ ⚑

Cruisers

Chair 8 offers the most by way of wide-open, uncrowded groomed runs. The natural half-pipe at the top of chair 4 (where they hold the Legendary Banked Slalom) is a good challenge for the hard-boot rider and freerider alike. Chair 6 has some nice groomed runs, but it's such a shame to stick to the groomed trails on this mountain that we'll say no more.

Freestylers

Almost every run on the mountain is a hit run when there's snow, so rage in style.

Grommets

Chairs 2 and 3 service a beginners' area that offers seclusion and good terrain to practice your turns on. Beginner lift, lesson, and rental packages are $40.

Nonbelievers

Mt. Baker's atmosphere, ambience, and attitude make it the place for a soul session. The terrain is the great equalizer, and skiers and boarders gear up for the mountain and not each other.

Ski White Pass

P.O. Box 354
Yakima, WA 98907

Phone: (509) 453-8731
Snowphone: (509) 672-3100
Elevation: base, 4,500'; top, 6,000'; vertical, 1,500'
Lifts: 4 chairs (1 high-speed quad) and a rope tow
Terrain Variety: 20% advanced, 60% intermediate, 20% beginner

The Season and Hours

The mountain opens in late November and operates through early April. Lift hours are 8:45 A.M. to 4:00 P.M. Night boarding until 10:00 P.M. is available on weekends from mid-December through early March.

Lift Tickets

Weekend—Adult/Senior/Junior: $29/$18/$18
Weekday—Adult/Senior/Junior: $18/$13/$13
Night—$10

Specials

Board on Wednesdays and Thursdays for $13.

Logistics

White Pass is located fifty miles west of Yakima. You can't miss the resort's parking lot, which sits smack-dab on the side of Highway 12. From the Seattle area, take Highway 410 to Highway 12, or take I-90 to I-82 through Yakima, then Highway 12 west.

The Local Scene

White Pass has always been proud of its smallness, lack of glitz, and local feel. But with the addition of a high-speed quad, it might get harder to keep the mountain a secret. In fact, it's the smallest area in the United States to employ a high-speed detachable lift. As a small mountain set away from the major metropolitan crowds, it offers some great terrain. Temple and Matt Cummings have been known to frequent the site, and it has a large contingent of local boarders who might show you some of the secret spots.

Where to Stay

At the mountain, the one and only lodge is the **Village Inn Condominiums**, (509) 672-3131. They have a big heated pool that can hold

WHITE PASS

EL. - 6,000'

Base Elevation - 4,500'

CHAIR 4

CHAIR 2

GREAT WHITE EXPRESS

CHAIR 1

RUNS

1. Holiday Cliff
2. Cascade
3. Holiday
4. Outhouse
5. Raven's Haven
6. Ptarmigan
7. Star Wars
8. Roller Cattrack
9. Mach V
10. North Peak
11. Midway
12. Upper Roller
13. Execution
14. Elevator Shaft
15. Cornice
16. Hourglass
17. Roller Cliff
18. Lower Roller
19. Poma Face
20. Near Side— Far Side

probably a hundred people. The nearest town with a wide variety of lodging choices is Packwood, about twenty minutes west of the mountain. Call the **Yakima Valley Visitors and Convention Bureau** at (509) 575-1300 and ask for information about lodging near White Pass. We like the **Tatoosh Motel,** (360) 494-5321; ask about their log house that sleeps ten and has a huge stone fireplace.

Tell Your Friends

We're under oath not to tell you too much about the Gravel Pits, except to say that it's an old rock quarry not far from White Pass where freestylers will spend all spring going fat off huge hits among the snow-covered rock piles and rusting machinery. Needless to say, there are no lifts.

The Mountain

The mountain is not big, and there are some slow chairs, but the high-speed quad will take you up to the top and a wide variety of terrain to explore. On a powder day the hits are numerous and forgiving, and there are all sorts of opportunities to get launched.

Freeriders

You'll see the Cornice on the lift ride up. With enough fresh snow, you can go as big as you want off this. Below, numerous huge hits are hidden in the trees. If you decide not to jump off the Cornice, the trees on the other side (between Roller Cattrack and Main Street) are spaced just right. This area is unofficially called Star Wars after the scene in *Return of the Jedi* where Luke, Leia, and the Miwoks ride their rocket bikes through the trees. This is the best place to find powder several days after a dump.

Good trees can also be found on Old Holiday, an abandoned trail right at the ski-area boundary. Hits are sprinkled throughout the area, and since no one goes there who doesn't know to, it's a good bet to find some snow. Another fun run, with lots of hits, leads you down the nose of the main ridge, called North Peak, and ends up in an area called the Chair Run, which drops you down Avalanche Chute—steep! There's a long list of spots that the right local will be able to show you. If the conditions are right, check out Buttons, a series of small cliffs and landings that lead down to the Rockslide Meadow. It's an intense descent, and Rockslide is a sure bet for good snow, especially a few days after the last dump.

Cruisers

Cascade is a big wide-open run coming down from the top that offers cruisers the opportunity to lay out big turns. The lower half of the mountain leads down to the chair, and while its pitch isn't that steep, there are nice areas to carve some GS turns. The backside usually isn't crowded, offering solitude for the easy rider.

Freestylers

If you turn left into the trees immediately off Outhouse (below the Cornice), you'll be lined up for a series of hits called the Quarter-Pipes. A traverse along the ridge at the top of the mountain also leads you to some good hits with good landings coming down. Hourglass is a good hit run, along with the cat track coming off Cascade and the hits along the lift poles at Lower Roller. With a little observation and exploration, you'll uncover all sorts of launches. The half-pipe, which doesn't get a lot of use because of its location, is just off the Elevator Shaft run, near the base of the mountain.

Grommets

The lower mountain has a wide-open beginners' meadow where there are almost no trees or poles that you could run into. Private instruction is available by the hour for individuals or groups of up to three students.

Nonbelievers

Skiers will feel perfectly at home on the mountain. In fact, Phil and Steve Mahre, two guys who know how to ski, learned their craft on these very slopes. Otherwise, White Pass is very close to Mt. Rainier National Park, where lots of alternative winter activities are available.

Stevens Pass

P.O. Box 98
Summit Stevens Pass
U.S. Highway 2
Skykomish, WA 98288

Phone: (360) 973-2441
Snowphone: (206) 634-1645 (Seattle); (360) 353-4400 (Everett)
Elevation: base, 4,061'; top, 5,845'; vertical, 1,784'
Lifts: 11 chairs
Terrain Variety: 35% advanced, 54% intermediate, 11% beginner

STEVENS PASS

EL. - 5,845'

Base Elevation - 4,061'

RUNS

1. Big Chief Bowl
2. Double Diamond
3. Tye Bowl
4. Skid Road
5. Parachute
6. Promenade
7. Hagen Hill
8. Rock Garden
9. Cloud 9
10. Meadows
11. Nancy Chute
12. Barrier Bowl
13. Windy Ridge
14. Housewives
15. Broadway
16. Showcase
17. Corona Bowl
18. Aquarius
19. Pegasus Gulch
20. Andromeda Face

7TH HEAVEN

SOUTHERN CROSS

JUPITER

BARRIER

BROOKS

HOGS BACK

BLUE JAY

DAISY

TYE MILL

BIG CHIEF

DOUBLE DIAMOND

The Season and Hours

The season runs from late November through early April. Lifts operate from 9:00 A.M. until 5:00 P.M. Night skiing is from 5:00 to 10:00 P.M.

Lift Tickets

All day on weekend, holiday—Adult/Senior/Child: $31/$26/$24

Half day on weekend, holiday—Adult/Senior/Child: $28/$23/$21

Monday, Tuesday—Adult/Senior/Child: $15/$15/$15

Wednesday–Friday—Adult/Senior/Child: $20/$20/$20

Night—Sunday–Thursday, $10; weekend, holiday, Adult/Senior/Child: $25/$20/$18

Specials

The Flex Ticket special makes every lift ticket you purchase good until 10:00 P.M.

Logistics

Stevens is located seventy-eight miles east of Seattle on Highway 2, along the Skykomish Valley. From Seattle, take I-5 to Highway 2. From Bellevue, take Highway 405, then Highway 522 to Highway 2.

The Local Scene

Stevens is a favorite among local snowboarders for its terrain, price, and laid-back atmosphere. For the most part, Stevens has been known as a family ski area where a lot of intermediate skiers from the metropolitan area make their weekend pilgrimages. It's also a favorite for day trips among Seattle-based boarders. As a result, there isn't really much of a locals' scene at the mountain. Many mountain employees live in the resort's housing or in Leavenworth, and most of them are snowboarders, so your best bet for gaining some local insight is to hang out around the food-service areas. There's a good board shop at the mountain, or stop in Gold Bar on the way up at the **Mountain Company**, (360) 793-0221, for any of your snowboarding needs. The **Soft Landing Lounge** in the West Lodge is a nice place to kick back after a day of boarding—watch the traffic stack up on the road going out and be glad you're not part of it.

Where to Stay

There is no lodging at the mountain (but RV hookups are available). Sixteen miles west in Skykomish, you'll find the **SkyRiver Inn**, (360) 677-2261. Thirty miles west in Sultan is the **Dutch Cup Motel**, (360) 793-2215. If you go east from the mountain, you'll find a wide selection of lodging at Lake Wenatchee and Leavenworth. Try these numbers for more information: **Bavarian Bedfinders,** (800) 323-2920; **Destination Leavenworth,** (800) 962-7359; **Lake Wenatchee Hide-a-ways,** (800) 883-2611; **Vacation Get-a-ways,** (800) 548-4808; and the **Leavenworth Chamber of Commerce,** (509) 548-5807.

The Mountain

With 1,125 acres that include a recently opened backside, Stevens offers terrain with continuous pitch to the base. You won't be faced with any shin-splint traverses, and the mountain contains a wide variety of terrain that will please every boarder's tastes: extreme descents, wide-open runs, glades, a terrain park, and bowls. Because the average skier here remains primarily on the runs, you can find good snow for many days after the last dump. This means there are all sorts of jumps with soft landings through the trees. Stevens receives probably the best accumulations of snow in the area, especially on the backside.

Freeriders

Seventh Heaven offers the best steeps, some sick lines through chutes, rock bands, jumps, trees, and powder. The descent isn't that long, but there are numerous paths to take off the top that will challenge every rider. Rock Garden and Cloud Nine also open up some lines that offer fat air and steep landings. Coming down off the Double Diamond chair to the skiers' left are some of the best trees on the mountain. Also, if you break hard left as you get off the chair, you can access the trees near the boundary on the other side of Big Chief Bowl. This entire area provides the best freeriding on the mountain, unless fresh snow has been falling. Then you need to race over to the backside. Because the groomers leave the backside pretty well alone, hits and drops are sprinkled over the faces. The Andromeda Face on the backside offers the best powder boarding on the mountain. Pegasus Gulch is a good place for some big tears. And going up in the Jupiter chair, you'll get a peek at Wally Rock on the right-hand side in the trees. It's about a fifteen-foot drop with a good landing if there's fresh snow—and if you don't zero in on your buddy's crater.

Cruisers

For some nice easy turning, Barrier Bowl coming down Windy Ridge is a good bomber run, and Showcase is a wide-open cruiser. You can find a steeper fall-line pitch on I-5 off the Big Chief chair. Off Hog's Back, try out International and Parachute, or if those are getting bumpy, move over to Blue Trail. Aquarius, the only groomed trail on the backside, sees a bit of traffic, but it's a good top-to-bottom run.

Freestylers

The best hits are found sprinkled through the trees below Schim's Meadow. The chutes coming off Windy Ridge also offer some good launches and landings. There's a half-pipe off the Brooks chair, along with a few groomers' specials. While the park still has a way to go, you won't have any trouble finding natural hits and kickers.

Grommets

If you're over eight years old and weigh more than seventy pounds, you qualify for the First-time Snowboarder package that includes lift, lesson, and rental ($30 on weekdays, $36 on weekends).

Nonbelievers

Stevens recently opened a Nordic center that offers fifteen groomed trails and over thirty kilometers of cross-country terrain. Skiers will have a good time on the mountain, as they've been doing for the last sixty years.

Chapter 4

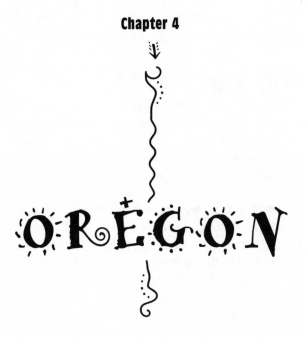

OREGON

A mountain has many sides, and depending on where you stand you'll see quite a few different faces. Oregon also possesses a quality of there being something unseen on the other side. The state is a study in extremes: a blend of ecoliberals and cowboys. The landscapes run from rain forest to high desert. And the mountains lie in between.

The Cascade Range is the result of a massive volcanic upheaval about fourteen million years ago, roughly corresponding to the first antagonisms between snowboarders and the Ski Patrol. Glaciers shaped the peaks and valleys (the Columbia River gorge is the result of glacial creeping), and their remnants are still present on the peaks at Lassen, Shasta, Bachelor, and Hood.

Oregon receives the wet Pacific storms that assault the West Coast during the winter, but because of the high elevations of the larger Cascade peaks, the snow that falls tends to be slightly colder and drier than the Washington-brand oatmeal. Not that you won't find it in Oregon, it's just that you also stand a chance of running into some dry powder on the eastern side of the range.

In spite of antigrowth policies in some areas, Oregon has been discovered by people from other states, and some of the smaller towns are currently experiencing growing pains associated with traffic, overdevelopment of residential areas, and allocations for public services. The state might someday have to impose a sales tax (over a few dead bodies), but for now it still embodies a certain low-key charm that snowboarders will enjoy, along with the killer boarding.

Backcountry Opportunities

Oregon's backcountry is found around the peaks of the Cascades, as there aren't many hills or ridges connecting the chain. The rim of Crater Lake is a popular spot in the spring, and unusual in that it's one of the few places where you do your hiking after you ride.

Just to the north, Mt. Bailey offers some spectacular terrain. If you don't have the dollars for a day of snowcat riding, there's a chance that you can work a barter with one of the many snowmachiners who hang out on the mountain. These folks are generally big, beefy men, and we imagine that a fine pilsner and a handful of beef jerky might get you a trip or two to the summit. Literally hundreds of snowmachine trails snake around Mt. Bailey and Mt. Jefferson, and with a little local knowledge you can find some truly spectacular fresh.

Mt. Bachelor has a backside complete with crevasses and a long hike out, but there's fresh out there and the adventuresome snowboarder might feel the urge to follow tracks to the backside. If you do decide to go around the mountain at Bachelor, hook up with someone

Oregon Survival Tips

1. *You can't pump your own gas.* When you pull into a service station, just stay in the car. It's crazy, we know, like out of a *Twilight Zone* episode where business is still based on customer service, but it's for real.

2. *You won't pay tax on your purchases.* If you know you're going to be traveling through Oregon, bring your grocery list, do your Christmas shopping, spend so much money there that your state will eliminate its sales tax just to get you home.

3. *When in doubt, drawl.* If you show up with your cap pulled down to your sunglasses, with pierced eyebrows, lips, and nose, tattoos across your arms and stomach, and that precoffee attitude, there's a chance that your very presence might displease a truck-driving patron of the gas station or grocery store to which fate has steered you. If you sense some tension, just say something like, "How y'all doing? Gotdamm it's col'." The glares will turn to grins, and before you know it everyone will be offering you a pinch from their can.

who's done it before, or you could be paying a thousand dollars an hour for rescue services.

The Three Sisters, the peaks west of Bend, are avalanche-ridden and windblown, but we've heard tales of people hiking up.

Mt. Hood Meadows has its own snowcat service that will take boarders to the upper bowls. Although access to this service requires the purchase of a lift ticket, it will give you a taste of ungroomed, steep ravines for a fraction of the cost of a daylong snowcat operation.

Finally, if you're riding at Timberline, there's a trail that goes down to Govy from the bottom of the Edelweiss chair. A good number of folks use this method of transportation in the afternoons, so if you haven't done it before, wait to follow someone down.

These are just a few tidbits that will give you an idea of the backcountry possibilities in Oregon. Your best bet is to hook up with the folks in the local board shop and let them fill you in on the particulars.

Hoodoo Ski Area

Box 20, Highway 20
Sisters, OR 97759

Phone: (503) 822-3799
Fax: (503) 822-3398
Snowphone: (800) 949-LIFT
Elevation: base, 4,668'; top, 5,703'; vertical, 1,035'
Lifts: 3 chairs
Terrain Variety: 30% advanced, 40% intermediate, 30% beginner

The Season and Hours

The season at the Doo opens the day after Thanksgiving and continues through the beginning of April, as conditions permit. Day lifts run from 9:00 A.M. to 4:00 P.M., and the night session lasts until 10:00 P.M.

Lift Tickets

Day—Adult/Junior: $22/$16
Late day (1:00–4:00 P.M.)—Adult/Junior: $17/$12
Marathon (9:00 A.M.–10:00 P.M.)—Adult/Junior: $26/$19
Swing (1:00–10:00 P.M.)—Adult/Junior: $22/$16
Night (4:00–10:00 P.M.)—Adult/Junior: $14/$10

Specials

You can ride free from 9:00 to 10:00 A.M. every morning to check out conditions. If you decide to stay, just go buy a lift ticket when someone notices that you're untagged. If you're going to be on the mountain more than seven days in the course of the season, you should join Club Hoodoo. No ritualistic sacrifices required, just $65 for a membership that will save you $9 on every lift ticket.

Logistics

The mountain is located on Highway 20 just east of its intersection with Highway 22. From Eugene, take Highway 126 eighty-three miles east to Highway 20. From Salem, take Highway 22 eighty-two miles south to Highway 20.

The Local Scene

Hoodoo is a small, family-oriented area that's a local stop for residents of Sisters, Salem, and Eugene. Day-trippers from these towns make up the majority of people on the mountain. The local snowboarding scene hasn't really flourished in the shadow of Mt. Bachelor, but this might change over the next few years as the mountain starts to develop a snowboarding program. For now, there's the town of Sisters twenty miles away; it contains one of the highest ice-cream-parlor-per-resident ratios in the state, along with a quaint downtown area.

Where to Stay

A few of the local hotels offer lodging-and-lift packages. A stay at the **Best Western Ponderosa Lodge**, (509) 549-1234, includes free lift tickets Monday through Friday. At the **Black Butte Ranch**, (800) 452-7455, ask for their special winter ski packages. If you stay at the **Sisters Inn and Mt. Shadow RV Park**, (503) 549-STAY and (503) 549-PARK, you'll get weekday lift tickets at half price. Some other choices are the **Blue Lake Resort**, (503) 595-6671, and the **Metolius River Lodges**, (800) 595-6290.

The Mountain

Hoodoo's a small mountain that has yet to build a niche for snowboarders. In the works are a snowboard park and half-pipe with a surface lift, but until those materialize, the offerings for snowboarders remain somewhat limited. The flat spots when you turn right off the Manzanita chair might necessitate some foot-out skating. Also, a trip down the backside run of Crater will lead you through a hillside of manzanitas to a catch line where again you'll be skating. This said, there's some fun to be had on the mountain. The runs off the Green and Red chairs offer some good pitch and pockets of interesting terrain.

Freeriders

A cornice wraps around the top of the mountain off the Green chair, and if there's been fresh snow to cover up the bumps, a jump down into Grandstand lets you go big. Take a right off the chair to a stand of dead trees at the top of Dive, which usually holds some good snow. There's another wind lip off Mambo, with good trees below it. A number of lines down Powder Valley will lead to several rock jumps you can spot off the lift. The Red chair accesses some good steeps off Angel's Flight and Gripper, but the second half of the run is a tuck to the lift. Avoid Crater at all costs unless you like hiking through a waist-high manzanita meadow.

Cruisers

Alpine riders will find the groomed areas on Mambo and Dive good places to carve their turns. Beneath the Green chair, check out Red

Sno-Parking in Oregon

Here's the deal: if you want to park your car in a plowed parking lot at an Oregon resort, you have to pony up for a Sno-Park permit. An annual permit costs $9, a three-day one costs $2.50, and the one-day version runs $1.50. The signs that announce the requirement of a Sno-Park permit are generally small, covered with snow, and impossible to read when you've got a parking lot engineer wildly flapping his arms. The sign doesn't say much, really—just that permits are required. It doesn't tell you where to get one or how much they cost, if it's a joke they play on out-of-staters, or what.

Our first experience with the Sno-Park permit came in Ashland. We didn't see the sign and just assumed that we didn't have to pay to park outdoors in a blizzard with a quarter-mile walk in front of us. The Mt. Ashland parking lot "attendants" (you know, baked jibbers pretending to have jobs) didn't bother to warn us, either. It was snowing, and we hurried to the mountain. At the end of the day, though, a yellow piece of paper was stuck under the windshield wiper of the truck, and in an instant—an instant!—all the fun we'd had that day got converted to effusive musings about the wankers that populate the world. A $50 fine! We're not paying, but still. . . .

On the way out, we spotted the sign. It was caked with snow that the wind had plastered to it. When they extradite us from South America, where we live now, this will be the backbone of our defense.

So here's why we're not paying the ticket. Not long after the incident, we picked up the official *Oregon Sno-Park Permits* brochure distributed by the Drive and Motor Vehicle Services of the Department of Transportation. It states that parking without a Sno-Park permit "may result in a $10 fine," but in Ashland we received a form with a $50 fine already typed in as scheduled bail. We figure they use these pretyped forms to gouge out-of-staters. But just in case we end up doing hard time over this incident, a word to the wise: buy your durn Sno-Park permit.

Valley. Off the Red chair, GS Racecourse and Slalom Course are fall-line pitches where you can open it up.

Freestylers

There's a series of frontside hits (regular-footed) on the wall coming down Backroad off the Green chair. The run is a traverse of a cat track, but if you keep your speed up you can have a good time working the hits. Until the park and pipe are built, work the hits under the Green chair and through the trees between Green and Manzanita.

Grommets

The runs off the Manzanita chair offer the best beginners' terrain. No snowboard learning program is in place yet, but the terrain on this mountain is well suited to people getting started on a board.

Nonbelievers

Skiers and pinheads will feel perfectly at home on the mountain. A large Nordic facility includes 15.8 kilometers of trails. Otherwise, Hoodoo is close to a number of stunning peaks, including the Three Sisters, Mt. Jefferson, and Mt. Washington.

Mt. Ashland

P.O. Box 220
Ashland, OR 97520

Phone: (503) 482-2897
Fax: (503) 482-3644
Snowphone: (503) 482-2754 (Ashland/Medford); (916) 221-7669 (Redding)
Elevation: base, 6,350'; top, 7,500'; vertical, 1,150'
Lifts: 4 chairs
Terrain Variety: 50% advanced, 35% intermediate, 15% beginner

The Season and Hours

Daily operations begin November 23 and go through April 2, after which the area opens on weekends only through April 16. The hours are 9:00 A.M.–4:00 P.M., with night boarding available off the Sonnet chair from 4:00 to 10:00 P.M.

Lift Tickets

Weekend—Adult/Senior/Child: $24/$16/$16
Weekday—Adult/Senior/Child: $16/$12/$12
Night—$12

MT. ASHLAND

EL. - 7,500'

Base Elevation - 6,350'

ARIEL DOUBLE

WINDSOR DOUBLE

COMER TRIPLE

SONNET

RUNS

1. South Side
2. The Bowl
3. Cornice
4. Upper Balcony
5. Lower Balcony
6. Ado
7. Juliet
8. Romeo
9. Bottom
10. Avon
11. Tempest
12. Winter
13. Upper Dream
14. Pistol
15. Dream
16. Caliban
17. Rodger's Way
18. All's Well
19. Betwixt
20. The Void

Specials

Ashland has special days when you get dollars off your lift ticket by dressing up funny—like a cowboy, or a character out of one of Shakespeare's plays. The baggy clothes favored by some riders can possibly be passed off as rodeo clown garb. In a pinch, tell the counterperson that your funky hat is reminiscent of Yorick, the king's jester in *Hamlet*.

Logistics

About five miles south of Ashland on I-5, take the Mt. Ashland exit (exit 6) and follow the signs eight miles to the mountain.

The Local Scene

Mt. Ashland is owned by the city of Ashland and operated by a non-profit management group. What results is a big family playground for central Oregon, where the feeling is relaxed and friendly. Ashland's claim to fame is its ongoing Shakespeare Festival, and in this spirit the lifts and runs are named for characters from Shakespeare's plays. Likewise, the architecture of the main lodge is based on some dysfunctional Elizabethan floor plan. Most of the local boarders reside in Ashland or Medford. The mountain hosts half-pipe and GS events, and the snowboarding scene is active and friendly.

Where to Stay

If you arrive in Ashland before mid-February, when the Shakespeare cycle starts up, you're in for some good off-season rates. Even afterwards, the city is geared up for tourism and most room rates are very reasonable. Call the **Southwest Oregon Reservation Service** at (800) 547-8052 and ask for a See and Ski package—a special rate that includes lift tickets and lodging.

Tell a Skier

'Tis better to be vile than vile esteem'd,
When not to be receives reproach of being,
And the just pleasure lost, which is so deem'd
Not by our feeling, but by others' seeing.
For why should others' false adulterate eyes
Give salutation to my sportive blood?

Shakespeare, "Sonnet 121"

The Mountain

The mountain is small by most standards, but there's such a wealth of terrain that every boarder will have a good time. A nice steep bowl with a fat wind lip, tree runs, and good cruiser territory are spread out over the mountain.

Freeriders

Freeriders will want to take a few plunges into the Bowl off the Ariel chair when it's open. A huge drop-off on top makes a perfect launching pad, and after a dump you can almost land on your head with no worries. But try not to land on your head. The Bowl has four main chutes that lead down around a cliff band, and quite a few different lines are available. Off the Ariel chair you'll find all sorts of trees to bounce through and hits sprinkled throughout. As you get farther down, the trees become more and more like car wash, so you may want to duck out midway down. The backside, aptly named South Side, contains nothing but goods. Wind-shaped lips and bumps are everywhere you look; they lead to the second parking lot, so it's a good run before lunch or at the end of the day.

Cruisers

Mt. Ashland doesn't have any flat spots, and the consistent pitch is great for cruisers. Avoid the run underneath the Ariel chair, which tends to get bumped out pretty quickly. Romeo, Winter, and Tempest are all good bets. The only downside is that if you're committed to staying on the groomed runs, you're going to feel like a twilight-zone victim after cruising the same runs over and over and over again.

Freestylers

Mt. Ashland has a natural terrain park in the Balcony. Here, the wind shapes a series of benches, rollers, and gaps that serve as perfect ramps and kickers. There's ample opportunity to go big, but check the landings first to make sure you're not flying into a procession of wind troughs. For more consistent landings, try the terrain park between the Romeo and Juliet runs that includes a half-pipe and some nice hits.

Grommets

The Snowboard Beginner package ($30) includes equipment rental, use of the Sonnet chair, and lesson. The Sonnet chair services a section of the mountain set aside for beginners.

Nonbelievers

Mt. Ashland has the feel of a neighborhood park, and skiers and snowboarders enjoy the mountain as much as families getting together for a barbecue. Ashland itself is a fine place for nonskiers to hang out; during the Shakespeare Festival, those with a cultural yearning can gorge on contemporary plays and Shakespearean classics.

Mt. Bachelor

P.O. Box 1031
Bend, OR 97709

Phone: (800) 829-2442, (503) 382-2607
Fax: (503) 382-4251
Snow and Activity Phone: (503) 382-7888
Elevation: base, 5,965'; top, 9,065'; vertical, 3,100'
Lifts: 6 express quads (3 triples, 1 double, 2 surface) covering 3,448 acres
(longest run 2 miles)
Terrain Variety: 25% expert, 35% advanced, 25% intermediate, 15% beginner

The Season and Hours

Bachelor receives an annual snowfall of 325 inches and traditionally
operates from early November through April. Camps and clinics are
offered through May.

Lift Tickets

All day—Adult/Youth (7–12)/Child: $33/$18/Free
Alpine point tickets: 200 points, $35; 400 points, $69

Point tickets are aimed at boarders and skiers who expect to put in
some short days, who prefer to get a late start, or who like to do only a
few runs during the day. Every time you ride a lift, some of your
points are deducted (for hard-core, skip-lunch riders, point tickets
aren't the answer). Multiday tickets are also available.

Specials

You can park your car in Bend, at the corner of Colorado and Simpson
avenues, and ride a free shuttle bus that runs all day to and from the
mountain (about twenty minutes away). Weeklong **High Cascade
Snowboard Camps**, (800) 334-4272, including adults-only and
women-only sessions, are offered several times during the season.

Logistics

Air service is provided by **United Express** and **Horizon Air** from
Seattle, Portland, and San Francisco to Redmond, about thirty minutes
north of Bend. By car, Bachelor is 162 miles from Portland. Drive
south on I-5 and take Highway 126 to Sisters; from there, take Highway 20 to Bend and follow the signs to Bachelor.

The Local Scene

Bachelor is a big upside-down snow cone that's the nexus of Oregon's
snowboarding scene as much as its geographic center. In 1990 there

MT. BACHELOR

EL. - 9,065'

Base Elevation - 5,965'

NORTHWEST EXPRESS (PLANNED)

OUTBACK EXPRESS

RED CHAIR

PINE MARTEN EXPRESS

SUNSHINE ACCELERATOR

SUMMIT EXPRESS

SKYLINER EXPRESS

SUNRISE EXPRESS

RAINBOW CHAIR

RUNS

1. Cow's Face
2. Beverly Hills
3. The Cirque
4. West Ridge
5. Flying Dutchman
6. Carnival
7. Cliffhanger
8. Dsq
9. Coffee
10. Canyon
11. Tippy Toe
12. Grotto
13. Leeway
14. Cinder Cone
15. Down Under
16. Boomerang
17. Kangaroo
18. Bushwacker
19. Summit Crossover
20. Chutes

were only two snowboarding shops in Bend (the nearest town to Bachelor), and Bend itself was just going through the first growing pains that come with a resort's sudden discovery as a snowy Shangri-la. The outskirts of Bend are leapfrogging into the ponderosa, with new malls, fast-food rows, condos, and all the other blights of human invasion. Now there are at least six full-blown board shops, all within a minute of each other on Century Drive.

Where to Stay

Call the **Central Oregon Recreation Association** at (800) 800-8334 to find out about good deals and to get its area recreation guide. One excellent spot is the **Mill Inn**, a bed-and-breakfast on the southwest side of Bend at 642 Northwest Colorado. From here, you're a short walk to the free shuttle bus that services the mountain, as well as within walking distance of the old downtown. They've even got a tuning bench for waxing your boards. A bunk room ($20 per person) is perfect for riders on a budget. Call (503) 389-9198 to put your name on a bunk.

Tell Your Friends

Without a doubt, the best eating and drinking deal in Bend—perhaps at any ski resort on the West Coast—is the **Deschutes Brewery and Public House** at 1044 Bond Street in the old downtown. We're talking massive burgers and fries ($3.50) and first-rate home-brewed lagers and ales on tap in numerous regular and seasonal flavors. The veggie burger and other meatless stuff is fine, too. This is an après-ski and locals' hangout and it packs to the rafters. If you're not there early, expect to quaff a Bachelor Bitter or a Broken Top Bock before your table opens up.

The Mountain

Despite Bend's malignant growth rate, Mt. Bachelor is still a big sweet mountain with a small-town feel. It's a dormant volcano in the Cascade chain, like Shasta and Hood, but unlike at those mountains, the lifts aren't confined to hilly shoulders far off Vulcan's throne. On those relatively rare days of calm on Bachelor, you can ride all the way to the 9,065-foot peak on the Summit Express quad, which provides a 360-degree vista of the surroundings and a virtually unlimited number of possible descents down the cone. Just north of Bachelor, the Three Sisters and Broken Top inspire dreams of epic days on untracked avalanche chutes and treeless volcanic craters. On the more common storm days, the trees on the lower half of the mountain provide shelter and a more secluded kind of happiness.

While the Summit Express is key to fully experiencing Mt. Bachelor, it's often on "weather hold." The good news is that the Ski Patrol is aggressive about getting it open during any break in the conditions. Be forewarned, however, that the Summit Express is the only lift we've ever seen where you're required to wear a hood or a hat. They're serious. No hat, no summit.

Freeriders

Bachelor is a freeriders' paradise. It's defined by big bowls cascading into eminently rideable tree glades. All along the edges of the bowls and through the glades are hits, drops, and powder pockets that will provide the freshie for days after a dump.

Cow's Face, on the east side of the cone, is a giant powder field dimpled by wind lips, gullies, and quarter-pipes; it's best after a good dump since high winds tend to wipe it bare. The frontside Cirque Bowl is the old north-facing crater of the volcano. It offers by far the steepest terrain on the mountain, including the only double-black chutes. After a good snow, when the bowl opens up, steep freaks will make the short climb to the peak from the top of the Summit chair and leap into this giant milk bowl. By traversing west across the crater, you'll reach a huge wind lip that offers unbeatable airs when the snow and the wind cooperate. On some days the wind blows so hard across the bowl that snow chunks the size of poodles go ripping across this ledge.

There are two ways to get to the western backside of Bachelor. First, when the Ski Patrol deems it safe, you can hike from the Summit Express across Bachelor's lunar peak to its western ridge and drop in. This is the most exposed, wind-blasted part of the whole mountain, and the top several hundred yards are often studded with knife-edged death cookies. Once you're past this gauntlet, Bachelor's best lies below. Big powder bowls and chutes are set off by wind lips and rolls. You'll often find quarter-pipes and natural kickers with perfect landings. As you enter the tree-lined lower half of the mountain, acres of untouched gullies that drain through the glades await you. If you find other people in here, they're almost sure to be boarders; this is terrain where few skiers dare to tread. To get out of the trees, you'll have to time your right turn to beat the catch line at the mountain's boundary. If you get it right, you'll end your three-thousand-foot descent right at the Outback Express chair.

Second, some of the best outback terrain is reachable by traversing hard to the west when you get off the Outback chair. If you want the whole mountain run, though, you'll have to make the long cat-track traverse back to the Summit Express. A Northwest Express quad is supposed to be installed to open up a vast swath of this backside tree terrain on Bachelor, but we hope it doesn't bring an end to raging days in undiscovered powder and trees. If Bachelor's managers have the boarders' interests at heart, they'll minimize the clear-cuts and leave this gorgeous area as wilderness terrain for good snow days.

There are miles of untracked terrain straight off the backside of Bachelor, but boarders beware: you'll pay for your epic powder run with a hellacious hike out on the backside catch line. This is definitely more of a travail than a traverse and, while Bachelor's management doesn't like to talk about it, many lost souls have had themselves rescued by the Ski Patrol back here. Anytime after a recent snow, the west-side trees are definitely a better bet.

Cruisers

Bachelor has some sixty named runs, most of which are precision-ground corduroy. Six high-speed quads guarantee top-to-bottom turns with a minimum of rest in between. The longest intermediate runs are down the Outback side, including Kangaroo and Down Under, while Healy Heights off the Summit Express is the widest, fastest groomed run on the mountain. Except for the permanent NASTAR course under the Yellow chair, we try to stay clear of the cruiser runs under Pine Marten just to avoid the crowd of out-of-control beginners near the base.

Freestylers

Bachelor hosts numerous snowboarding events (it was the kickoff site for the 1995 FIS Snowboard World Cup), and the Rattlesnake Park terrain garden is in a constant state of evolution and modification to meet the demands of freestyle events. The Rainbow chair, a slow double farthest to the east, is the secret hit lift. A natural whoop-de-do half-pipe in a creek bed, fallen trees, and lots of big humps and mounds lurk in the woods off the Flying Dutchman and Roostertail runs. Watch for the fat camel's hump halfway down the Carnival run.

Grommets

Bachelor aggressively pursues the beginners' market; a beginners' board-ticket-lesson package is $50. The rental shop has over three hundred boards, but that's not a huge number considering the size of the mountain. Rentals from the shops in Bend may prove a better deal, especially for multiple days if you're not a beginner. Lessons are taught on the Home Run hill near the West Village lodge, while new boarders working on their skills will want to check out Skyliner under the Skyline Express chair and the long Leeway run that winds down from the Pine Marten Express past Bachelor's baby cinder cone. Intermediate runs are everywhere on the lower mountain.

Nonbelievers

Bachelor's big on family business: it has eight day lodges, day care for up to 120 kids (reservations recommended), snow play and lessons for kids as young as three, a really massive eight-thousand-square-foot retail shop, and packages for all levels of skiers. Since the mountain is served continuously by the free shuttle to and from Bend, nonskiers in spring can conveniently bail down the mountain for a round of golf on one of Bend's countless courses.

Mt. Bailey Snowcats

Mt. Bailey Snowcats
Diamond Lake, OR 97731

Phone: (800) 733-7593
Elevation: base, 5,400'; top, 8,363'; vertical, 2,963'
Terrain Variety: advanced intermediate to expert

The Season and Hours

Mt. Bailey Snowcats operates from November through April, depending on conditions and interest. You have to be there to meet the cat crew and guides well before dawn, and the cat will run all day, or until you've logged your fifteen thousand feet.

Cost

A one-day pass is $160 and a two-day package that includes meals and lodging runs $422. Three- and five-day packages are also available for $609 and $905 respectively (meals and lodging included). The snowcat carries a maximum of twelve riders and needs a minimum of six to go out. The Bailey operation is in the process of integrating a newer, faster snowcat, which will help move boarders up the mountain. Once the new cat is phased in, Bailey's price structure will change to guarantee fifteen thousand vertical feet, with everyone pitching in for extra rides. Given the small capacity of the current operation, you need to call at least a month in advance to make reservations.

A day on Bailey is costly, but it's far cheaper than the $500 a day you'll pay to go heli boarding. At any rate, it's hard to put a price on an awesome mountain of totally untracked powder.

Logistics

Diamond Lake Resort, the starting point for a Bailey day, is about seven miles from the northern entrance to Crater Lake National Park. To get there from Medford, drive seventy-five miles via Highway 62 and Highway 230 and go north a few miles on Highway 138. The resort is about one hundred miles from Bend, but be forewarned that Highway 97 is an infamous speed trap. Air travel is available to the Bend/Redmond airport with an Amtrak link to Chemult, but you may be better off renting a car in Redmond and driving.

Right Place, Right Time

By the time you read this, Bailey may be two years from becoming a major ski resort, with lifts, lodges, grooming machines, ski patrols, boundary lines, ski bums—you name it. Today it's just a mountain, with a snowcat, a "road" to the summit, a couple of guides, some wide-open snowfields and bowls, plenty of trees, and a bunch of avalanche chutes.

About once a season fate smiles and you find yourself with fresh powder, blue skies, and no crowds. When we arrived in the premorning dark, we could not have declared that we'd found the promised land. Hordes of snowmobiles were parked outside the Diamond Lake Lodge. The place looked like a biker bar where every Harley just happened to be on skids. After plunking down 160 beans, the day's contingent departed in a van to the takeoff spot. Here we were handed an avalanche beeper with a brief explanation on how to use it. Then we all piled into the snowcat and headed out on one of the three-hundred-odd miles of snowmobile trails maintained by the Diamond Lake Resort.

Our particular snowmobile track had been rated one of the best in Oregon for a reason—it took us more or less straight to the top of Mt. Bailey, offering a knockout view of the Cascades in every direction. During the day, we took turns riding up front in the warm cab of the snowcat. The driver, a boarder named Scott, was quick to point out that as the cat lumbered up and over the tree line, the landscape changed from forest to moonscape, with rocks and ice wind blasted into eerie white monsters. "Kind of spooky, you know, but cool" was how he described it.

The final hundred feet of the ascent culminated in a stomach-twisting crawl onto the picnic-bench-sized peak. From here, we got a jaw-dropping look at what lay in store for the rest of the day. The mountain falls away in every direction—and virtually all of it is rideable, even the aptly named Avalanche Chute, which drops on a continuous forty-five-degree slope for over two thousand vertical feet.

When you are in the right place at the right time, you know it. The sky was ice blue, the air was still, and Oz was shaking his head and grinning. It had dumped about eighteen inches over the last two days, and the snow was the dry champagne powder that makes the eastern Cascades a place to be revered.

Rick "Oz" Oswald is the head of the snowcat operation and the lead guide on the mountain. On the first run of the day, Oz led us down one of the easier chutes in order to evaluate everyone's skill level and decide where the rest of the day would happen. About midway

The Local Scene

Diamond Lake Resort caters primarily to snowmachiners during the winter, so you'll be sharing your space with lots of biker types and a small crowd of older locals. There aren't any snowboarders who hang out here, with the exception of one or two of the snowcat drivers. The average Bailey cat rider is a middle-aged businessman from Seattle or Portland looking for the best powder money can buy close to home. The restaurant at the lodge serves good, big food with average resort prices, and the bar where everyone gathers after a hard day's boarding

down, instead of cutting toward a shallower pitch, Oz decided we were all ready to rock, so he took a right turn and led us into a steep tree-lined chute. Grins abounded. We were into the goods.

Every time we came to a new chute that posed a threat of a slide, Oz or our other guide, Neil, would make the first run to cut the face. A couple of times, Oz gave us strict instructions to hold up behind him, and proceeded to lob a stick of dynamite over the edge, while we stood there with hands over our ears and mouths gaping wide. With one bomb he let loose a small-but-respectable slide, reminding everybody that soft fluffy snow isn't quite so innocuous as it seems. During the cat rides he told us about the four slides he'd been caught in, and how his beacon and a buddy had come into play in a couple. When a few of us stopped at the bottom of an avalanche path to watch the others come down, he told us this wasn't a good idea. Oz was looking out for us. We were glad he was there.

Now don't think that Mt. Bailey is all about logistics and precautions. Most of the day we flew down huge snowfields, brought on ice-cream headaches in insanely steep chutes full of dry powder, launched off of cornices and wind drifts, and snaked our way through the old-growth trees. The sensation of riding through totally untouched deep powder

with only a handful of other people on the mountain is hard to describe, but impossible to forget.

At the end of every run, we hit a catch-line trail. This was a long traverse with a significant number of flats and small uphills. It's unofficially mandatory that you carry collapsible backcountry ski poles for pushing through the flats. We neglected to bring these and had to borrow regular poles from our guides to manage the traverse, which was not an optimal setup. The catch line brings you back to a warming hut at the end of every run and a big lunch at midday.

During our day, we logged about fourteen thousand vertical feet, but the excitement of private untracked powder made it feel like twice that, and left us all groping for the oxygen bottle.

The master plan for Mt. Bailey calls for a major resort, starting with a few lifts and eventually working up to a Mt. Bachelor–style full-service operation. The plan hinges on the whims of the Forest Service and on public opinion, which currently frowns on clear-cuts, resort building on mountaintops, and potential threats to Diamond Lake's water table. In fact, no new resort has been built on U.S. National Forest land in over fifteen years.

We recommend getting to Bailey before any of these proposed changes come to pass. You and the mountain may never be the same.

is a good place to get a draft. Otherwise, things here are pretty quiet; only sixty-five people live in Diamond Lake year-round.

Where to Stay

The **Diamond Lake Resort** is about it. Rates are similar to what you'd find in Medford or Bend and you don't have to be on the road by 4:00 A.M., as you would if you were leaving from one of those places.

Safety Talk

As with any responsible backcountry operation, you'll get a brief lesson on the use of the avalanche transceiver you're issued at the start of the day. You'll also be told to follow your guide's instructions. Other than that, you're expected to use your head and watch out for unmarked obstacles (that is, *all* obstacles), to ride all the way into the big trees at the bottom of avalanche chutes, and to exercise a certain degree of common sense. One unusual hazard is the "hot hole"—you should resist the temptation to jump over these volcanic steam vents that pock the mountain's surface. Other than that, you've got a whole mountain of unrestricted, unmolested terrain to explore.

Things to Know

Bring collapsible poles! While a day on Bailey is boarder heaven, it can be the opposite if you're not prepared for the catch-line traverse at the bottom. We can't emphasize enough how big a help the ski poles are for this. You'll find that fifteen thousand feet of vertical feel more like forty thousand feet if you have to skate the traverse track without any upper-body help. We also recommend bringing a camera. The view from Bailey's summit is tremendous, and you'll rarely get a better chance at great shots of your friends making first tracks.

The Mountain

Bailey is a big, juicy volcano with rideable terrain over nearly 360 degrees of its cone. With a bald top and trees ringing the lower half, it looks and feels quite a bit like nearby Mt. Bachelor, except that on an average day on Bailey, you're sharing the mountain with only a dozen other human beings, a few mutant semihuman snowmobilers, and an endless dream of untouched powder. The mountain gets as much or more snow than any other mountain in Oregon, and there's almost no one to take advantage of it.

Bailey can be roughly divided into three areas. The *face* is a wall of steeps that drops into a massive natural bowl. The *chutes* are a series of avalanche gullies—with names such as Parachute, Devil's Drop, Refrigerator Door, and the Magnificent Seven—that fan out across the northwest slope. (Rumor has it that with the proper tip to the guide, you can get one of the chutes named after your group.) The south side's avalanche *bowl* is a twenty-five-hundred-foot, forty-five-degree face flanked by long, rolling tree glades and ridges. The lower half of the mountain drops into dense forest where snowboarders on gunny powder boards will have to be on their toes to snake through the tight trees.

Intermediate riders would have a good time here, but unless you're with a group of like-minded riders, you may have a hard time keeping up. On the other hand, riders intimidated by Bailey's terrain could easily take the cat up and ride down on the untracked powder next to the road to meet up with the rest of the group at the bottom. In general, however, if you're not an advanced or expert rider, you probably won't get your money's worth out of a Bailey day.

Freeriders

Bring your powder board—but leave the Mutumbo-sized Dough Boy at home or you'll have serious trouble negotiating the tight trees at the base.

Cruisers

Be warned that hard boots will transform the catch-trail traverse from a headache into a migraine.

Freestylers

There are no half-pipes or terrain parks here, but natural hits are everywhere. Bonkers with sawed-off trick boards should consider renting or borrowing a good-sized board to keep their speed up in the pow. And leave the plumber's-crack pants at home—you'll be swimming through pow all day, so dress for it.

Grommets

Bailey's no place for beginners. To have a good time here, you have to be comfortable in deep powder, steep steeps, and tight trees—sometimes all three at once. If part of your clan is hell-bent for Bailey, have them drop you off at Mt. Ashland or Mt. Bachelor, work on your turns, and save your snowcat money for next year.

Nonbelievers

Skiers can borrow a pair of Bailey's fat-boys, which make all the difference for negotiating the mountain's powder. Capable powder skiers will have almost as much fun as boarders here. Alternative adventures in the area include a trip to Crater Lake or a snowmobile tour, which the folks at the Diamond Lake Resort will be happy to arrange for a fee.

Mt. Hood Meadows

P.O. Box 470, Highway 35
Mt. Hood, OR 97041-0470

Phone: (503) 337-2222
Snowphone: (503) 227-SNOW
Elevation: base, 4,523'; top, 7,300'; vertical, 2,777'
Lifts: 9 lifts (2 high-speed quads)
Terrain Variety: 35% advanced, 50% intermediate, 15% beginner

The Season and Hours

You can ride Meadows from mid-November through mid-May, with
the lifts opening at 9:00 A.M. and running until 4:00 P.M. on Mondays
and Tuesdays. The rest of the week, you can ride until 10:00 P.M. on
the twenty runs lit for night skiing. The Mt. Hood Express is the
Northwest's only night-operating high-speed quad—which moves
night boarding a little closer to a good idea.

Lift Tickets

Shift (9:00 A.M.–4:00 P.M., 11:00 A.M.–7:00 P.M., or 1:00–10:00 P.M.): $32
Night: $14
Half day (12:00–4:00 P.M.): $27
Child (6 and under): $6
Junior (7–12) or Senior (65+): $20

Specials

The shift tickets sound like work, but they actually help maximize
your dollars and time on the snow. You can find probably the best
snowcat deal in the nation at the top of the Cascade chair. For $12 a
ride, or five trips for $50, you add 1,020 vertical feet to the mountain
and gain access to the steeps and powder bowls of Upper Heather
Canyon. You purchase tickets at the top of the Cascade chair, but call
first to see if the cat is running—weather and snow conditions pro-
hibit operations a lot of the time.

Logistics, the Local Scene, Where to Stay

See the Mt. Hood Mystique sidebar on page 92.

The Mountain

Mt. Hood Meadows resort at Mt. Hood offers the most area, best
steeps, and greatest diversity of terrain on the volcano. The main face,
a big bowl with runs separated by glades, is serviced by the Mt. Hood

MT. HOOD MEADOWS

EL. - 7,300'

Base Elevation - 4,523'

SNOWCAT SUPERBOWL

SHOOTING STAR CHAIR

HOOD RIVER MEADOWS

YELLOW CHAIR

MT. HOOD EXPRESS

BLUE CHAIR

CASCADE EXPRESS

DAISY

BUTTERCUP

RED CHAIR

RUNS

1. Texas Trails
2. Boulevard
3. Marmot Ridge
4. Arena
5. Excitable Boy
6. Upper Elevator
7. Outer Limits
8. Andromeda Bowl
9. Chunky Swirly
10. South Canyon
11. Fire Weed
12. Four Bowl
13. Waterfall
14. Upper Face
15. Jacob's Ladder
16. Powder Keg
17. Ram's Head
18. Titan
19. Kinnickinick
20. Outrigger

The Mt. Hood Mystique

Want to ride powder in June? You can do it at Mt. Hood. Hood receives three to four hundred inches of snow annually, and being the highest of the Cascade peaks at eleven thousand feet, its upper snowfields remain year-round. The mountain also lies within sixty miles of Portland, so during the winter it's the destination of most urbanites. Mt. Hood's reputation has grown over the years, mostly owing to its summer activities. Beginning in June, throngs of out-of-school snowboarders descend on Government Camp and Timberline to receive instruction in the holy art of snowboarding.

Logistics

Mt. Hood sits an hour east of Portland. If you're traveling from the north, take I-5 to I-205 just north of Vancouver, Washington, cross the Columbia River, and take I-84 east to exit 64 in Hood River. Follow Highway 35 thirty-six miles to Mt. Hood Meadows, or continue on to the intersection with Highway 26 about six miles down the road. You'll find Mt. Hood SkiBowl at this intersection. If you continue through Government Camp on Highway 26, you'll see the signs for Timberline in about five miles. When you're approaching the mountain from the south, take I-205 to Highway 26. Go though the towns of Gresham, Sandy, Brightwood, Zigzag, and Rhododendron (the last four are possible lodging opportunities) on the way to Government Camp.

The Local Scene

Government Camp, or Govy, is the small town at the base of the mountain where you'll find food, lodging, and nightlife. Don't go there expecting the glitz and big crowds of a resort destination—Govy has three bars, a few restaurants, and a couple of stop signs.

If you're of legal age, you may want to check out the Rathskeller, which claims most of the local snowboarders' business. There's no sign above the door, but it's across the street from Charlie's, the other bar in the neighborhood where an "older" crowd hangs out. At the Rathskeller, you'll find a battered but functional foosball table, two pool tables where you pay a quarter to play, a propane kiln of a heater, a couple of fireplaces, pitchers of good beer, and food. On Tuesday nights they hold a pool tournament starting about 8:30 or 9:00 where two dollars gets you into a single-elimination, winner-take-all contest. Mt. Hood Brewing Co., located next to the Mt. Hood Inn, attracts an upper-scale crowd and serves six of its own malted barley creations, as well as moderately priced bar food. A stay in Govy isn't complete without a malt or stack of pancakes at Huckleberry's, the only twenty-four-hour eatery in town.

Where to Stay

You'll find the best deal in town at Huckleberry's, (503) 272-3325, in the middle of Government Camp, where standard rooms that sleep one to six people start at $45. The Mt. Hood Inn also offers a dorm-style facility that sleeps groups of up to fourteen. Some other Govy lodgings are:

England's Lodging, (503) 272-3350

Falcon's Crest Inn, (800) 624-7384

Mt. Hood Inn, (800) 443-7777

Mt. Hood Manor, (800) 514-3440

Palmer Lodge, (800) 575-4464

Summit Meadows Cabins, (503) 272-3494

Thunderhead Lodge,
(800) 859-8493

Timberline Lodge, (800) 547-1406

Trillum Lake Basin Cabins,
(503) 272-0151

Trollhaugen, (503) 272-3223

View House, (503) 272-3295

As you drive down the hill, you'll find that the prices per night go down as well. It's all a big *Psycho* flashback as you pass these places:

Boulder Creek Retreat, Brightwood,
(503) 655-3491

Brightwood Guesthouse, Brightwood, (503) 622-5783

Cedar Grove Cottage, Welches,
(503) 557-8292

Doublegate Inn B&B, Welches,
(503) 622-4859

Fernwood at Alder Creek, Sandy,
(503) 622-3570

Mountain House, Welches,
(503) 622-5155

Mt. Hood Village—Oregon's Finest
Public Campground, Welches,
(503) 622-4011

Old Welches Inn B&B,
(503) 622-3754

Resort at the Mountain, Welches,
(800) 622-3101

Shamrock Motel Inn, Sandy,
(503) 622-4911

Snowline Motel, Rhododendron,
(503) 622-3137

Udderly Heaven, Zigzag,
(503) 296-8400

If you're looking to rent a house or cabin for a few days, contact these folks:

Cascade Property Management,
Welches, (503) 622-5688

Mountain Retreats, Welches,
(503) 622-3212

Mt. Hood Leisure Country, Inc.,
Welches, (800) 625-4042

Summer at Hood

Mt. Hood has become an international mecca for summer snowboard training. Palmer snowfield at Timberline attracts a handful of hard-core alpine riders and hordes of freestylers lining up to session the pipes and parks. Photographers congregate to document the events, and the crowds flock to the hits where they're stationed. The most asked question is, "Are you from Transworld?" Camera crews gather footage for snowboarding videos and shampoo commercials.

The source of this carnivalesque atmosphere can be linked directly to the four summer camps being conducted on the snowfield. In addition to building pipes and hits and putting a couple of hundred riders on the snow, the camps bring up the pros, the biggies, the heroes-to-all-groms, who are on hand to give instruction or make a guest appearance way up in the air. Their presence hypes everyone up—campers, photographers, Ski Patrol—and in the ensuing infection, you'll see riders being all they can be and more. The camps also provide an off-snow circus that includes trampoline training, skate ramps, wakeboarding, paintball, and more.

The Palmer chair at Timberline is open to more than just camp participants, and if you're in the area and needing to get on the snow, the opportunity awaits you. The morning snow is firm and groomed, nice for carving, especially when your edges have some bite to them. As the sun warms things up, the snow gets soft. By afternoon it's either forgiving or slushy, depending on the weather, and this is the best time of the day to practice your freestyle moves.

(continued on next page)

If you can raise the required cash to attend a snowboard camp, you're guaranteed to improve your skills. Each of the camps listed below lines up pro riders as instructors, and even more world-famous personages make guest appearances from time to time. Here's the info that will get you started on the ultimate summer camp experience:

High Cascade Snowboard Camps, P.O. Box 6622, Bend, OR 97708. Phone: (800) 334-4272; fax: (503) 389-6371. The camp costs $950 for an eight-day session and $1,165 for a ten-day adventure. Prices include lodging, meals, instruction, and off-snow fun. There are lots of big-name pro instructors, along with off-snow paintball, mountain biking, and a water park. High Cascade also offers an adult snowboard camp for those over twenty-one years of age, and a women-only camp. Both are held at Mt. Bachelor during early and late spring.

Mt. Hood Snowboard Camp, 4457 Southeast Wynnwood Drive, Hillsboro, OR 97123. Phone: (503) 693-6725; (800) 247-5552 (brochure). The camp owns its own hotel, a fortress in Rhododendron right across from the Dairy Queen. Among the attractions are half-pipes, racecourses, a park, and off-snow activities that include skateboarding, river surfing, and hot tubbing among others. Call for prices.

United States Snowboard Training Center Snowboard Camp, P.O. Box 360, Brightwood, OR 97011. Phone: (800) 325-4430. This camp runs $895 for an eight-day session and is geared toward the serious competing rider. Campers receive technical instruction in both gate and freestyle events. In August the camp goes international, with camps in Santiago, Chile, and Wanaka, New Zealand. The price might go up for these expatriate sessions.

Windell's Shred the World Snowboard Camp, P.O. Box 628, Welches, OR 97067. Phone: (800) 765-7669. For $850 you buy an eight-day session with mega on- and off-snow activities. The park at Windell's includes half-pipes, spines, tabletops, a twenty-two-foot mailbox, rails, fun boxes, picnic tables, and a sound system.

Express, one of two high-speed quads. You'll find that the express chairs are where the crowds are, so you'll want to spend some time exploring the canyons serviced by the Shooting Star and Hood River Meadows chairs—the terrain is comparable, but the areas usually don't get zooed out.

The other detachable chair is the Cascade Express, which opens up the upper mountain. This chair frequently remains on weather hold because of wind and avalanche danger, but when it runs it gives riders access to the best terrain on the mountain. If it's closed when you arrive, ask for a status report every time you ride a chair, and when it opens, make a run for it.

Because of its numerous canyons, gullies, ridges, and chutes, Meadows is a natural snowboarder's playground. You'll find that most of the locals list this as their favorite spot to ride.

Freeriders

Freeriders will find their heart's content of terrain at Meadows. When the top is open, you're into the goods. The runs we recommend off the Cascade Express include a jump off the Cornice, which lies off the Texas Trails run; a run through the wind lips between Boulevard and Gulch; Upper Elevator (many nice rocks); and, of course, Heather Canyon, which offers steeps, wind lips, big rock drops, and a good accumulation of powder. At the bottom of the Canyon, you'll hit a series of creeks and gullies whose hips offer some fine launching pads. Before you head down Heather, though, take note that once you're in, you're committed to riding to the bottom, which includes a painful traverse down the Heather run-out. You'll end up at the Hood River Meadows chair, which has some tight tree runs and good pitch in all but a few spots.

You can find more trees by dropping into Shooting Star Canyon off Discovery. Here, you're able to make three or four turns on the wall before you hit the easy-cruising zone that leads back to the lift. The main face, serviced by the Mt. Hood Express, contains good steeps, trees, and hits along the borders. You can find rock jumps in Bowls 2–5. There are some gullies that a little exploration will reveal between Middle Fork and North Canyon. And if you've got an extra twelve bucks, it's well spent on a snowcat ride to Upper Heather.

Cruisers

On the lower mountain, alpinists will want to session the Hood River Meadows chair. The runs are groomed leg-burners, and when the morning sun hits them you can really open it up. When the upper mountain opens, Boulevard is a crowded yet well-groomed choice. Other places to lay out some turns are Breeze Way, Powder Keg, and Middle Fork on the main face.

Freestylers

To find what is probably the best hit run, turn left going off the Mt. Hood Express lift and come down Chunky Swirly, where you'll find hits and kickers to session. The run leads to South Canyon, where in the trees you are guaranteed to find some good launching pads complete with landings.

Meadows has constructed a half-pipe off the Red chair in the beginners' meadow. Because of the amount of snow the mountain receives, the walls are usually built up and ready for you to go big. The real fun, though, can be found in the hits spread out over the mountain. The wind lips off Boulevard on the upper mountain form a natural snowboard park. The wind lips, gaps, and drops off Catacombs also offer plenty of opportunity for play. There are rock hits in the bowls on the main face, as well as in the trees between the Mt. Hood Express and the Yellow chair.

Grommets

A learn-to-ride package ($40) covers a ninety-minute lesson, rentals, and a lift ticket that allows you to session the runs off the Buttercup chair all day long. Afterwards, you can tell your friends how Buttercup was going off.

Nonbelievers

Meadows promotes its thousands of acres of intermediate trails as what its skiers enjoy most. Add to that fifteen kilometers of groomed Nordic trails, an adaptive ski school, and NASTAR racing and you've got a mountain that can please most tastes.

Mt. Hood SkiBowl

87000 East Highway 26
Government Camp, OR 97028

Phone: (503) 222-2695
Snowphone: (503) 222-2695
Elevation: base, 3,566'; top, 5,066'; vertical, 1,500'
Lifts: 4 doubles and 5 rope tows
Terrain Variety: 30% advanced, 50% intermediate, 20% beginner

The Season and Hours

SkiBowl opens in late November and operates through the beginning of April, as conditions permit. On Mondays and Tuesdays, the lifts run from 1:00 P.M. till 10:00 P.M. Wednesdays through Fridays they open at 9:00 A.M., and on weekends they begin running at 8:30 A.M. Night boarding is a value here: you can ride until 11:00 P.M. Friday and Saturday nights.

Lift Tickets

Weekday all day/day and night: $18/$28
Weekend all day/day and night: $23/$28
Half day: $19
All day and night Juniors/Seniors: $18
All night only Juniors/Seniors: $11
Night: $13

Specials

If you want to session the snowboard park only, you pay $15 for access to the Cascade chair and the half-pipe surface tow. For the half-pipe tow only, you pay a mere $10. The night boarding for $13 is a value, especially when you consider that it's only an hour's drive from Portland.

Logistics, the Local Scene, Where to Stay

See the Mt. Hood Mystique sidebar on page 92.

The Mountain

People may chuckle when you mention SkiBowl, but the locals at Mt. Hood know that it has the best steeps in the area. The problem is, a lot of times when it's snowing on Timberline and Meadows, SkiBowl's getting rained on. Its base sits about a thousand feet below the other resorts, so the snow doesn't pile up as high and its season doesn't stretch out into the late spring. But when there's snow, the place goes off. The mountain is divided into SkiBowl East and SkiBowl West. The snowboard park and half-pipe are located in East, while the best terrain on the mountain lies off the West peaks. The upper mountain at West is a series of bowls spreading out toward the Outback—SkiBowl's best ungroomed terrain. When the Outback is open, you can find powder turns, tree glades, and some nice rock jumps. The skiers tend to stay near the Upper Bowl chair where they can bounce through head-high moguls and high-five each other a lot. If you're not sure what's going off, the lift-ops are friendly folks who will send you in the right direction.

Freeriders

Go to the Outback. You'll have to take your board off and walk ten minutes out the Tom Dick Peak, but the hike is practically flat and you'll get a great view of Mirror Lake from up there. From Tom Dick, you have a number of options for lines, all of which are worth exploring. Another way into the Outback is to take the West Boundary trail and drop in off the ridge. The traverse coming out on Gunsight Notch isn't that much fun, but you regular-foots will find a series of toe-side hits on the sidewall to keep you from falling asleep. The best snow on the mountain piles up on the West Wall run. If you're into rock jumps, look for launches to your right while riding the Upper Bowl chair. The big cliff band on the lower mountain is unrideable for the most part, so unless you have a rock-proof base, don't even bother. The main face gets bumped out pretty quickly, but after a big snow you'll be able to find a number of lines between the East and West walls.

Cruisers

Canyon, a big wide groomer coming down off the Upper Bowl chair, has great pitch for some high-speed turns. Anywhere the groomers have been in the Upper Bowl is a good bet for some steep turns. The lower mountain is an easy, wide-open area, and after enduring the traverse to East, you'll find Racer, Challenger, and Skidaddle, groomed runs that keep mostly to the fall line.

Freestylers

You can find the board park at SkiBowl East on the appropriately named Boarder Garden run. The terrain park varies depending on snow conditions, but when the snow is big, so are the hits. Tabletops, gaps, a spine, and a half-pipe make up the terrain obstacles.

Grommets

Groms can get into a First-timer Snowboard package for $32 that includes a ninety-minute group lesson, equipment rental, and an all-day rope-tow pass (yikes!). Once you're linking turns, the lower mountain at West is wide-open and offers enough pitch to move you along. The Skidaddle, Roundhouse, and Bunny Basin runs at East are other good places to wire your basic moves.

Nonbelievers

Bump skiers flock to the Upper Bowl at West, and we've seen pinheads and young children dotting the slopes to create that ever-elusive "family feel." SkiBowl has a snow park that features an Extreme Inner Tube Hill. It also touts its Mobile Rapid Riser, a bungee liftoff that accelerates you eighty feet into the air, pulling 2.5 G's. You bounce around like a cat toy for a while before it's over.

Timberline Ski Area

Timberline Lodge
Timberline, OR 97028

> **Phone:** (503) 272-3311 (local); (503) 231-7979 (Portland)
> **Fax:** (503) 272-3710
> **Snowphone:** (503) 222-2211
> **Elevation:** base, 4,349' (winter), 6,000' (summer); top, 7,000' (winter), 8,500' (summer); vertical, 2,651' (winter), 2,500' (summer)
> **Lifts:** 6 lifts, 1 high-speed quad
> **Terrain Variety:** 20% advanced, 50% intermediate, 30% beginner

The Season and Hours

You can ride Timberline for nine months out of the year, with the seasons of operation split into winter and summer. Winter season begins in early November and extends through April. Summer riding on the Palmer Snowfield starts on weekends in mid-May, with full-time operations from June through Labor Day. Hours are 9:00 A.M.–5:00 P.M. Night lifts run Wednesday through Saturday until 9:00 P.M.

Lift Tickets

Day/night (9:00 A.M.–closing)—Adult/Child: $28/$17
Day (9:00 A.M.–5:00 P.M.)—Adult/Child: $26/$16
Early (9:00 A.M.–1:00 P.M.)—Adult/Child: $24/$14
Late (1:00 P.M.–closing)—Adult/Child: $24/$14
Late late (4:00 P.M.–closing)—Adult/Child: $13/$11
Betsy chair only (9:00 A.M.–closing)—Adult/Child: $14/$10

Specials

Purchasing a lift ticket gets you a free board check. Timberline also offers lift, meal, and lodging packages at the Lodge and at Silcox Hut. Call (800) 547-1406.

Logistics, the Local Scene

See the Mt. Hood Mystique sidebar on page 92.

Where to Stay

If you feel strangely uncomfortable in the shadow of the **Lodge** at Timberline, it may be that you recognize it from the movie *The Shining*. Room rates run from $60 for a chalet to $160 for a room with a fireplace. You can find a better bargain at the **Silcox Hut**, a stone-and-timber structure that serves as midmountain bunkhouse. For $65 a night you get round-trip snowcat transportation, bunk, dinner and breakfast, and all taxes and gratuities. Bring your sleeping bag.

The Mountain

The Palmer Snowfield at Timberline is largely responsible for Mt. Hood's reputation as a snowboarding destination. From June through August, summer campers flock to the upper elevations, where they build half-pipes and terrain parks, set up gates for races, and conduct a large number of off-snow activities in the afternoons. The winter terrain at Timberline doesn't include this section of the mountain, and as a result you'll find the terrain lacking in challenging steeps. Numerous gullies and wind lips liven up the mountain, though, and it's a fun place to play.

Freeriders

The mountain off the Magic Mile Super Express contains wide-open powder fields that are filled with wind lips and drops. When you head down Molly's Run, keep your speed up off the lift or you'll have to hike over the roller. From there, though, you can take several lines back toward the Victoria Station chair; these lines include some cat-track and rock jumps, as well as a few tree turns. West Pitch and Cut Off also contain some rock drops.

Cruisers

The gentle pitch of the slopes at Timberline prohibits any serious bombing, but some very nice cruiser terrain lies off the Magic Mile Super Express. Here you can take Coffel's Run down to the base of the Blossom chair in a long slow-burner. The other groomed runs funnel you back to the express chair and allow you to maximize your vertical. The Main Run underneath the Victoria Station chair, although some-times crowded, adds to the list of longer cruisers.

Freestylers

The Bone Zone off the Blossom chair offers a series of gullies that make a natural snowboarder playground. About every twenty feet there's a wall of hip hit to pop off of. If you turn left off the Blossom chair, you'll find the Paint Brush run near the boundary. Here, a series of wind lips set you up for some smaller hits and drops (don't go big unless you've scouted the landing). Hits line up going down Main Run Victoria, and a permanent half-pipe is located next to the Betsy chair. The serious freestyling goes off during the summer sessions, when multiple half-pipes and terrain parks spring up all over the Palmer Snowfield.

Grommets

Lesson packages that include board-and-boot rental plus lift ticket range from $40 to $55. This is a great mountain to learn the basics—from turning to tricks. The Puci chair services the least intimidating terrain on the lower mountain, and every winter chair includes a greenie escape route.

Nonbelievers

The setting at Timberline, from the main lodge to the day lodges to the easygoing terrain, creates a friendly environment with a touch of class. Skiing remains the most popular winter activity here, and day lodge–dwellers don't have it bad, either.

Willamette Pass

P.O. Box 5509
Eugene, OR 97405

Phone: (503) 484-5030 or (800) 444-5030
Fax: (503) 484-5030, ext. 250
Snowphone: (503) 345-SNOW
Elevation: base, 5,120'; top, 6,683'; vertical, 1,563'
Lifts: 5 chairs (four triples, one double) covering 1,100 acres
Terrain Variety: 35% advanced, 45% intermediate, 20% beginner

The Season and Hours

The mountain opens in mid-November and operates through April. The recent doubling of snowmaking capacity will keep conditions consistent throughout the season. The lifts run from 9:00 A.M. to 4:00 P.M., with twilight and night boarding available on Fridays and Saturdays until 9:00 P.M.

Lift Tickets

Day (9:00 A.M.–4:00 P.M.)—Adult/Youth/Senior: $22/$16/$11
Half day (12:30–4:00 P.M.)—Adult/Youth/Senior: $16/$11/$8
Twilight (12:30–9:00 P.M.)—Adult/Youth/Senior: $22/$16/$11
Night (4:00–9:00 P.M.)—Adult/Youth/Senior: $16/$10/$8

Specials

Those on a tight schedule or budget can board by the hour at Willamette—$9 for the first two hours, and additional hours for $4.50. On Tuesdays, you can buy a lift ticket for $10. If you plan to make Willamette your regular mountain for the season, it's a good idea to shell out $59 and join Club Vertical. You'll have earned that back after your fifth visit, and after eighteen trips to the mountain, you ride for free.

Logistics

Willamette is located at milepost 62 on Highway 58. From Eugene, take I-5 south to Highway 58. From Klamath Falls, take Highway 97 north to Highway 58. You can also take the **Snapple Weekday Express** from Eugene to Willamette Pass for $10 ($8 for Club Vertical members). Meet at the Elks Club parking lot on Centennial across from Autzen Stadium at 7:30 A.M.

The Local Scene

Willamette Pass remains somewhat isolated in terms of nearby communities, but it's not a secret spot anymore. The mountain's managers have created a snowboard haven for residents of Eugene and central Oregon by actively promoting a snowboard competition series that includes gate events, slope style, and half-pipe. Their partner for these events is **Boardsports** in Eugene ([503] 484-2588), a full-service snowboard shop. If you're driving back to Eugene after a day of riding, you might want to stop by **KC's Tavern** in Oakridge (behind the Dairy Queen) for pizza and microbrews on tap.

Where to Stay

Several resorts offer lodging-and-lift packages that start at about $42 midweek. In Cascade Summit (within seven miles on Highway 58), choose from **Crescent Lake Resort**, (503) 433-2505; **Odell Lake Resort**, (503) 433-2540; **Shelter Cove Resort**, (503) 433-2548; and **Willamette Pass Inn**, (503) 433-2211. In Oakridge (twenty-seven miles west of the mountain), along with an assortment of restaurants, grills, and fast-food outlets, you'll find: **Cascade Motel**, (503) 782-2602; **Hall's Motel**, (503) 782-2611; **Oakridge Best Western**, (503) 782-2212; **Oakridge Motel**, (503) 782-3430; **Ridgeview Motel**, (503) 782-3430; and **Westfir Lodge B&B**, (503) 782-3103. If you drive east to Highway 97 and then toward Gilchrist, these resorts are good bets: **Sunriver Resort**, (800) 962-1770, and **Woodsman Motel**, (503) 433-2710.

The Mountain

The people at Willamette have done everyone a favor by not cutting down all their trees. The runs are separated by wide glades that make you feel like you're into secret spots when you're riding the main face. The resort encompasses a backside that you can't see from the parking lot, adding to the sense of discovery you'll experience the first few times you ride here. The face off Eagle Peak includes some steep pitches up top and nice trees to navigate, and the creatively named Peak 2 doubles the mountain's terrain. You'll have a good time cruising runs off both peaks, but you'll find that snowboarders congregate mostly on the backside where they can session the trees and terrain park.

Freeriders

There are a few chances for extreme drops, but you'll have to content yourself with turning through the trees and looking for hits. If there's been snow, the brave and the foolish can give the chair crowd a show along the big rock band under the Peak 2 chair. Also, a traverse down the first part of Where's Waldo will lead you to a cliff section that usually has a good accumulation of snow underneath, although there aren't any lines down through it that anyone but Spiderman could make. If you traverse all the way around the nose of the cliff, you'll find yourself in a tight steep chute that opens up after a couple of turns (at least when the snow's filled it up wide enough to turn through). Any of the runs down the Peak 2 chair will get you into the great tree glades at Willamette—the trees on the backside are spaced out perfectly for boarding through. On the frontside, the trees are a little tighter, but still a lot of fun. Check out the glades off RIS, Timburr, and High Lead. In general, the snow on the backside's a little better, but after a big dump (which happens often) you really can't go wrong.

Cruisers

The groomers get out every night, and as a result you'll find no lack of cruiser runs. Lower Timburr and Rough Cut off Eagle Peak were cut along fall-line pitches and are good leg-burners. The boundary runs off both peak chairs are traversing cruisers where you can make some easy turns through the wide lanes. Skiers tend to bump out the steeper runs closer to the chairs, but because the pitches aren't extreme, the bumps aren't big and they're not that tough to turn through. Willamette puts on GS and slalom races throughout the season, so put on your hard boots, pay your ten bucks, and get famous.

Freestylers

The new terrain park off the Northern Exposure run on the backside is a welcome addition to the mountain. With a competition-class half-pipe and a series of hits that get as big as the snow will allow, Willamette is well on its way to establishing a quality terrain park. For sidewall hits, come down Rosary around the frontside. If you keep your speed up, you'll be able to find hits as long as your calves hold up. There are also a couple of lines on the Rough Cut run where you can bust some smaller hits.

Grommets

The First-Timer Snowboard package ($41) includes lesson, rentals, and lift ticket for the Sleepy Hollow slope. By George, the run serviced by the Midway lift, is a big, wide-open, tree-free zone that's ideal for riders perfecting their turns.

Nonbelievers

Skiers and snowboarders interact well on the mountain, and the management appears committed to providing a quality product for both groups. For flatlanders, a snowcat is dedicated to grooming the twenty kilometers of Nordic trails. And if you've got young'uns in tow, the lodge offers day-care services.

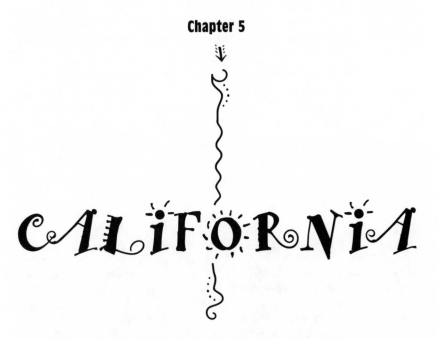

Chapter 5

CALIFORNIA

As far as snowboarders are concerned, California is really four or five different states.

Shasta, a towering, solitary giant in California's extreme north, embodies the state of grace. Only a tiny wrinkle of its dome is serviced by ski lifts. The rest is accessible only by crampon- or snowshoe-covered boot.

The next state, the North Lake Tahoe area, is the status quo. In many ways this region sets the standard for snowboarding on the West Coast. With a high elevation and heavy snowfall punctuated by California sun storms, Tahoe's north shore is more consistently good for boarding than anywhere else from Alyeska to Pasadena. Squaw Valley, Northstar, Mt. Rose, Diamond Peak, Boreal Ridge, Donner Ski Ranch, and Sugar Bowl are all outstanding snowboarding spots in their own right. Having them all together in a tiny area gives snowboarders almost too many choices.

South Lake Tahoe is in a state of decadence. This region, which includes Heavenly Valley, Sierra Ski Ranch, and Kirkwood, is a boom land of cheap motels, bars, and casinos. The mountains offer excellent boarding if you can get out of bed the morning after.

The central region is a state divided. The central Sierra includes Bear Valley, Dodge Ridge, Badger Pass, and Sierra Summit on the west slope and June Mountain and Mammoth Mountain on the east slope. The west-side resorts are small, family-oriented hills, while the east side has a serious case of "you can't get there from here." Six to eight hours from the nearest California cities, Mammoth and June are big, bold, Colorado-style mountains that get cold, dry snow and legions of weekend warriors from the Los Angeles basin.

Finally, we arrive at the state of chaos. The southern region includes Mt. Baldy, Bear Mountain, Snow Valley, Snow Summit, Mountain High, Ski Sunrise, Mt. Waterman, and Kratka Ridge. Like many Southern California stories, this is one of too many people trying to bite the same slice of pie. The southern resorts are handicapped in the first place by too little snow and too much sun (bad for your skin). Throw in ten million people within an hour or two's driving distance,

Winter Storm Lingo

Weather is what makes the snowboarder a scientist. An ability to judge cloud cover, wind, and the sun's effect on snow can make the difference between spending all day shaving ice and finding a good stash of powder or corn. A weather radio is always a good investment. The frequency is automatically set up to receive broadcasts from the National Weather Service, which has relay stations to cover just about everywhere a person can go. Because radios don't provide a weatherperson with pointer and satellite map, you have to rely more on your understanding of winter-storm definitions to paint an accurate picture of the conditions.

Snow flurries or *snow showers* are defined as snow falling for short, intermittent periods. Snowfall during the flurries may briefly reduce visibility to an eighth of a mile or less, but accumulations from snow flurries are generally low.

Snow squalls are brief, intense dumps of snow and are comparable to summer rain showers. They are generally accompanied by gusty winds.

Blowing snow and *drifting snow* usually occur together. "Blowing snow" is defined as snow lifted from the surface by the wind and blown through the air to a degree that visibility is greatly restricted. "Drifting snow" is used in forecasts to indicate that strong winds will blow falling snow into significant drifts.

Blizzards are these cool ice-cream concoctions at the Dairy Queen served upside down. We asked one DQ queen to serve it upright and she told us she couldn't. Blizzards are also the most dramatic and dangerous of all winter storms, characterized by strong winds bearing large amounts of snow. Most of the snow accompanying a blizzard is in the form of fine, powdery particles that the wind blows with such force that at times visibility is only a few yards.

Avalanche is a word that snowboarders should truly fear. Because you're strapped into your board, your chances of escaping an avalanche once you're in one is close to zero. Avalanches occur and there just aren't enough chairs on the lifts, not to mention the difficulties of finding untracked swaths of silky white stuff. The result is a surf-style attitude that almost exactly mirrors the one at the beach a few miles away. Some resorts, like Bear Mountain, have attempted to stem the inevitable crowd conflicts by segregating boarders and skiers. To some extent, this has worked. But boarding in the southern mountains remains more of a skate-park rumble than a solitary trip in the woods.

Backcountry Opportunities

Spring is the time to explore California's abundant backcountry. The skies are generally sunny, and the snow corns out to perfection. While there are numerous spots for a hike in the Tahoe area and along the Sierra, we'll leave finding those to you. The more obvious places will

when snow becomes destabilized (because of temperature changes, weight, and pressure) and then suddenly moves down the mountain. Backcountry travel is not recommended during periods of high avalanche danger.

Winter storm watch alerts the public that a storm is forming or has formed, and is approaching the area. The storm has a potential to produce heavy snow, often accompanied by high winds, and to create blizzard conditions over mountain passes and other traveled areas. Winter storm watches are usually issued twenty-four to thirty-six hours in advance of the storm.

Winter storm warning means that the storm is imminent and you'd better load up on videos because television reception is going to be the worst. Also, immediate action should be taken to protect such things as life and property. The winter storm warning is normally issued within twelve hours of the storm, although many times the warning is issued concurrently with the storm in progress.

A *traveler's advisory* may be issued for less severe storms that do not meet winter storm criteria for heavy snow. Usually issued within twelve hours of the impending storm, they alert motorists that they're going to be putting on their chains at some point during the drive, and that roads will be slow going because of low visibility and slippery conditions.

A *blizzard warning* is used when wind speeds of thirty-five miles per hour or greater are sustained for three hours or more, with considerable falling or blowing snow. The conditions occur over mountain passes and other wind-prone areas during winter storms.

An *avalanche warning bulletin* is issued by the U.S. Forest Service whenever it is determined that avalanche danger is high or extreme. The conditions normally occur within twenty-four hours of a heavy snowfall, before the snow has had a chance to stabilize. Strong winds and rapidly changing temperatures are also critical in determining avalanche danger.

give you the heart-pounding thrill of a long hike and an unmarked face. And because they're more obvious, the rescue teams will have a better chance of finding you if something goes wrong and you have to bunk down for a while.

Mt. Shasta is probably the most accessible of the backcountry spots in California. In the spring, droves of local boarders in snowcats, snowmobiles, or snowshoes ascend the mountain's southern ridges and board down. Most locals climb about halfway to Shasta's 14,162-foot summit and ride down into the Old Mt. Shasta Ski Bowl (once the site of a ski resort, now wiped out by a massive avalanche), making a couple of hard-earned runs in a day. Other potentially excellent runs include Avalanche Gulch, the Heart, Green Butte Ridge, and West Face Gully. Still other popular backcountry runs are Sun Bowl and Powder Bowl.

While we've heard of lots of people climbing to the summit and riding down Shasta's big upper snowfields and glaciers, we also know at least one teleskier who got chased down by a good-sized slide while doing this, so watch your butt and be prepared for a serious mountain climb complete with crevasses and blue ice, even in summer. The weather can turn vicious on the mountain at the drop of a hat, with hundred-mile-per-hour winds being common. So in addition to carrying avalanche safety equipment, including crampons, ice axes, and possibly ropes, you'll need to make the climb sufficiently prepared to bivouac for the night if necessary. Legend has it that a couple of snowcats poach trips onto Shasta's upper reaches, but these are strictly unofficial—and probably unauthorized—and if you want to get in on them, you'll have to go there and figure out the deal for yourself.

Moving to the south, you'll also find spring snowboarding at Mt. Lassen, the southernmost major peak of the Cascade chain. The mountain used to have a small ski resort at its base until inaccessibility and avalanches closed it down. Currently, a Nordic center occupies the former resort, and during the winter and spring you'll find an abundance of snow and very few people there. Your best bet is to check with the locals at the Nordic center, who undoubtably have some tele-experience in the area, or with the Forest Service if you're planning a route on one of the other faces. To reach Mt. Lassen, take I-5 north from Sacramento (about one hundred miles), turn east on Highway 36, drive to the town of Mineral, and turn north on Highway 86, which leads you there.

The Sierra High Route in central California is getting more exposure by the day. What saves this east-west route from becoming a highway of polypropylene is the fact that there are no warming huts along the way. Used primarily by teleskiers, but equally suited to snowshoes or a backcountry snowboard, the route allows you access to some of the most spectacular terrain in the world. If you start near Mt. Whitney on the eastern side of the Sierra, you follow the boundary between Kings Canyon National Park to the north and Sequoia National Park to the south. Mt. Williamson, Mt. Tindall, and Colby Ridge are a few of the places you'll pass. If you decide to take on the High Route, know what you're doing—bone up on your mountaineering, avalanche safety, and winter-camping knowledge. Be prepared for rapidly changing conditions, and remember that the more the sun shines, the less stable the snow becomes.

Probably the best way to familiarize yourself with California's backcountry is to let an experienced guide show it to you the first time. The money you pay for the trip is well worth it when you consider the hazards out there. **Sierras Guides Alliance**, (510) 653-3628, runs snowboarding excursions in the eastern Sierra near Carson Pass, Mammoth Lakes, and June Lake. For learning the basics, or acquiring the advanced knowledge needed to do serious touring, your best bet is to contact **Sierra Ski Touring** at (714) 934-4495, where you can learn from David Beck, the guru of the Sierra.

One important thing to know about getting the fresh in California is that, unlike in Oregon and Washington, it's a crime to go out of bounds from a ski area. We've heard stories of boarders getting met by the sheriff when they come out at the road, and the fine is four figures big. Unless you're one of those snowboarders with a lot of money (are there folks like that?), use your good judgment when contemplating civil disobedience.

Northern California and Nevada

North Lake Tahoe

Where to Stay

North Lake Tahoe, forming a triangle from Truckee to Incline Village to Homewood, is a giant resort community containing hundreds of hotels and motels and thousands of rental condominiums and cabins. Choosing a place to stay depends on your tastes and where you plan to ride. Start by contacting the **Tahoe North Visitor's and Convention Bureau** at (800) 824-6348; fax: (916) 581-4081. The bureau can also arrange air transportation, rental cars, and lift tickets.

In general, any ski area in the North Lake Tahoe region will be only fifteen or twenty minutes from wherever you happen to stay. Sometimes, however, Donner Ski Ranch, Boreal, and Sugar Bowl, which are on the other side of Donner Pass, get cut off by big storms. If you plan to ride at one of these sites, your best bet is to stay in one of the many rental cabins at Donner Lake.

Northstar and Squaw Valley are their own little self-contained communities, so if you're staying in one of their hotels or condos, you won't have to look far to find some kind of food to go with your lodging.

If gambling is your thing, it's best to stay in the Kings Beach, Crystal Bay, or Incline Village area. From here, you're a couple of minutes from the few forlorn little North Shore casinos (a far cry from South Lake Tahoe's glitz). From this corner of the triangle, it's an easy reach to Mt. Rose, Diamond Peak, and Northstar.

If you're planning to ride at Squaw or Homewood, staying at Donner Lake, Squaw Valley, or Tahoe City makes sense.

Where to Eat

Truckee is really a pretty dull freeway pit stop, but if you like shopping in touristy boutiques, the main drag in Truckee is all right. We prefer the **Truckee Brewery**, which is well known for its beer on tap. Dining in Truckee is a lose-lose situation. We have eaten in every Mexican restaurant in town and cannot recommend any of them. The other option is pizza, and our favorite in this topping-rich category is **The**

Station in central Truckee. You'll find it by looking for the railroad car in a parking lot.

In Tahoe City, we like to eat at the **Nawty Dog**, a small pub with good grub located on Highway 28 just east of the "Y" (across from the fire station). There are some hip bars with dancing and evening activities in Tahoe City—unlike in Truckee, where things shrivel up and die around 7:00 P.M.

South Lake Tahoe

You know you're on the road to South Lake Tahoe when, after the fifteenth billboard, you begin trying to remember the book you once read on blackjack. *Hit on fifteen if the dealer's showing royalty. Hold when the dealer's got a five. Don't lose more than forty bucks. Quit when you've paid off your credit card bill. Bet big to impress the small-nosed beauties on the other side of the table. Lose like you don't need the money. Win like it happens all the time.* Wild thoughts. Crazy thoughts. (Gamblers Anonymous: [916] 583-8941).

Little-Vegas-by-the-Lake gained its reputation from its casinos, but there's also some of the best snowboarding in the region to be found at North Lake Tahoe's redheaded stepsister. Located at Stateline, Heavenly is the only resort where you can enter another state in the middle of a run. Sierra-at-Tahoe has some of the best tree boarding to be found in California, and Kirkwood is a mountain that features natural terrain every bit as challenging as Squaw. Desolation Wilderness to the west is a popular summer spot for trout fishing and backpacking, and on the drive to Kirkwood you'll see that there's more to South Lake than high kilowatt readings. A lot of Bay Area residents are in the habit of staying on the interstate and going up to North Lake. If you haven't checked out the spots to the south, our advice is to do so. It's just so durn beautiful!

The hotel-littered strip that connects California and Nevada isn't. In fact, it's a major eyesore, given its proximity to the most beautiful lake on the continent. The blessing, though, is the large number of cheap hotels that snowboarders seem to favor over all others. There's plenty of fast food, convenience stores, and rental shops on every block. The **Village Mountain Surf Shop** is a good full-service board shop (3553 Lake Tahoe Boulevard; [916] 541-2726), and **Vertical Sports** offers tuning and rentals (2318 Lake Tahoe Boulevard; [916] 542-1411). Just down the street are the gaming parlors where you can gamble the night away, drink for free, and talk to all the other folks who've come to put the casinos out of business.

Chaining Up

One fact of life for boarders in the Tahoe area is snow chains. Unless you've got *4WD* stenciled on the side of your car, you'll need to put on chains at some point during the winter. Unlike other states, California actually enforces the chain requirements—in the form of two guys decked out in rain suits, freezing their behinds off, looking at tires and either nodding at you or pointing you over to the chain-up area. They've heard all sorts of explanations about the traction qualities of certain tires and how they make a particular car "just as good as four-wheel drive," so don't try to snow them. They're pros. They know drive trains and tires. That's their job.

When you're herded to the chain-up area, you'll see more lackeys wearing yellow rain suits—except these are holding up pieces of cardboard with the words *Chains—$20* drawn in Magic Marker. They're not selling chains—they're offering to put them on. Now most of our snowboarding bros are usually scraping to come up with lift ticket money. If you're in that boat and want to avoid the added expense of paying someone to do something that, while unpleasant, you can easily do yourself, here are a few suggestions to make chaining up less painful:

1. Carry chains. You don't want to backtrack to the nearest hardware store and pay a premium for chains. Buy your chains in the late spring at a good distance from a mountain pass, put them in your car, then forget about them until you need them.

2. Carry extra links, extra crosspieces, a tool for chain repair, and rubber chain tighteners. Some of the chain packages come with these included, but check when you buy your chains, and if they're not in there, buy them.

3. Keep a bath mat, a cheap Costco rain suit, or some other form of tarp in the car. Odds are you'll be on your knees, if not your back, during installation, and it will be dumping hard. Also, you'll need a flashlight and a pair of gloves (this is one of the few times it's okay for a snowboarder to not wear mittens) for fumbling around with the fasteners. You can do it without gloves, but on those days when you lose all feeling in your fingertips after thirty seconds of fondling cold steel, you might prefer to be a Boy Scout. Even if your buddies give you grief, you won't be riding the last hour to the mountain with a wet strip down your back and bleeding fingers that have no feeling.

4. Once you know you're going to need to chain up, start searching for an overpass. It will probably be the only dry place around. Gas stations are another option, and a good portion of gas station attendants are friendly toward snowboarders, although some get a little antsy if you're chaining up in front of their

Where to Stay

Most of the hotels at South Lake Tahoe belong to the **Visitor's Bureau at Tahoe** service. By calling (800) 288-2463 and telling the agent where you want to stay or how much you want to spend, you can get information on several lodges and book a reservation, all with a single phone call. There are lodging options to fit every budget, taste, and size of group.

pumps. In this case, designate another member of your party to perform an extensive fluids check routine while you're taking care of business in the wheel wells.

5. If you're on the highway, the most important thing is to *get your car completely off the road.* If another car hits you while you're hugging an R-14 165, you might lose a hand or two. Also, *don't park on a hill or curve.* Again, if a car swerves into you, you're toast. Butterside-up, butterside-down, it doesn't matter. Toast is toast.

6. Keep your headlights on.

7. When you're installing the chains, remember that there are left and right chains. Also, there's a top and bottom. You don't want the chains to dig through your tires, leaving you with two flats in the middle of a snowstorm, so take a minute to make sure you're set up.

8. Each set of tire chains comes with instructions, only some of which were written for people. Some general rules to fall back on after you've burned the instructions for warmth:

a. Make sure that the hook is on the inside and the latch is on the outside of each tire.

b. The sharp edges of the links, where they are crimped shut, should face away from your tires.

c. Place the chains over the tops of the tires.

d. Drive in reverse slowly so the wheels back into the chains about one-quarter of a revolution.

e. Hook the inside chain first, using your flashlight to help you accomplish this task.

f. Latch the outside chain, taking up as much slack as possible.

g. For rear-wheel installation, place the last crosspiece toward the front of the tire and drive the car slowly forward into the chain.

h. Put the rubber chain tighteners on.

We've heard that this method is quicker and simpler than laying the chains out and driving onto them, or jacking up the car to wrap the chains on. The most important thing, though, is to stay on the road once you've installed your chains. There is no bigger bummer than spending a day digging out of a ditch or waiting for a tow truck (many hours) while everyone else is getting into the fresh. If you live near the mountains or find yourself spending a good number of days up there, invest in snowboard stocks so you can buy a truck with four-wheel drive.

⇧　⇩　⇧

If you want to get away from the bright lights, you'll do no better than **Richardson's Resort**, (800) 544-1801, on the west shore near Emerald Bay, about three miles north of the Y intersection on Highway 89. Richardson's has a main lodge as well as seventeen four-season cabins. You won't find televisions or phones in the rooms, but the downstairs common area with huge fireplace and tables is a great spot to hang out after a long day of riding. The place has the feel of a New England artists' colony, but without the admission requirement. The cabins, well-spaced from each other, provide a good place for groups of four or more to kick back around a fireplace and make some noise or have one of those candlelight moments. At Richardson's marina, you can score some killer pasta or comida americana at the **Beacon Restaurant.** For beer on tap, run down the road two miles to **Dixon's,** the locals' choice when they want to knock back a fine lager.

For the honeymooning snowboarders, the **Inn by the Lake,** (916) 542-0330, is an upscale hotel with king-sized beds, phones in the bathrooms, and all the croissants you can eat at the continental breakfast. On the other end of the spectrum, you'll find about twenty hotels along Highway 50 with signs in the windows advertising a queen-sized bed for about $20 midweek. Several casinos—among them, Harrah's, Harvey's, and Caesar's Palace—offer midweek lodging-and-lift specials. For information, call the **Visitor's Bureau at Tahoe** (here's the number again: [800] 288-2463).

Boreal Ridge

P.O. Box 39
Truckee, CA 96160

Phone: (916) 426-3666
Elevation: base, 7,200'; top, 7,800'; vertical, 600'
Lifts: 9 chairs (2 quads, 2 triples, 5 doubles)
Terrain Variety: 15% advanced, 55% intermediate, 30% beginner

The Season and Hours

Boreal Ridge is open from early November through late April, depending on conditions and interest. Hours are 9:00 A.M. to 9:00 P.M. (night skiing begins in late November).

Lift Tickets

All day—Adult/Senior/Child: $33/$10/$10
Afternoon—Adult/Senior/Child: $25/$10/$10
Night—Adult/Senior/Child: $16/$10/$10

Specials

All-day tickets and afternoon tickets are good until 9:00 P.M. Night boarding begins at 4:30 P.M., Tuesdays through Thursdays. All prices are substantially lower after New Year's Day.

Logistics

Boreal is the easiest resort to get to in the Tahoe area. It's just off I-80 ninety miles east of Sacramento.

The Local Scene

Snowboarding completely transformed Boreal Ridge. Once a quiet little hill where busloads of schoolkids learned how to ski, Boreal is now famous as Jibbassic Park. The jibbers' park pretty much defines the local scene, with lots of hot riders cutting their teeth on Boreal's terrain. Jibbers means young riders—the average age here is about fifteen. The skiers that make up the other half of the people on the mountain also tend to be kids. The whole place has a kind of after-school-pep-rally vibe.

Where to Stay

See the North Lake Tahoe introduction on page 110.

Tell Your Friends

After a good dump, bail the jib park and hit the backside. It's not big, but you'll find some good hits and fun lines through the trees.

The Mountain

Boreal Ridge, as the name suggests, isn't much of a mountain. Top to bottom, it's only 600 feet high. On the other hand, few snowboard-oriented playgrounds compare. Boreal has been an innovator in snowboard park development, and Jibbassic Park is a masterpiece of hit making.

Freeriders

Jibbers rule. This is no place for freeriders.

Cruisers

Boreal's packed and groomed most of the time, so cruisers will have fun here even though the runs are too short to really dial in. It's a good place for new cruisers on a budget to practice their skills, though.

Freestylers

Two half-pipes (one for morning, one for afternoon) and a small terrain park are warmups for the huge terrain garden that is Jibbassic Park. Ramps, banks, snow rails, kickers, and gaps of every description await. The park starts near the top of the ridge and runs almost all the way to the lift at the base.

Contests are held here regularly, and even when no judges are in attendance, there's an ongoing jibbers' fest in the park.

New boarders are advised to use caution when riding in Jibbassic. Some of the hits are *T. rex*–sized.

Grommets

Boreal has a highly active lesson program and plenty of room for beginners to learn.

Nonbelievers

While parents may decide to sit out the Boreal skiing experience, there's fine cross-country skiing just down the road near Soda Springs, and skiing with lots of kids probably isn't so bad anyway. It's about a twenty-minute drive to Truckee, assuming good weather over Donner Summit.

Diamond Peak

1210 Ski Way
Incline Village, NV 89451

Phone: (702) 831-3249
Fax: (702) 832-1281
Snowphone: (702) 831-3211
Elevation: base, 6,700'; top, 8,540'; vertical, 1,840'
Lifts: 7 chairs (1 quad, 6 doubles) covering 655 acres
Terrain Variety: 33% advanced, 49% intermediate, 18% beginner

The Season and Hours

Lifts operate from 9:00 A.M. to 4:00 P.M. daily from early December through mid-April.

Diamond Peak

Two for one $49 First Time Beginner Snowboard Package, valid non-holiday, Monday through Friday. Package includes two-hour group snowboard lesson, lift ticket to the School House Beginner Chair, snowboard and boot rental ($250 deposit or credit card deposit required). Present coupon at Guest Services Window. CODE 316.

Do not tear this coupon out of the book. You must present this book to get the discount.
RESORTS: Please cancel this coupon by crossing it out of the book.

DiAMOND PEAK

EL. - 8,540'

Base Elevation - 6,700'

RUNS

1. Solitude Canyon
2. Golden Eagle Bowl
3. The Great Flume
4. Crystal Ridge
5. Thunder/Lightning
6. Diamond Back
7. Battle Born
8. Sunnyside
9. Powder
10. Luggie's
11. Freeway
12. Spillway
13. Lodgepole
14. Penguin/Delight
15. Wiggle
16. Showoff
17. Slalom Glade
18. O. God
19. G.S.
20. School Yard

Lift Tickets

All day—Adult/Child/Senior/Beginner Lift: $35/$14/$14/$12
Half day—Adult/Child/Senior/Beginner Lift: $27/$11/$11/$12

Children age five and under and seniors age seventy and over ride for free.

Tickets for two consecutive days are available, as well as family packages that provide a discount on the purchase of an adult and a child ticket. Diamond Peak guarantees its lift tickets—if within an hour you decide the conditions aren't up to snuff, you can exchange your lift ticket for a voucher good for another day.

Specials

Diamond Peak offers some midweek specials such as free group lessons and free rental with the purchase of a lift ticket. Call the resort to find out about its current offerings.

Logistics

From I-80, take Highway 267 south to Highway 28 and follow it east into Nevada. Just past Incline Village, turn north on Country Club Drive to Ski Way, then follow the signs to Diamond Peak.

The Local Scene

Diamond Peak bills itself as Lake Tahoe's "premier family resort." As a result, its snowboarding scene is under a lot of watchful eyes. Thankfully, the mountain's management recognizes that, as in many families, skiers and snowboarders can coexist here. Diamond Peak has always fostered snowboarding—it was the first Tahoe resort to build a half-pipe. A couple of years ago, in order to involve local riders in the snowboarding program, the resort held focus groups geared toward finding out what snowboarders wanted on the mountain. As a result of these meetings, the half-pipe is gone and a snowboard park has opened. Riders can check out shovels to build hits and work on transitions.

Because of the family environment, the après-boarding scene isn't quite as happening as in some other areas. Diamond Peak borders the upscale communities of Incline Village and Crystal Bay, where you can find a wide array of restaurants and some bars. Those of you looking for a little more excitement can experience twenty-four-hour Nevada-style gaming at a variety of resort-casino hotels. For equipment needs, there's **Buddha's Board Shop** in the Raley's complex just down the hill from the mountain.

Where to Stay

Several lodging-and-lift packages are available in the area. The **Hyatt's** Hot Ski package goes for $69 ([702] 832-1234), and families staying at **Incline Village** will ride free at Diamond Peak, with packages starting at about $46 per person per day. The **Tahoe Biltmore**, (800) 245-8667, offers lodging-and-lift deals starting at $35 a head. Other packages are available; for information or reservations, call (800) GO-TAHOE.

The Mountain

Formerly named Ski Incline, the resort doubled its size in 1987, adding mostly advanced terrain. The name was changed to Diamond Peak to reflect the mountain's new character. The majority of the runs lie between two ridges that funnel everyone back toward the lodge. As a result, it's hard to get lost. In keeping with its family image, the resort has closed three of its runs on the lower mountain to snowboarders: Penguin, Wiggle, and Delight. These are intermediate runs where the ski school takes a lot of learning skiers. In the interest of parity, snowboarders have their own terrain park on Upper Showoff. Snowmaking covers 75 percent of the terrain, which allows Diamond Peak to provide consistent coverage all season long.

Freeriders

Freeriders will want to take the Crystal quad to the top of the mountain. From there, you've got any number of lines to explore. Solitude Canyon is where you'll find the best accumulations of powder and some nice trees. Off Crystal Ridge, check out the trees beneath the chair, and between Lightning and Diamond Back. A number of rocks, hits, and stumps sprinkled throughout Golden Eagle Bowl give you some chances to go big. You'll find that the upper mountain offers great ungroomed terrain, including two canyons filled with opportunities for exploration and fun.

Cruisers

The Crystal Ridge run is a long, steep cruiser where you can open up the throttle all the way. The Great Flume, also off the Crystal chair, is a mile-and-a-half-long run that drains you to the bottom. For some shorter but steeper turning, check out GS, Slalom Glade, and FIS off the Lake View chair. The groomers keep a nice corduroy on these runs, and off-season work on the slopes has paid off in the form of some really smooth pitches to turn down.

Freestylers

You can access the snowboard park on Upper Showoff by riding the Lake View chair. Groomers have shaped several hits that include gaps, tabletops, quarter-pipes, and a spine when there's sufficient snow. On the upper mountain, you'll find a nice lineup of hits coming down the Great Flume. Solitude Canyon and Golden Eagle Bowl provide additional opportunities for some big launches.

Grommets

Beginner snowboard packages (age thirteen and up) include a two-hour lesson, rentals, and beginners' chair lift ticket. Because of a limited number of rental boards, the beginner package is available Monday–Friday, nonholidays only.

Nonbelievers

Just a few miles above Incline Village is Diamond Peak's cross-country center, with over thirty-five kilometers of groomed track and skating lanes. Of course, skiers are pretty much welcome on the mountain. In early and late season, nonskiing members of the family can get a tee time at one of Incline Village's golf courses.

Donner Ski Ranch

P.O. Box 66
Norden, CA 95724

Phone: (916) 426-3635
Snowphone: (916) 426-3635
Elevation: base, 7,031'; top, 7,751'; vertical, 720'
Lifts: 6 chairs (1 triple, 5 doubles)
Terrain Variety: 25% advanced, 50% intermediate, 25% beginner

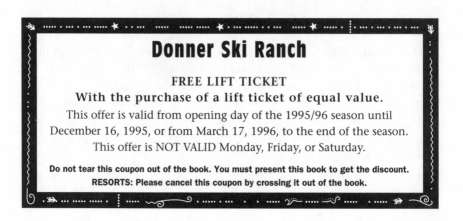

Donner Ski Ranch

FREE LIFT TICKET
With the purchase of a lift ticket of equal value.
This offer is valid from opening day of the 1995/96 season until December 16, 1995, or from March 17, 1996, to the end of the season. This offer is NOT VALID Monday, Friday, or Saturday.

Do not tear this coupon out of the book. You must present this book to get the discount.
RESORTS: Please cancel this coupon by crossing it out of the book.

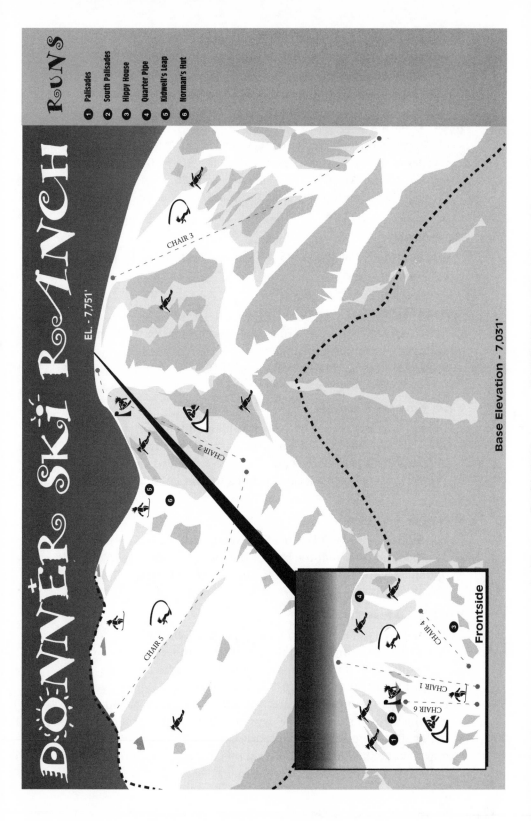

DÖNNER Ski RANCH

RUNS

1 Palisades
2 South Palisades
3 Hippy House
4 Quarter Pipe
5 Kidwell's Leap
6 Norman's Hut

EL. - 7,751'

CHAIR 3

CHAIR 2

CHAIR 5

Base Elevation - 7,031'

CHAIR 4

CHAIR 1

CHAIR 6

Frontside

The Season and Hours

The season at Donner Ski Ranch runs from October 31 through May 31. Lift hours are 9:00 A.M.–4:00 P.M. Evening skiing is 4:00–7:00 P.M. Half days start at 12:30 P.M.

Lift Tickets

All day on weekend—Adult/Senior/Youth/Child: $20/$10/$10/$5
Half day on weekend—Adult/Senior/Youth/Child: $16/$10/$10/$5
Midweek—Adult/Senior/Youth/Child: $10/$5/$5/$5
Evening—Adult/Senior/Youth/Child :$5/$5/$5/$5

Specials

The beginner's package is $45. School packages and other promotions are available.

Logistics

Drive eighty-five miles east of Sacramento on I-80 and take the Soda Springs exit. Donner Ski Ranch is 3.5 miles from the freeway on Soda Springs Road, just past Sugar Bowl.

The Local Scene

Donner Ski Ranch is one of the best values in the Tahoe area. While not as big as Sugar Bowl or other nearby resorts, it has the advantage of $10 midweek lift tickets, along with some first-rate snowboarding terrain. It's a funky cross between a locals' ski hill and a rippin' snowboarders' spot.

Where to Stay

The **Summit House** at Donner Ski Ranch, (916) 426-3622, provides accommodations right at the base of the mountain. For other lodging options, see the North Lake Tahoe introduction on page 110.

Tell Your Friends

Along with a terrain park and half-pipe, you'll find a few serious cliff drops that have compressed the vertebrae of more than one overly aggro rider. Don Bostick, a walking institution who organizes and judges many of the snowboarding competitions at Donner, Boreal Ridge, and other nearby ski areas, is one of those snowboarders who's walking an inch shorter these days from a flat landing off one of Donner's cliffs. If you're looking into the competitive scene in Tahoe, track down Don at his Donner Ski Ranch office or say hi to him in between heats at the judges' stand.

If you sneak through the trees on the southwest side of the ski area, you'll end up on the road, near Sugar Bowl. Check ahead, but a shuttle usually runs by here regularly and will carry you back to the Donner ski area. According to Bostick, the natural half-pipe down here is the historic birthplace of the 360.

The Mountain

Donner actually has one and a half hills. From the lodge, you can look up the front face of the first hill, also called "frontside," but once you're on top of this one, you'll be looking down the "backside," which is actually two peaks. With a few exceptions, the most interesting terrain is on the backside.

Freeriders

Freeriders will spend most of their time on the backside if the snow's packed, although on powder days, the main face has the longest runs and some of the best steeps, particularly on either side of the notorious cliff band that's just uphill from the lodge. The South Palisades, to the left of chair 1 and beyond the cliffs, is a great spot for big hits. A huge cat-track drop coming off the top on the right side of chair 1 is often called Kidwell's Leap. On powder days, epic, unlimited air is possible here.

Cruisers

Cruisers will find several long, fast, groomed runs on the mountain. Kidwell's is a popular one, as are numerous tracks off the backside.

Freestylers

Some tree slides and good hits are scattered throughout the mountain, particularly under chair 3. While it changes from year to year, 1995 featured half-pipes on both the front and back sides. There are some steep bump runs on the expert section of the backside below chair 2. To the left of chair 5, as you're facing uphill, seek out the fat jumps near the area boundary.

Grommets

Donner Ski Ranch has an active school program and plenty of terrain for beginners to try their wings, although the learning area and much of the traffic under chair 1 tend to overlap, and occasionally collide.

Nonbelievers

Skiing, like snowboarding, is a low-tech activity at Donner. You'll see far more skiers in jeans than in fancy ski outfits on this hill. Cross-country skiers can scoot down to the Norden cross-country area, a couple of miles back toward the freeway.

Heavenly Ski Resort

P.O. Box 2180
Stateline, NV 89449

Phone: (702) 586-7000
Fax: (702) 588-5517
Snowphone: (916) 541-SKII or (712) 586-7000
Elevation: base, 6,540' (California), 7,200' (Nevada); top, 10,040'; vertical, 3,500' (California), 2,840 (Nevada)
Lifts: 24 (1 aerial tram, 3 high-speed quads, 8 triples, 7 doubles, 5 surface lifts) covering 4,800 acres
Terrain Variety: 35% advanced, 45% intermediate, 20% beginner

The Season and Hours

Lifts operate 9:00 A.M.–4:00 P.M. Monday through Friday, and 8:30 A.M.–4:00 P.M. on weekends and holidays. The season begins in mid-November and extends through late April.

Lift Tickets

All day—Adult/Youth/Child/Under 7: $42/$30/$18/Free
Half day—Adult/Youth/Child/Under 7: $29/$25/$12/Free

Specials

Call (800) 2-HEAVEN for current information on the resort's lodging-and-lift and lodging-lift-and-lesson packages.

Logistics

Heavenly is located at the top of Ski Run Boulevard, off Highway 50. If you're a Californian, head for the state line and turn right just before reaching Nevada. The Nevada base lodges are located off Kingsbury Grade (Highway 207); just follow the signs.

There's a free shuttle service to the mountain from Heavenly Ski bus stops, located near most of the lodging properties. The buses run every twenty to thirty minutes from 8:00 A.M. to 5:30 P.M. daily.

The Local Scene

Being the largest Tahoe-area mountain and sitting on the border of Nevada, Heavenly is the stop for the biathletes competing in boarding and gaming. It's not a locals' mountain, and because there's so much terrain, you won't find groups of boarders collecting in any one area.

HEAVENLY

EL. - 10,040'

Base Elevation - 6,540'

WEST BOWL
GUNBARREL
AERIAL TRAMWAY
WORLD CUP
POWDERBOWL
WATERFALL
GROOVE
CANYON
PATSY'S
RIDGE
SKY EXPRESS
DIPPER EXPRESS
COMET EXPRESS
OLYMPIC
NORTH BOWL
STAGECOACH
MOTT CANYON
GALAXY

Heavenly's nightlife happens in Nevada. The nearest shop that can outfit you with equipment, apparel, and rentals is the **Boardinghouse**, next to Long's Drugs on Highway 50.

Where to Stay

Heavenly operates a complete travel and reservation service that you can access by calling (800) 2-HEAVEN. With over 11,500 lodging units from which to choose, from five-star casino suites to basic motel units, they'll be able to set you up with something.

The Mountain

Heavenly's a big place. It takes two states to hold the mountain, it's that dang big. What you'll find on the mountain is an endless supply of tree runs, good cruisers, and some challenging steeps in Mott Canyon. On a powder day you can do no wrong at Heavenly, and on the sunny days you'll find some good turning on the groomed runs. The one important thing to remember when navigating Heavenly is to return to the state where your car is parked before the lifts close.

Freeriders

It's no secret that Mott Canyon holds the best terrain on the mountain if you like steeps, powder, and some nice hits and lips to launch from. The canyon is protected from the wind, and you'll find that snow accumulates here like nowhere else on the mountain. If you're a tree lover, Heavenly has the goods. Basically, everywhere you look there's a good stand of well-spaced trees, so we don't have to tell you where to go. Some locals told us that you can find snow near the boundary areas, such as off the Powder Bowl and West Bowl chairs, many days after a dump. The trees coming down off Olympic Downhill are filled with rocks, logs, and drops every few yards, and in fresh snow you can find no better place on the mountain for some goofing off.

You do want to stay out of Killebrew Canyon, even though there are some good steeps. The traverse out will take all the joy out of the experience.

Cruisers

The groomers on the mountain keep a large number of trails well polished. On the California side, try out the runs coming off the Canyon chair—Canyon, Steamboat, and Rusutsu. When it's groomed, Ellies off the Sky Express chair will give you a steep fall-line pitch on the mountain to turn down. For some longer burners, the Nevada side offers the Olympic Downhill (roller and banks make this a fun one), the Big Dipper off the Upper Express, and the Perimeter and Galaxy runs off the Galaxy chair.

Freestylers

New in 1995 was a snowboard park located off the Olympic Downhill on the Nevada side. They're still perfecting the architecture and layout, but the managers are committed to building a quality park and have the resources to do it. If you're looking for hits, just about every run on the mountain has some sidewall hits. The tree runs also open up some good jumps and bonks. Check out the rocks on the boundary side of West Bowl (California side), and the hits sprinkled through the trees underneath the North Bowl chair in Nevada.

Grommets

Go to the Shred Ready snowboard school at the Boulder Lodge or California Lodge for beginning, group, and private snowboard rentals. A Shred Ready beginner snowboard package ($35) includes a three-hour lesson and beginner lift access (you have to take care of your own rentals).

Nonbelievers

To ski here, you just have to rent a pair of skis from one of the shops in town. But to get lucky at the tables, you have to believe.

Kirkwood

P.O. Box 1
Kirkwood, CA 95646

Phone: (209) 258-6000
Fax: (209) 258-8899
Snowphone: (415) 989-SNOW (San Francisco); (510) 939-SNOW (East Bay); (408) 236-SNOW (South Bay); (916) 448-SNOW (Sacramento, Tahoe); (209) 258-3000 (all other areas)
Elevation: base, 7,800'; top, 9,800'; vertical, 2,000'
Lifts: 11, none high-speed
Terrain Variety: 35% advanced, 50% intermediate, 15% beginner

The Season and Hours

The season runs mid-November through May. Lifts operate from 8:30 A.M. to 4:30 P.M. daily.

KIRKWOOD

THIMBLE PEAK
9,800'

Base Elevation - 7,800'

RuNS

1. Sentinel Bowl
2. Rabbit Run
3. Sentinel
4. Jim's
5. Chamoix
6. Firebowl
7. Stump Run
8. Free 'n' Easy
9. Olympic
10. Monte Wolfe
11. The Drain
12. The Sisters
13. Wagon Wheel Bowl
14. Notch Chute
15. Eagle Bowl
16. Shotgun
17. Cold Shoulder
18. Larry's Lip
19. Hully Gully
20. The Wave

To Palisades Bowl

9 BUNNY

7 HOLE IN THE WALL

6 CORNICE

5 SOLITUDE

11 THE REUT

10 WAGON WHEEL ("THE WALL")

1. SNOW KIRK

2. CAPLES CREST

3. IRON HORSE

4. SUNRISE

Lift Tickets

All day—Adult/Young Adult (13–24)/children: $42/$30/$18
Learn-to-Ski Program: $30
Mighty Mountain Children's All-Day Ski School: $50

If you purchase your tickets through BASS, you'll save $5 off Adult and Learn-to-Ski lift tickets and $10 off a Mighty Mountain ticket. The numbers for Californians are: (510) 762-BASS, (408) 998-BASS, (707) 546-BASS, (916) 923-BASS, and (209) 226-BASS. Outside of California, call (800) 225-BASS.

Specials

If you plan to board Kirkwood more than four days in a season, stop by the Avid Skier Center in the main lodge and get an Avid Skier card, which entitles you to a free day of boarding after you pay for four.

Logistics

Getting to Kirkwood isn't always possible when the storms hit the Tahoe area, and chain requirements are a fact of life if you don't own a four-wheel drive. Once you reach the mountain, though, you'll know that the drive was worth it. From the Bay Area, take I-580 east to I-205, then get on Highway 88 just before Stockton and follow it to Kirkwood. If snow has been falling, your best bet is to take Highway 50 toward Lake Tahoe, turn south on Highway 89 and then south on Highway 88.

The Local Scene

Set apart from the South Lake Tahoe sprawl, Kirkwood has a unique feel among Tahoe resorts—something akin to an alpine getaway. On the winding drive up, you'll see nothing but mountains until you reach the gas station and the Kirkwood Inn. Apart from these structures, the area is wonderfully underdeveloped save for the lodge and condos. The **Kirkwood Inn**, which has stood for about 130 years, is a good place to stop on the way in or out. A full bar, beer on tap, big food, fireplace, and the wood-floor ambience provide any number of reasons for a visit. At the resort, the **Red Cliffs Main Lodge** offers homemade soups, sandwiches, barbecue, and comida mexicana, all served up by snowboarders posing as food-service technicians. **Zak's Bar** is a place to get a beer, or for a more "tasteful" venue, check out the **Cornice Restaurant and Bar.**

The refreshingly low-glitz scene might be changing in the next few years. Telluride Ski Company recently acquired a major interest in Kirkwood, with an eye to developing more than one hundred acres of private land at the resort's base. The developers maintain that preservation of the pristine wilderness environment will remain a top priority (just below making a return on their investment). Whether or not the base area turns into a zoo, all snowboarders should check out Kirkwood's terrain, which is some of the best in the Tahoe area.

Where to Stay

There are over one hundred condos and hotel rooms to choose from near the slopes; they start at $65 for two people and go up from there. Call **Kirkwood Central Reservations** at (800) 967-7500 for information and reservations. If you want to rent a cabin or privately owned condominium, call **Kirkwood Real Estate** at (209) 258-7777.

The Mountain

Among the Tahoe resorts, Kirkwood owns the highest base elevation by about a thousand feet. When the weatherbabe is saying El Niño every other sentence (Pineapple Storm in the others), this higher elevation translates into a better chance for snow when the other mountains are getting rain. The mountain has volcanic origins, and as a result a unique series of natural gullies and chutes stream down the faces. For snowboarders, these natural half-pipes provide the opportunity to line up hits off the hips, tear big turns on the walls, or carve some high-banking turns. For purposes of discussion, you can divide the mountain into three faces: the backside (Sunrise chair), the main face, and the Sentinel Bowl area. The main face is where most of the snowboarders hang out, but you're not doing the mountain justice if you don't explore the intermittent trees, abundance of steeps, chutes, and cliffs, big bowls, and cruisers. Kirkwood will bring out the Lewis and Clark in you, and in the process will put all your abilities to the test.

Freeriders

The mountain probably first erupted with freeriders in mind. There's such a large variety of terrain that in order to get to any particular feature, you have to negotiate so many terrain changes that riding here will make a freerider of anyone. Here are the things, though, that you shouldn't miss. In the center of the main face, a series of chutes feed down into the Drain. The Drain itself is one of the best playgrounds on the mountain, with high walls and consistently spaced hits all the way down. Above these chutes is a cliff band called the Sisters that features some extreme jumping opportunities, and the steeps beneath them are seldom bumped out. The trees on the main face come in narrow bands between the runs, but they are spaced out for some short glade runs.

On the Sentinel face, the cliffs above Sentinel Bowl coming down into Jim's are perhaps the most photographed on the mountain. Here you can easily find fifty- or sixty-foot drops, or less extreme descents off the wind lip at the top of the bowl. The landing is steep and the run-out sufficient to avoid the trees below unless you get on that back foot and lose mental functions. When the gates are open to Palisades Bowl, the traverse is pretty darn close to being worth it.

On the backside, the Wave is a big wind lip where you can go as big as you want. When snow has been falling, this will do more for your ego than one of those Publishers Clearing House letters. Just remember to cut hard to the left after your victory drop to avoid the flats beneath Fawn's Ridge. The rock band off Larry's Lip is a big lunker, and a scouting run would be time well spent.

Cruisers

The cruiser runs are steep, twisting, and for the most part filled with a good number of rollers and banks to keep things interesting. On the main face, the groomers hit Lower Monte Wolfe and Racecourse religiously, and you'll usually be in for some good turning off the Solitude chair (chair 5). On the backside, the snowcats maintain a trail coming down Hully Gully that's a steep fall-line pitch. You'll also find a run down Cold Shoulder a good opportunity to lay out some turns. Coming down from Sentinel Bowl, they keep the Sentinel run groomed, and this links up nicely to Stump Run (sometimes a little bumpy) and Free 'n' Easy, a wide-open run where you can carry some speed. The Hole in the Wall chair (chair 7) services the best intermediate area on the mountain where you can lay down the arcs.

Freestylers

The Drain, formed millions of years ago, proves that order and intention were ingredients of its creation. The Drain is a natural half-pipe that the chutes coming down from the Sisters feed into. Here you'll quickly see the series of hits that line up. The takeoffs are well formed, the landings are steep, and the pitch keeps you moving. After a few runs you'll have the lines wired. Another run that's essential to check out is Snowsnake Gully. The walls aren't as high as in the Drain, but the hips are Polynesian and more pronounced, and the hits line up nicely. You'll find more of the same in Lost Cabin Gully, and for the most part if you stay between chairs 5 and 11, you'll have no trouble finding your share of hits. There's talk of a snowboard park off chair 2 for the 1995–96 season. If it's not there, make sure you pay a visit to the main office and fill out a comment card and demand one.

Grommets

The Bunny chair (chair 9) services a beginners' area, which is set off from the rest of the runs for some peaceful, easy learning. The Learn-to-Snowboard package (rentals, lift, two-hour lesson) goes for $50. After you're dialed into the basics, chair 7 features the best intermediate run for taking your skills to the next level.

Nonbelievers

In addition to being a mountain that's unanimously popular with skiers, Kirkwood's Nordic area is one of the most extensive and most beautiful areas in the region. Eighty kilometers of trails, a warming hut, and its own professional Ski Patrol are just a few features.

Mt. Rose

22222 Mt. Rose Highway
Reno, NV 89511

Phone: (800) 754-7673 or (702) 849-0704
Fax: (702) 849-9080
Snowphone: (702) 849-0706
Elevation: base, 8,260'; top, 9,700'; vertical, 1,440'
Lifts: 2 quads, 3 triples
Terrain Variety: 35% advanced, 35% intermediate, 30% beginner

The Season and Hours

The mountain opens in mid-November and operates through mid-April, with lifts running from 9:00 A.M. to 4:00 P.M. daily.

Lift Tickets

All day—Adult/Child: $32/$23
Half day—Adult/Child: $14/$8

Specials

A group of two adults and one or two children ride for $70 any day of the week. Midweek specials include a free group workshop on Tuesdays and free rental equipment on Wednesdays (not offered on holidays). Beginner lesson packages are also available.

Logistics

Mt. Rose is only fifteen minutes from Incline Village, on Tahoe's North Shore. From the Reno airport, it's a twenty-five-minute drive. To get

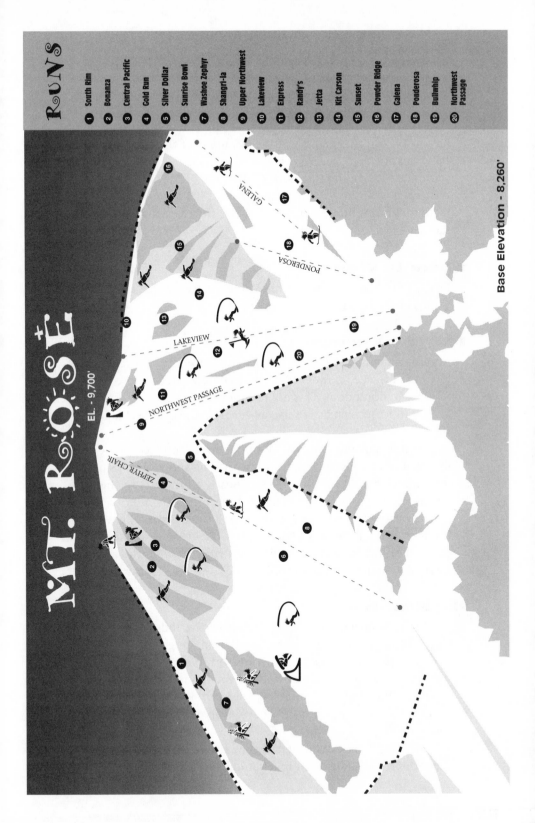

MT. ROSE
EL. - 9,700'

Base Elevation - 8,260'

RUNS
1. South Rim
2. Bonanza
3. Central Pacific
4. Gold Run
5. Silver Dollar
6. Sunrise Bowl
7. Washoe Zephyr
8. Shangri-la
9. Upper Northwest
10. Lakeview
11. Express
12. Randy's
13. Jetta
14. Kit Carson
15. Sunset
16. Powder Ridge
17. Galena
18. Ponderosa
19. Bullwhip
20. Northwest Passage

ZEPHYR CHAIR

NORTHWEST PASSAGE

LAKEVIEW

GALENA

PONDEROSA

there from Reno, take Highway 395 south, then go west on Highway 431 toward Incline Village.

The Local Scene

Mt. Rose has legendary status with snowboarders, even though the Mt. Rose that's often featured in snowboarding videos is the backcountry area just down the road. Nevertheless, many of the area's best riders hang out at Rose.

Because it's on the east slope of the Sierra, Rose gets good, dry snow compared with the rest of Tahoe. There's a hard-core snowboard race team that trains on Rose, particularly on the steep runs under the Ramsey's lift.

Where to Stay

Plenty of lodging is available in Incline Village, as well as in some big, gaudy, cheap hotels in Reno. Take your pick.

Tell Your Friends

In case you're tempted to jump over the fence into the steep, sweet-looking untracked powder that's wedged between the Rose and the Slide sides, don't do it. This is a notorious avalanche chute that's been known to let loose massive slab avalanches, the deadliest kind of slides.

If you're hankering for an out-of-bounds experience, we've been told that in rare perfect conditions with a big snowpack, it's possible to ride from the top of the Slide side nearly all the way to Highway 395 (but if anybody asks, you didn't hear it from us).

The nearby Mt. Rose recreation area (located across Highway 431 from Mt. Rose ski area) is a backcountry boarder's dreamland. Knowledgeable snowboarders can find some switchback shuttles and easy hikes that open up thousands of acres of untracked snow.

The Mountain

The Mt. Rose area used to be separate from the Slide Mountain ski area on the other side of the hill, but it's all been merged into a single park now. This is great for boarders, because on those spring days when the snow conditions live or die by the sun, you can move from the southern-exposure Slide side to the north-facing Rose side to stay with the best conditions. Likewise, on stormy days, everyone smart will flee to the Slide side to get out of the wind.

Rose is a big mountain that's prime for freeriding and carving, but a giant new half-pipe, built in a natural curved gully, and a giant snowboard park where it's possible to get twenty or thirty feet of vertical air definitely round out its potential as an all-around boarder's haven.

Freeriders

Freeriders will find all kinds of terrain on the Mt. Rose side, including trees along the edges of the runs between the Northwest Passage chair and the Lakeview chair. Next to the lower Lakeview run there's a natural terrain garden with wind lips and kickers.

On the Slide side, you can traverse over toward the closed area and ride the trees just along its boundary into Shangri-la. Here, too, big hits with excellent landing zones await. Right below the top of the Zephyr chair, look for a steep rock outcropping that constitutes a drop for the crazed few.

Finally, on powder days after a storm, make the hard traverse from the top of the Zephyr chair all the way over to South Rim. There you'll find a wide tree glade that leads down to the Washoe Zephyr run.

Cruisers

Cruisers will love Mt. Rose. The Rose side has lots of expert groomed runs, including Greg's, which has some huge rolling airs in the middle if you're going all out. The Slide side has wider intermediate runs ideal for big laid-out turns.

Freestylers

A snowboard park was under construction when we were there (well below the Bonzai run). The half-pipe, which curves around a bend, is unique. It looks possible to get some fat air over the inside bend of this corner.

The tabletops they were building at Rose can only be described as mammoth. One boarder, on a test run, stuck a method with an easy twenty-five feet of vertical as we stood with our mouths gaping.

Grommets

Rose's beginners' area pretty much dominates the bottom half of the Mt. Rose side. The Ponderosa and Galena chairs are exclusively devoted to beginners. More advanced riders are expected to stay to one side of the incredibly wide Easy Street run.

Nonbelievers

Skiers will be quite at home at Rose: there are lots of groomed trails and not a few mogul fields. Like many of the areas in the South Lake Tahoe region, Rose is in close proximity to a host of indoor entertainments. Snow parks and cross-country ski trails are also abundant in the area.

Mt. Shasta Ski Park

104 Siskiyou Avenue
Mt. Shasta, CA 96067

Phone: (916) 926-8610
Fax: (916) 926-8607
Snowphone: (916) 926-8686
Elevation: base, 5,500'; top, 6,600'; vertical, 1,100'
Lifts: 2 double chairs
Terrain Variety: 20% advanced, 60% intermediate, 20% beginner

The Season and Hours

The resort is open from November through April, depending on conditions and interest. Lift hours are 8:30 A.M.–4:00 P.M.

Lift Tickets

Weekend—Adult/Senior/Junior/Pup: $26/$17/$17/$3
Afternoon (12:30–4:00 P.M.)—Adult/Senior/Junior/Pup: $17/$12/$12/$3
Night (4:00–10:00 P.M.)—Adult/Senior/Junior/Pup: $17/$12/$12/$3
Day and night (9:00 A.M.–10:00 P.M.)—Adult/Senior/Junior/Pup: $32/$23/$23/$5
Three days—Adult/Senior/Junior/Pup: $68/$42/$42/$7

Specials

Monday through Friday, an adult ticket is $21; on Tuesdays, all lift tickets are $16. Two-for-one night skiing is a special on Wednesdays and Thursdays. Discounted spring rates kick in around March 20.

Logistics

The turnoff to Mt. Shasta Ski Park is about 4.5 hours north of Sacramento on I-5. From Medford, Oregon, it's one hundred miles south. Just south of the town of Mt. Shasta, take the Highway 89 turnoff toward the town of McCloud. Look for the turnoff to the mountain a few miles in from I-5.

The Local Scene

Shasta's a long way from the big cities, and the resulting atmosphere is decidedly down-home. Off the mountain, you'll find the usual assortment of pizza huts and burger stands, but Shasta's not exactly hopping after hours. For cheap grub, stop by the **Bagel Cafe** on Alma Street in the town of Mt. Shasta. **Willy's** is the hangout for good beer. And don't forget that Saturday is Fiesta Night at the **Shasta Ski Park Cafe**—get a free Mexican dinner with the price of a night-skiing lift ticket.

Where to Stay

You'll find lots of hotels and budget motels in Mt. Shasta and nearby Dunsmuir. There are also a couple of nice bed-and-breakfasts in McCloud. Call the **Ski Park Lodge** at (916) 926-8610 for recommendations.

The Mountain

Shasta, arguably the most spectacular peak in the Cascade chain, is the northernmost ski mountain in California. Boarders here come from Chico, Redding, and the other towns of the north Sacramento Valley. The mountain's glacier-capped peak is visible from as far away as Sacramento on rare clear days.

Mt. Shasta Ski Park is a small operation located on the southern shoulder of the Shasta peak, a few miles outside the town of Mt. Shasta. This park replaced an older operation, the Old Mt. Shasta Ski Bowl, which was wiped off the map by a big avalanche.

Shasta currently runs two lifts. The beginners' lift services a big beginner slope with enough area and variety to keep most grommets going for days. The main lift runs up the middle of the steepest face on the mountain. Off to its sides, you'll find the mountain's hits and otherwise interesting terrain. Although the lift-serviced part of the mountain is pretty small, boarders can put in some great days here by looking for the goods along the edges.

Shasta has an excellent grooming operation, and cruisers will find plenty of silky-smooth, wide-open ground for carving fat turns.

Mt. Shasta Ski Park

$1 off a weekday lift ticket (all ages).
Valid Monday through Friday, non-holiday only.

$1 off night lift ticket. Valid every night-skiing night.

**Do not tear this coupon out of the book. You must present this book to get the discount.
RESORTS: Please cancel this coupon by crossing it out of the book.**

Freeriders

Down the boarders' left side of the face serviced by the main lift, you'll find the best rideable glade of trees. Midway down the right side, an outcropping of rocks offers a mess of steep drop-offs. On both sides, you'll find plenty of snow-covered rocks and other fun kickers.

Hard-core freeriders should investigate the backcountry riding on Shasta. When avalanche conditions permit, there's awesome riding to be had on the mountain's upper bowls.

Cruisers

Cruisers will feel right at home on Shasta, since almost the whole rideable part of the mountain is wide-open groomed faces.

Freestylers

In the trees on the run farthest to the right, look for the semisecret chute, probably the rippin'est natural terrain on the mountain. The Shasta groomers will also lay a half-pipe in this area when there's enough snow to build it up.

Grommets

Shasta's a great place to hone your skills. The beginners' hill is almost untouched by high-speed skiers and boarders.

Nonbelievers

Because Shasta is a small hill and it's such a locals' scene, skiers and boarders share the slopes pretty much in harmony.

Northstar-at-Tahoe

P.O. Box 2499
Truckee, CA 96160

Phone: (916) 562-1010; (800) 466-6784 (lodging)
Fax: (916) 562-2215
Snowphone: (916) 562-1330
Elevation: base, 6,330'; top, 8,610'; vertical, 2,280'
Lifts: 1 gondola, 4 express quads, 2 triples, 4 doubles
Terrain Variety: 25% advanced, 50% intermediate, 25% beginner

The Season and Hours

The season runs from November through April, depending on conditions and interest. Lift hours are 8:30 A.M.–4:00 P.M.

NORTHSTAR·AT·TAHOE

RUNS

1. Crouse Alley
2. Powder Bowl
3. Dutchman
4. East Ridge
5. Cat's Face
6. Pinball
7. Corridor
8. Springboard
9. Jibboom
10. The Gully
11. Boondocks
12. Main Street
13. Village Run
14. West Ridge
15. Challenger
16. Sierra Grande
17. Burnout
18. Rapids
19. Iron Horse
20. Back Door

MT. PLUTO
8,610'

BACKSIDE EXPRESS QUAD

LOOKOUT DOUBLE

BEARPAW CHAIR

CHIPMUNK

BEAR CUB

BIG SPRINGS GONDOLA

COMSTOCK EXPRESS QUAD

ARROW EXPRESS QUAD

RENDEZVOUS TRIPLE

ECHO TRIPLE CHAIR

VISTA EXPRESS QUAD

Base Elevation - 6,330'

Lift Tickets

Day—Adult/Senior/Child: $42/$21/$18
Afternoon (after 12:30 P.M.)—Adult/Senior/Child: $28/$21/$12

Seniors age seventy and over ride for $5.

Specials

Multiday ticket discounts are available. Club Vertical is a promotional program that's actually worth something if you go to Northstar more than a few times a season. For $69 you buy a Club Vert wristband that entitles you to a lift ticket and a $5 discount on all subsequent lift tickets. It also gets you into a special lift line that's often far shorter than the one the rest of those poor plebs must stand in. Moreover, the special line leads to a gate that's activated by your computer chip to tell you how many runs you've made on that lift. Throughout the season, Northstar will mail you notices of how many vertical feet you've logged and whether you're entitled to any freebies for your efforts. The chachkas start at seventy-five thousand vertical feet.

Northstar offers literally dozens of special packages, clinics, room-and-lift rates, and other promotions, many of which change annually. Have them mail or fax you a brochure.

Logistics

The turnoff to Northstar is halfway between Truckee and Kings Beach on Highway 267. Take this road about two miles up the hill to the big, multilevel parking lot. Valet parking is available. The rest of us take the hayride down from the lot.

The Local Scene

Snowboarders at Northstar are well outnumbered by intermediate skiers, many of whom stay in the condos scattered throughout the village and at the base of the mountain. Unlike other nearby North Lake Tahoe areas that have tight cliques of hard-core skiers, boarders, and beautiful people, Northstar is a very laid-back, family-vacation resort. It's one of the few remaining really big mountains where skiers sharing the lift frequently ask questions like, "Do very many places allow skiboarding?"

Before you arrive at the mountain, make sure you're carrying some extra bolts and nuts for your bindings, and a strap or two if your bindings are over a month old. There's no snowboard shop at the base of the mountain, and if you have equipment problems you may have to drive back into town to get functional again.

Where to Stay

Northstar has a gaggle of condos on the mountain (fifty-five hundred beds total), ranging from one-person studios to crowd-sized casas grandes. Lodging-lift-air packages and stay-and-ski-free packages can be a great value, particularly for groups. Call group sales at (916) 562-2265. Lodging is also available in Truckee; see the North Lake Tahoe introduction on page 110.

The Mountain

According to our expert skier friends, Northstar is pretty flat. We laugh when they tell us this, however, because the backside of Northstar after a good dump has to be one of the greatest in-bounds snowboard-ing spots in the world. ("Sure," you say, "after a big dump, Divisadero Street in San Francisco is also one of the greatest snowboarding spots in the world.")

Before you start dissing this statement, try to imagine 1,860 vertical feet of wide-open trees with a constant top-to-bottom pitch and three feet of fresh powder. Open this up with a single high-speed, top-to-bottom quad chair. Limit the crowd to a few clued-in snowboarders and a lot of intermediate skiers who don't know the meaning of trees. Then imagine yourself one of the few happy riders.

With an early start, it's no great trick to lay down forty thousand vertical feet a day by riding the Backside Express quad. That's twice what you can expect to do in a $500 day of heli boarding, assuming your legs can handle that many turns, your teeth can filter enough oxygen out of that many face shots, and your heart can survive the many big hits off fat wind rolls and buried stumps. If what you're after is copious miles of fresh tracks, this is the place.

Squaw Valley, Northstar's nearest comparable competitor, blows Northstar's doors off if you're comparing for steepness and terrain va-riety, but Squaw's steeps typically get rutted out in an afternoon, while Northstar's backside trees can stay good for days. We can think of other runs that are more gnarly, more interesting, more fun, or more remote, but it's hard to think of another place where you can expect to get in more powder turns in a day.

With the exception of the upper ridge, which is about a fifth of the frontside, Northstar *is* pretty flat. On the other hand, the whole mountain is a cruiser's dream. The backside has half a dozen long intermediate groomed runs with continuous steep pitch where we wouldn't be surprised to see a boarder with good legs rack up fifty thousand vert in a long day. Also good for intermediates are the long, velvety groomed runs that lead one into another all over the frontside of the mountain.

More advanced riders will want to haunt the trees off the top third of the mountain under the Comstock, Rendezvous, and Vista Express chairs that climb the upper ridge.

Freeriders

Freeriders will beeline to the backside after a snowfall. The Challenger run winds along the park boundary and hits a monstrous lip about a third of the way down. This spot is ripe for practicing 360s and other tricks, but have someone scout your landing unless you want to go the way of the space shuttle. This area leads down into the most untouched part of the mountain, including some wide-open glades with hits and small trees scattered everywhere. Halfway down the Railsplitter run, drop into the woods on the right to find a steep, hidden, tree-studded bowl. By riding down the West Ridge run a ways, then dropping back into the backside on the left, you'll get into another woodsy area that takes a long time to get bumped out.

Every boarder will want to avoid the so-called Back Door run from the top of the Lookout chair to the backside. This is a long, miserable traverse trail that's usually iced out, dangerous, and no fun.

Cruisers

With dozens of long, groomed runs for every ability level, Northstar is a mecca for hard-boot carvers. Experts will ride the Backside chair and stick to the many steep, groomed runs on that side, while riders looking for a mellower slope will favor the Vista Express quad and the Sunshine, Pinball, and Logger's Loop runs.

Freestylers

Northstar has an on-again, off-again half-pipe and an evolving terrain park in the Pinball area off the Vista Express chair. There are hits all over the mountain in the trees, but by far the best hit terrain is in the backside trees and off the Down Under run near the base of the Backside chair. Depending on the snow, you may also find good hits near the top and bottom of the Comstock Express chair.

Grommets

The resort's huge beginners' program is centered on the Chipmunk chair near the midmountain day lodge. While the mountain is incomparable as playground for intermediates and powder sluts, and has a great setup for rank beginners, there's only one long green trail: the Village run. Stretching from the day lodge to the base village, it's as unavoidable as it is endless—an icy people mover that's too flat for anything but perfecting your tailbone slams. All things considered, it's probably the most dangerous run on the mountain.

Nonbelievers

In the winter, you can ski, take telemark or cross-country ski lessons, or check out the miles of groomed Nordic ski trails (if $15 doesn't seem like too much to pay for a long-footed walk in the woods). The Northstar village lives up to its name, with day care, watering holes, several choices of dining, and miscellaneous money-spending opportunities. Special events are scattered throughout the season, so call ahead for details.

Sierra-at-Tahoe

1111 Sierra-at-Tahoe Road
Twin Bridges, CA 95735

Phone: (916) 659-7453
Fax: (916) 659-7749
Snowphone: (916) 659-7475
Elevation: base, 6,640'; top, 8,852'; vertical, 2,212'
Lifts: 10 (3 high-speed quads, 1 triple, 5 doubles, 1 surface) covering 2,000 acres
Terrain Variety: 25% advanced, 50% intermediate, 25% beginner

The Season and Hours

The lifts operate 9:00 A.M.–4:00 P.M. on weekdays, and 8:30 A.M.–4:00 P.M. on weekends. The season runs from mid-November through April.

Lift Tickets

All day—Adult/Teen/Child/Senior: $37/$27/$17/$17
Half day—Adult/Teen/Child/Senior: $25/$20/$13/$13

On Sundays, if you redeem your ticket by 2:30 P.M., you'll receive a $15 credit toward your next midweek visit.

Specials

Join Club Vertical for discounts on lift tickets and free prizes just for riding. You can also purchase two- and three-day tickets for further discounts. If you're visiting the mountain midweek, ask about discounts that have included Wild Women, Out-of-Staters, and free snowboard lessons.

SIERRA·A·AT·TAHOE

Huckleberry Peak
8,852'

SENSATION
TAHOE KING
NOB HILL
ROCK GARDEN
SLINGSHOT
PUMA
LYNX
EL DORADO
SHORT STUFF

Base Elevation - 6,640'

RUNS

1. Sugar 'n' Spice
2. Dynamite
3. Preacher's Passion
4. East About
5. Castle
6. Snowshoe
7. Jackrabbit
8. Snowboard Alley
9. Smokey
10. Coyote
11. Main
12. Sleigh Ride
13. Dogwood
14. Clipper
15. Powder Horn
16. Horsetail
17. Bashful
18. Pyramid
19. Marmot
20. West Bowl

Logistics

Sierra-at-Tahoe is located on Highway 50, about forty-five miles east of Placerville, California. It's easy to find. If you're staying in South Lake, call (916) 541-7548 for information on the complimentary shuttle bus.

The Local Scene

With the creation of its Snowboard Alley park, Sierra-at-Tahoe has generated a strong local following of boarders who hang out in the park or in the trees, much like those threatening characters you see haunting Central Park on TV, except these are snowboarders. At the mountain, you can start your day in the **Bake Shop** by powering down some coffee and muffins. The **Sierra Pub** stays open until 6:00 P.M. for a post-session beer. Since there are no other bars or restaurants close by the resort, you'll have to create your own scene wherever you're staying.

Where to Stay

See the South Lake Tahoe introduction on page 111.

Bum's Tip

Buy the bread bowl of chowder, load it with Saltines, and you won't need to eat for the rest of the day.

The Mountain

The mountain can be divided into three sides. The *West Bowl* offers a variety of wide cruisers and some nice steeps and trees. Going up the Sensation chair to *Huckleberry Peak,* you'll see any number of lines to take through the trees. The *Backside* offers mostly beginner and intermediate runs, but this is also where you'll find the board park. There are some really nice drops, steeps, and trees on the mountain, as well as wide cruisers and beginning terrain. As dumb as this sounds, we're going to say it: the mountain has something for everyone.

Freeriders

On the way up on the Nob Hill chair, if you look to your right about midway up, you'll be able to see a clearing in the trees where the Ice Cliffs are. Depending on the coverage, you can go really, really big there off three ledges with good landings. The one downside: we hit the ice cliffs early in the morning and followed the one pair of ski tracks out. We had to posthole the last forty yards or so. There may be a better way out, and if there is you'll find it by staying left after you clear the cliffs.

You'll want to spend a good part of the day sessioning the Sensation chair. The tree runs on both sides are fantastic—steep, long, through well-spaced trees. If you go left off the lift, toward Preacher's

Passion and Castle, you'll be heading into the windward side of the mountain where wind lips build up for all sorts of interesting hits. Going right off the lift, you'll be able to find fresh turns through the trees if you head down Sugar 'n' Spice for a ways before cutting in.

Cruisers

The cruising terrain isn't mondo steep, but there are some nice wide-open runs to turn down. Coming down the West Bowl, you'll want to check out Clipper first, then move out toward Powder Horn and Dogwood. These are basically the only solid cruisers on the mountain for getting your speed up. If you're a bump boarder, give the runs off Sensation a try.

Freestylers

Go to the Backside and hang out in Snowboard Alley park. There are some nice, big hits that you can let loose on, as well as some good quarter-pipe hits, a spine, and some gaps. The hits change throughout the year, but the architect is a snowboard park guru who keeps everything spaced out well and the landings are in good shape. You can find sidewall hits on Sugar 'n' Spice, but your calves will ache by the end of the run. Castle usually has some nice wind lips to hit off of, and you can find a good rock just below the Sensation chair coming down Dynamite.

Grommets

A one-day beginner session runs $37 for a two-hour lesson, rentals, and beginner's lift ticket. Two-day sessions go for $67 (full lift), and the ThreePeat is $97.

Nonbelievers

The skier-boarder situation appears very laid-back: skiers hang out on the runs; boarders hang out at the park or in the trees. Everyone seems pretty happy.

Ski Homewood

P.O. Box 165
Homewood, CA 96141

Phone: (916) 525-2992
Snowphone: (916) 525-2900
Elevation: base, 6,230'; top, 7,880'; vertical, 1,650'
Lifts: 2 doubles, 2 triples, 1 quad, 5 surface
Terrain Variety: 35% advanced, 50% intermediate, 15% beginner

The Season and Hours

Homewood opens in December and operates through April. Lifts run from 8:30 A.M. to 4:00 P.M. daily.

Lift Tickets

All day—Adult/Senior/Youth/Child: $32/$12/$11/Free
Half day—Adult/Senior/Youth/Child: $24/$10/$9/Free

Specials

Children under age eight ride free with an adult. A poma-lift-only ticket is $10 for all ages. Wednesdays are 2-for-1 lift tickets, and multi-day lift packages and lesson packages are available.

Logistics

Homewood is located on the west shore of Lake Tahoe, next to the picturesque village of Emerald Bay. To get there, take Highway 89 from Truckee and continue south past Tahoe City. It's about six miles out of Tahoe City.

The Local Scene

Looks can be deceiving. Homewood, from the north parking lot, appears to be a "dinky patch of nuthin'." The parking lot itself looks like it would hold about a hundred cars, and four of the five lifts you can see from there only go about a quarter of the way up the hill. One lift, however—the Madden triple—disappears over the top and into the unknown. This is the part of Homewood that's worth knowing.

Riders here have a quiet, knowing look behind their goatees and powder goggles. They tend to travel in pairs rather than packs. Generally, they don't say very much. Homewood is a freerider's dream, and

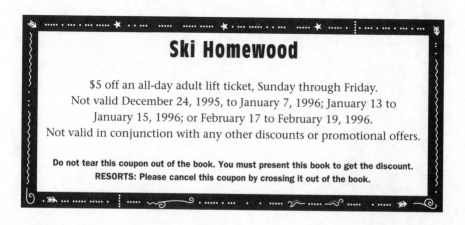

Ski Homewood

$5 off an all-day adult lift ticket, Sunday through Friday.
Not valid December 24, 1995, to January 7, 1996; January 13 to January 15, 1996; or February 17 to February 19, 1996.
Not valid in conjunction with any other discounts or promotional offers.

Do not tear this coupon out of the book. You must present this book to get the discount.
RESORTS: Please cancel this coupon by crossing it out of the book.

HOMEWOOD

EL. - 7,880'

Base Elevation - 6,230'

RUNS

1. Rainbow Ridge
2. Homeward Bound
3. Quail Face
4. Hobbit Land
5. The Glades
6. Hidden Vein
7. Ego Alley
8. Dutch Treat
9. Smooth Cruise
10. Lake Louise
11. Nugget
12. Bonanza
13. Woody Fellers
14. Tailings
15. Jimmy's Run
16. Glory Hole
17. Racecourse
18. The Face
19. Main Cirque
20. Wally's Folly

THE QUAD

TAILINGS T-BAR

ELLIS TRIPLE

QUAIL DOUBLE

MADDEN TRIPLE

SOUTH PLATTER

NORTH PLATTER

SPRING DOUBLE

ALPINE PLATTER

the boarders here seem to be weaving their way through the trees, even when they're riding the lifts.

Where to Stay

The most convenient place to stay is on Tahoe's northwest shore, but Homewood is close enough to the south side to stay in one of South Lake Tahoe's supercheap motels if you're willing to drive a little farther. It can be a difficult or impossible drive from the South Lake, however, right after a dump (when Homewood's at its finest).

The Mountain

Homewood is a wrinkled, convoluted mess of a "mountain." It can roughly be divided into five areas: the north face, the frontside, the backside, Hobbit Land, and South Side. Assuming you're parking in the North Lot and riding up from there, you'll start out on the Madden triple, which carries you up over the aptly named Face (you can unload midmountain to ride this mogul field) to Rainbow Ridge. Rainbow Ridge divides the mountain into the frontside and the backside. A chair called simply the Quad services the backside, which is a series of groomed runs separated by wide swaths of tight, rideable trees. The frontside and Hobbit Land are serviced by a chair called the Ellis triple. The steepest groomed terrain is on the frontside, while Hobbit Land is a giant playground of open trees, powder fields, and hits. When the Ski Patrol deems it safe to open, you can traverse above Hobbit Land to the top of Quail Face. This is a giant, open avalanche bowl that's a powder boarder's dream.

From Quail Face, you can ride down to Sunny Side, then down to the Quail chair at the South Lot parking area. To get to this chair from the base of the Ellis triple, you have to make a long, sometimes foot-out traverse.

Freeriders

Freeriders will love the whole mountain, especially the trees on the backside, frontside, and Hobbit Land. Quail Face is a steep powder lover's dream. On the backside, ride the trees alongside Juniper and Nugget. Also don't miss the tree run called Woody Fellers that drops down off Rainbow Ridge. Halfway down any of the groomed runs on the backside, look for the potentially huge kicker off the cat track. All of Hobbit Land, between the groomed trails, is a giant tree slalom.

Cruisers

Cruisers will head for the backside groomed runs, like Lake Louise and Bonanza. For one of the longest cruising runs, take the High Grade trail all the way down to Ego Alley, which winds up at the base of the Ellis triple chair.

Freestylers

The Sluice Box is a cat track that intersects the runs off the Quad chair. Here you will have the chance to go extremely big with a nice groomed slope to land on. Homewood's terrain park is located on Juniper where the hits are big, though spaced a little tight. The only downside to sessioning the park is that you have a long, uninteresting traverse back to the Quad chair. Homewood is more a woodsperson's mountain, and when it's been snowing you won't see the boarders for the trees.

Grommets

Beginners are well served by the four beginners' lifts near the North Lot and one near the South Lot. There is one long beginners' trail that starts on Rainbow Ridge and zigzags down the mountain to the South Lot, but otherwise, this is really an intermediate-to-expert mountain.

Nonbelievers

Skiers will enjoy Homewood, especially the moguls and groomed areas near the South Lot and North Lot. This is one of the few resorts, however, where we'd say the terrain is really made for boarders.

Squaw Valley USA

1960 Squaw Valley Road
Olympic Valley, CA 96146

Phone: (916) 583-6985; (800) 545-4350 (reservations)
Fax: (916) 583-5970
Snowphone: (916) 583-6955
Elevation: base, 6,200'; top (Granite Chief; there are five other peaks), 9,050'; vertical, 2,850'
Lifts: 150-person cable car, 1 gondola, 3 quads, 8 triples, 15 doubles, 5 surface lifts
Terrain Variety: 30% expert/advanced, 45% intermediate, 25% beginner

The Season and Hours

The season runs from Thanksgiving through April, 8:30 A.M. to 4:00 P.M. Half days begin at 1:00 P.M.

Lift Tickets

All day—Adult/Senior/Child: $43/$5/$5
Half day—Adult/Senior/Child: $29/$5/$5

SQUAW VALLEY

SNOW KING
7,550'

KT-22
8,200'

SQUAW PEAK
8,900'

EMIGRANT
8,700'

GRANITE CHIEF
9,050'

GRANITE CHIEF

SHIRLEY LAKE EXPRESS

SOLITUDE

SILVERADO

BROADWAY

EAST BROADWAY

LINKS

BAILEY'S

BROKEN ARROW
8,020'

MAYNE

GOLD COAST

EMIGRANT

SIBERIA EXPRESS

RIVIERA

HIGH CAMP

SUPER GONDOLA

CABLE CAR

HEADWALL

SQUAW ONE EXPRESS

EXHIBITION

KT-22

OLYMPIC LADY

RED DOG

SQUAW CREEK

Base Elevation - 6,200'

RUNS

1. The Mountain Run
2. Half Pipe
3. Big Hits/Steeps
4. Massive Cornice
5. Hike to peak
6. Shirley Lake
7. Gold Coast People Watching
8. Squaw Creek Resort

Specials

Ice-skating, a pool and spa, and cable-car rides are extras.

Logistics

Squaw Valley is about halfway between Truckee and Tahoe City on Highway 89.

The Local Scene

Squaw's "local scene" is like a world beat. This is a major tourist destination and glamour resort, with a large contingent of local yupsters and well-to-do condo owners tossed in. Since it's also one of the biggest, baddest mountains anywhere, a huge number of boarders ride Squaw as well. If there's any serious deterrent to riding Squaw, it's the hefty ticket price.

Where to Stay

Squaw is a major resort hotel operation in its own right, with condos, houses, lodges, and a big high-rise hotel all within walking distance of the lifts. The Squaw Valley area has lots of privately owned rental units as well. For accommodations outside the valley, see the North Lake Tahoe introduction on page 110.

Tell Your Friends

Squaw has a full-sized ice-skating rink, a bungee jumping tower, and an ongoing international ski fashion festival. Ever since the Olympic skiing competition was held here in 1964, the area has served as one of the best lessons to nations the world over in how to really cash in on an international sporting event. Many of the staff at Squaw are on exchange from New Zealand. Kiwis are renowned for their ability to wear funny glasses, load people onto ski lifts, and hitch rides into town.

The Mountain

What Squaw seriously lacks in down-home feel and cheapness, it makes up for in size, variety, and quality of snowboarding terrain. If what you like is steep drops, rocky chutes, long runs, and thousands of fun hits, Squaw more than atones for the fact that its parking lot often resembles the world's biggest mall on the night before Christmas. There's plenty of radical steep stuff, which accounts for Squaw's legendary status, and for the aggro boarder, the real fun is on the fringes: the Palisades, the chutes off the top of Granite Chief, the cornices on the upper ridges, the chutes on the backside, and the woods near

Shirley Lake. Everywhere you look, you'll see a mix of steep drops, hanging lips, and juicy outcroppings just waiting to be bashed. Every boarder will find plenty to like about Squaw, and just about every salty snowboarder ends up putting in a good deal of time here.

Squaw is six major peaks: Snow King (elevation, 7,550 feet), KT-22 (8,200 feet), Squaw (8,900 feet), Emigrant (8,700 feet), Granite Chief (9,050 feet), and Broken Arrow (8,020 feet). With a few exceptions, the area is almost all big, open bowls, so few of the individual runs are named. The key to riding Squaw is knowing which peak has the best snow on any given day. It's impossible to ride the whole mountain in a day, so we usually stick to one area for a couple of hours, then switch when we need a change or the lift lines build up.

Freeriders

Squaw is the quintessential freeriders' mountain. Some of the best areas are the trees and hits near the Shirley Lake and Solitude lifts and the steep chutes under the Silverado chair.

A great run is to ride the KT-22 lift, traverse around the backside of the peak, and drop in off the ridge, looking for the great chutes and gullies below.

An area that's often deserted is Snow King, below the Squaw Creek chair. This offers some of the best tree riding at Squaw, although it's at a very low elevation compared to the upper runs, and the snow softens up early when it's warm.

Two all-time classic freeriding areas are the rocky ledges and steep chutes off Broken Arrow and the cornice and chutes off the upper part of Granite Chief, which you can get to only by hiking up.

Although it's hell at the end of the day, when it funnels thousands of skiers out of the woodwork, one of the funnest runs at midday is right down the middle Mountain Run. There's a huge natural creekbed half-pipe in here that's amazingly one of the last places to get tracked. Great kickers abound off the edges of the cat tracks.

Cruisers

Cruisers will lay dozens of miles of tracks in a day at Squaw. One of the best cruising runs, and the longest you can take, is to ride the Emigrant lift to the summit, then blow past the High Camp lodge on your way down the Mountain Run. Many carvers will hang out on the Mainline, Gold Coast, and Newport lifts and carve up the huge bowls under Squaw Peak and Emigrant Peak.

Rippin' cat tracks also come down off Red Dog and Olympic Lady, and racecourses are set near the base lodge on the Snow King side.

Freestylers

Squaw maintains an excellent half-pipe and a smallish terrain park under the Riviera chair. It's kind of silly to spend forty-three bucks to hang out in a half-pipe for a day when Squaw is such a huge mountain begging to be explored, but, hey, who are we to judge?

Grommets

Squaw's enormous ski school is based at High Camp, and this area has a huge beginners' snowfield. This may not be the homiest place to send your kids to school, but it's hard to fit Granite Chief into a one-room schoolhouse.

Nonbelievers

You don't want to snowboard? No problem. Tie a rubber band to your ankles and jump off a scaffold. How about putting slats on your feet and jumping off a cliff? If that doesn't interest you, go skating on thin ice and then take a swim. Speak seventeen languages over barbecued chicken, and scream when the cable car takes a "little swing" over Broken Arrow. It all happens at Squaw every day and people seem to enjoy it.

Sugar Bowl Ski Resort

P.O. Box 5
Norden, CA 95724

Phone: (916) 426-3651
Snowphone: (916) 426-3847
Elevation: base, 6,883'; top, 8,383'; vertical, 1,500'
Lifts: 3 quads (1 express), 5 doubles
Terrain Variety: 45% advanced, 40% intermediate, 15% beginner

The Season and Hours

Open 9:00 A.M.–4:00 P.M., November–April, depending on conditions and demand.

Lift Tickets

Weekend, holiday—Adult/Child: $37/$10
Half day any day—Adult/Child: $24/$10
Two days—Adult: $65
Midweek—Senior: $17
Gondola—Adult/Child: $5/$3

SUGAR BOWL

EL. - 8,383'

Base Elevation - 6,883'

RUNS

1. Fuller's Folly
2. Silver Belt
3. The '58s
4. Lake View
5. Chutes
6. Carl's Nose
7. Harriet's Hollow
8. Trailblazer
9. Christmas Tree
10. Sugar Bowl
11. East Face
12. Disney Nose
13. Avalanche
14. Eagle
15. Montgomery
16. Mad Dog
17. Crow's Face
18. MacTavish
19. Bacon's Gully
20. Lonesome Pine

SILVER BELT

CHRISTMAS TREE

JEROME HILL EXPRESS QUAD

NOB HILL

GONDOLA

VILLAGE CHAIR

MT. DISNEY

MEADOW

CROW'S NEST

Specials

Group and private lessons are offered for all levels. Sugar Bowl has numerous ski-lodging packages if you stay at its European-style hotel.

Logistics

Sugar Bowl is ninety miles east of Sacramento on I-80. Take the Soda Springs/Norden exit (the sign is often buried by snow) and follow the road about two miles to the ski area. If the main parking lot is full, continue another half-mile to the Mt. Judah parking lot, directly across the street from Donner Ski Ranch.

The Local Scene

Sugar Bowl is popular with boarders, many of whom make day trips from Sacramento and other valley towns. Since it's bigger than nearby Donner Summit and Boreal Ridge, it tends to draw more of a freeriding crowd. Still, it's a bargain compared to Northstar and Squaw farther east, and it tends to attract riders more into the small-and-funky scene than the glitzy-and-big destination.

Where to Stay

Sugar Bowl has its own cush old-fashioned hotel on the mountain. It's also within easy driving distance of Donner Lake and Truckee (assuming Donner Pass isn't closed by a blizzard, which happens several times a season). For more information on this area, see the North Lake Tahoe introduction on page 110.

When it comes to après-ski, choose the **Chalet** over the **Belt Room.** This bar reaches out to the snowboarder, from its placement in its own shack away from the main lodge, to the pool table and jukebox. It's a good mellow place far from the stretch-pants snow bunnies and Ernies. We've yet to find an exciting place to hang out in Norden, however.

The Mountain

Even though it's relatively small, Sugar Bowl has the look and feel of a big mountain. Along with Mt. Disney and Mt. Lincoln, the resort recently added a new peak, Mt. Judah, to the lift-serviced terrain. None of the runs off any of the peaks is more than a few minutes long, but Mt. Lincoln in particular offers big, steep terrain and a natural playground of hits and chutes that make Sugar Bowl a freeriders' fun zone.

It's hard to explain exactly what it is that makes Sugar Bowl a great snowboarding mountain. It has a good all-around balance of steeps, natural terrain, hits, and groomed runs, plus a series of chutes that will challenge the most extreme riders. It also has a down-home, friendly atmosphere that hits you even before you ride the gondola across the valley to the mountain.

Freeriders

Sugar Bowl's mountains are serviced by eight chairs, but most boarders looking for steep terrain will focus on two: the Silver Belt quad that runs up the center of Mt. Lincoln and the Mt. Disney double chair. As you ride the upper half of Silver Belt, you'll see Sugar Bowl's best directly below you. Silver Belt Canyon, a huge natural half-pipe lined by big rocks and hits, is an epic, experts-only run. It gets skied out pretty quickly once it opens, so arrive here early after a dump. Just east of this, Fuller's Folly winds through the woods and ends up above some big rock drops and chutes (watch out!). By riding farther over and turning down Chute 1, you'll be able to drop in and muster your courage above Carl's Nose—a big rock launch that's probably broken the face of more than one guy named Carl.

If you hike/traverse west from the top of the Silver Belt, you'll get to the '58. This band of cliffs and rock spires is threaded by some sick chutes and drops that are rarely ridden.

There are a couple of semisecret freeriding areas that get much less pressure than any other part of the mountain—Sugar Bowl and East Face, both of which require a short hike over the back of the hill from the Mt. Disney chair. When the snow's been falling and blowing, a good-sized cornice can develop at the top of East Face, and the run is plenty steep for face shots in the powder. At the bottom of this run, you'll have to ride the Silver Belt chair up Mt. Lincoln, or gun it over the long, flat Union Street run (sometimes a foot-out traverse) to get back to the Mt. Disney chair; come to think of it, this may explain why East Face gets so little pressure. When there's recent snow, one of the best steep powder runs is Bacon's Gully, also on the east side off the Disney chair.

The other semisecret spot is on Sugar Bowl's far-west side off the Crow's Nest chair. Traverse as far as you can to the left once off the chair, then drop into the trees. It's a short run with a fairly long flat section at the end, but it's worth it if you're hungry for some turns and hits in the trees.

Cruisers

The classic cruising runs at Sugar Bowl are on Mt. Lincoln—down Chute 2 or Lake View, then winding down the mountain through Henderson's Ridge and Chase Ridge. This loop brings you back to the

Silver Belt chair and sets you up for a fast top-to-bottom leg drainer. On days when the wind is whipping Mt. Lincoln or the chair is zooed out, you can alternate between the Crow's Nest lift and the Mt. Disney chair, which are usually less crowded.

The runs on the frontside of Mt. Disney are wide open and great for carving big turns, although if you carry much speed you'll eat up the vertical in a hurry.

Freestylers

Being in sight of Boreal Ridge and Donner Ski Ranch has probably made it a bit futile for Sugar Bowl to get into the jib-park business, so the mountain is pretty much all-natural terrain. On the other hand, the hits in Silver Belt Canyon and down through Broken Ankle, off the Jerome Hill chair, are good fun. The cat-track launches halfway up the Crow's Nest chair are ripe for picking fat airs, but post a lookout for people before your reentry.

Grommets

Sugar Bowl's a fine place to learn snowboarding (the authors both cut their teeth there). Lessons, and most of your first couple of days, take place on the Meadow run off the Meadow chair, an area rarely visited by high-speed skiers and boarders. There are lots of beginners' runs between the Christmas Tree and Jerome Hill chairs, and more adventurous beginners can wander off onto the many adjacent blue runs.

Nonbelievers

Sugar Bowl has great skiing conditions and a positive attitude toward boarder-skier relations. With a good balance of groomed and natural terrain, it seems to keep everybody happy. Sugar Bowl is also adjacent to the massive Norden cross-country ski area and about a fifteen-minute drive from Truckee and Donner. Nonskiers will enjoy the rustic atmosphere of the lodge and hotel.

Central California

The central California snowboarding scene is an exercise in navigation. Some of the best boarding in the state lies technically in the central part, at Mammoth and June, but central Californians have to drive farther than anyone else to get there. Mountain passes through the Sierra close after the first major storm and stay closed through April or May. To reach the eastern slopes of the Sierra, you have to either drive through Carson City, Nevada, or detour down to Bakersfield and then back up and around.

The resorts in the western central Sierra—Dodge Ridge, Sierra Summit, Bear Valley, and Badger Pass—are more locals' hangouts than destination resorts. As a result, you won't find the amped-up snowboarding scene of the Tahoe and Big Bear areas. You will find a number of dedicated riders, though, who make snowboarding at these mountains much more of a soul session than a fashion show.

While the central Sierra receives as much snow as the San Bernardino Mountains (much more snow on the eastern slopes), there aren't the same population centers to generate the big crowds, or the big dollars for the resorts. You won't find brass toilet seats or trains circling the parking lots—just many people escaping the valley, getting their turns in, having some fun.

Badger Pass

Yosemite Concession Services
Yosemite National Park, CA 95389

Phone: (209) 372-1332
Snowphone: (209) 372-1000
Elevation: base, 7,200'; top, 8,000'; vertical, 800'
Lifts: 1 triple, 2 doubles, 1 rope tow
Terrain Variety: 15% advanced, 50% intermediate, 35% beginner

The Season and Hours

The season begins on Thanksgiving and ends on April 4. Lifts operate from 9:00 A.M. to 4:30 P.M. daily.

Lift Tickets

Weekend all day—Adult/Child/Senior/Military: $28/$13/Free/$20
Weekend half day—Adult/Child/Senior/Military: $20/$9/Free/$9

Ask Dr. Jumper

Pain is a part of snowboarding. It begins with the first day on a board, when you're butt-slamming and head-planting your way to good form. Pain also besets the seasoned snowboarder with a good deal of frequency. Riders cursed by day jobs tend to ride hard on the weekends, and in the process stress muscles that aren't exercised on a daily basis. And anytime you're busting big air, playing near-miss in the trees, or perfecting a new trick, the odds are you're going to rattle molars, tweak a joint or two, and wake up the next morning feeling like a slow matador.

The best way to deal with pain is simply to ignore it, tough it out, pretend like you're one of those Jeremiah Johnson types who eats a lot of beef jerky. Denial has made America the great, dysfunctional country that it is. Another approach is to treat the pain. For advice on these matters, we've consulted an expert: Mike Jumper, M.D., a real doctor licensed in California (a.k.a. Dr. Jumper). Dr. Jumper doesn't snowboard yet, but he does know quite a bit about the management of pain.

The Big Picture

There are two very basic things you need to do to avoid injury: stay fit and stay hydrated. Do your training, which should include aerobic fitness and flexibility work, before you go up the mountain. Also, the stronger your muscles, the more they protect the joints from sprains and tears. Once you're on the mountain, remember that even if you don't think you're sweating, you are losing water. Dehydration slows your reflexes and causes you to lose strength, stamina, and coordination. Each of these symptoms increases your chances of injury.

Joint Injuries

Sprains are common in snowboarding, mostly in the upper body (wrists, elbows, shoulders, fingers), although the knees become vulnerable when you're spinning or starfishing down a slope. There's some hot/cold controversy as to how best to treat a sprain, but we'll clear the air with this edict from Dr. Jumper: treat with ice for the first twenty-four hours, then with heat the next day. Icing constricts the blood vessels and prevents blood from gathering in the joint. When you are icing, avoid treating the injury for longer than forty-five minutes at a time—the body will rush blood to the area to increase the temperature, thereby increasing swelling. After the first day, heat loosens up the joint, thereby relieving pain. Dr. Jumper says a hot tub will work just fine for heat treatment.

If you have a sprain, you might want to take acetaminophen (Tylenol) to control the pain, as well as an anti-inflammatory (naproxen or ibuprofen). These will complement the local therapy with cold and heat, which is by far the most important process to speed up your recovery.

Contusions

For the bruise (big and small), treat immediately with cold to prevent blood gathering at the injury, and then control pain with acetaminophen. Don't take aspirin—it's a platelet inhibitor that will actually increase the swelling and make your big green bruise spread out that much wider.

If you think you've broken something, stabilize the limb and ask someone to get help. If you try to ride down the hill with, say, a broken arm, a single fall could increase the severity of the break, or worse, rupture an artery, turning a bad situation into a life-threatening crisis. It's better to go on a sled ride with the Ski Patrol (you can hurl insults at them and then say you were delirious with pain) than try to navigate the out-of-control skiers on the bunny slopes near the lodge. Of course, if you sprained your pinky, don't be a weenie.

Soreness

Especially at the beginning of the season, you might experience that I've-been-in-a-car-crash feeling, character-ized by an allover, generalized hurt. This is your body telling you, via the buildup of lactic acids in the muscles, that you've pushed yourself hard. Dr. Jumper doesn't recommend it, but we've heard that a fine pilsner will take the edge off that pain. What Dr. J does advocate is treatment with Tylenol or Motrin, then a dip in the hot tub to get your circulation active. Hydration is another key to over-coming soreness. A good simple rule is: if it hurts, drink some water.

Hangovers

For some people, a hangover is the most common form of injury in snowboarding. For others, alcohol is the most common treatment of other injuries. Alcohol does have the ability to liquefy neuromem-branes and inhibit neurotransmitters, but on the downside it takes all the pain that you didn't feel and doubles it up for you the next morning.

A lot of people have their own home remedies for dull-witted mornings, but the most effective remedy is to pound water (hydrate) before you go to bed. If you do that, you give your body a fighting chance to flush the toxins out of your system. We've heard from some people that multivitamins are good to take while you're pounding water, as well as a cou-ple of Tylenol. If you forget to hydrate yourself and wake up feeling bad, there's nothing better than a freshly cut mango or two. Works like magic.

Some other things you should carry in your medicine bag are Alka-Seltzer, which will help settle the stomach (al-though long-term use disintegrates the lining of the stomach) and Pepto-Bismol. The bismuth in Pepto-Bismol binds toxins from certain bacteria that contribute to the symptoms of a hang-over, and basically pulls all the gnarly stuff out of your GI tract.

Drugs

Most snowboarders are somewhat reluc-tant to use drugs, but sometimes the pain is too much to bear. Here's a run-down on over-the-counter analgesics:

1. *Naproxen.* Found in Aleve as well as in prescription doses, naproxen is the longest-lasting anti-inflamma-tory and works best on joint strains and chronic joint pain (bursitis, arthritis). It can rag out your stom-ach if you haven't had anything to eat, and if you pop naproxen every day of the season, you run the risk of your kidneys shutting down be-fore the snow melts. But nothing works better for a joint that's not feeling right.

2. *Ibuprofen.* The supermarkets do a good job of supplying big tubs of generic or store-brand ibuprofen, and no responsible snowboarder travels without a bottle of this. Advil, Motrin, and Nuprin are some of the brand-name forms of the drug. Ibuprofen is used to treat in-flammation, muscle soreness, and swelling from bruises (ibuprofen's moderate antiplatelet effect should be mitigated through ice treat-ments). It and naproxen are the drugs to take for inflammatory reac-tions stemming from damage to muscles and soft tissues. You can also take ibuprofen in concert with (continued on next page)

acetaminophen for a pain-relief, inflammation-relief one-two punch.

3. *Aspirin.* This is the least expensive of pain relievers and functions much like ibuprofen in that it works well on inflammation. Aspirin can be hard on the stomach if it's not buffered, and because it's a platelet inhibitor, it will increase swelling and bruising if you take it in response to a contusion.

4. *Acetaminophen.* This is the drug that will actually lessen the sense of pain. While the drugs mentioned so far act more on the part of the body that has sustained the injury, acetaminophen (found in Tylenol) shuts down some of the pain receptors in the brain. It also reduces fever and is easy on the stomach (important when treating injuries incurred off the slopes). Acetaminophen is less effective for muscle aches, and it does little for inflammation. It's also highly toxic if taken in large doses, so don't play by "the bigger the pain, the bigger the pill" philosophy.

⇧ ⇩ ⇧

Midweek all day—Adult/Child/Senior/Military: $22/$13/Free/$16
Midweek half day—Adult/Child/Senior/Military: $19.50/$9/Free/$8

Lift-ticket prices do not include entrance to the park, which is $5 per vehicle plus $3 per person.

Specials

Beginners' packages are available. Persons exactly forty years old ski/ride free. Families staying in any of Yosemite's overnight accommodations ride for free at Badger Pass the following day (except on holidays). Call (209) 454-0555. Special child-care packages are also offered.

Logistics

Badger Pass is inside Yosemite National Park. From Fresno, follow Highway 41 to the south entrance of Yosemite. Take Wawona Road to Chinquapin, then take Glacier Point Road to Badger Pass (where the road ends in winter). Alternatively, from Merced, you can take Highway 140, which enters Yosemite at El Portal; from here, you wind through Yosemite Valley until you come to Wawona Road heading south. Take this to Glacier Point Road.

The Local Scene

There's no good reason to go to Badger Pass if all you want to do is snowboard. But if you're interested in seeing Yosemite at its most beautiful (especially free of tour-bus traffic jams and smog) *and* getting in a little boarding, it's a perfect destination. For families with kids who want to cross-country ski out to Dewey Point for a scenic picnic while mom and dad rage on snowboards on the hill, it's also a fine destination. Actually, you'll find mostly kids on the mountain, along with the occasional Coarsegold and Oakhurst local.

Where to Stay

Even in winter, there are many options for visitors who want to stay in or near the park. Call (209) 252-4848. For lodging outside the park, try the **Southern Yosemite Visitor Center,** (209) 683-4636 or (800) 208-2434.

Tell Your Friends

Strap on a pair of snowshoes or skis and hoof out to Dewey Point (about five miles). It's an absolutely incredible view in the winter.

The Mountain

Badger is a small mountain with a small mountain feel. It's a great place to ride if you're a beginner, or if you're tuning your intermediate skills. It's not that exciting if you're a hot rider looking for lots of big hits and chills.

Freeriders

Work on your fakie riding. Practice your 180s and 360s. Get ready for big days on big mountains.

Cruisers

Badger Pass is mostly groomed runs, so cruisers will style here. It's a pretty short mountain top-to-bottom, so expect to spend more time on the lift than on the hill.

Freestylers

Hits are sprinkled around. You'll have no trouble finding them.

Grommets

This is an A-1 spot for beginners. Badger is serious about lesson programs, and there's plenty of room for first-timers to maneuver. Because of its location, when you get tired of butt slams, you can take a break from boarding and hoof out to Dewey to see the sights or cruise into the valley.

Nonbelievers

For the family with cross-country skiers and snowboarders in the same station wagon, Badger Pass is an ideal destination. Hard-core backcountry skiers should inquire about the overnight Glacier Point trip with a stay in the backcountry cabin there. Other activities include guided snowshoe walks, snow play for kids, and ice-skating at Curry Village; call (209) 372-1445.

Bear Valley

P.O. Box 5038
Bear Valley, CA 95233

Phone: (209) 753-2301
Fax: (209) 753-6421
Snowphone: (209) 753-2308
Elevation: base, 6,600'; top, 8,495'; vertical, 1,895'
Lifts: 11 (2 triples, 7 doubles, 2 surface)
Terrain Variety: 30% advanced, 40% intermediate, 30% beginner

The Season and Hours

Mid-November through April, 8:30 A.M.–4:00 P.M. Half days begin at 12:30 P.M.

Lift Tickets

All day—Adult/Child: $28/$12
Half day—Adult/Child: $20/$10

Children age six and under and seniors age sixty-five and over ride for free.

Specials

Return an adult all-day ticket by noon and receive a $5 discount on your next all-day ticket.

Logistics

From the San Francisco Bay Area, follow I-580 to Highway 205, then take the Highway 120 east cutoff to Manteca. Proceed north on Highway 99 to Highway 4 east and follow this to the ski area, about four miles past Bear Valley village.

The Local Scene

Because Bear Valley is almost exactly between Tahoe and Yosemite, most of the boarders on the mountain originate in the South Bay area and the Sacramento Valley. As such, Bear Valley has much more of a

BEAR VALLEY

EL. - 8,495'

Base Elevation - 6,600'

RUNS

1. Water Tank
2. Sugar
3. Feather Duster
4. NASTAR
5. Tuck's Run
6. Home Run
7. Spring Gap
8. Groovy Gully
9. Mokelumne West
10. West Ridge
11. Slot
12. Red Baron
13. Flying Serpent
14. Parasite Pitch
15. Chutes
16. Tortilla Flat
17. Strawberry Fields
18. Westworld
19. Shady Grove
20. Bear Boogie

HIBERNATION CHAIR

POOH BEAR CHAIR

GRIZZLY CHAIR

KODIAK CHAIR

BEAR CHAIR

KUMA CHAIR

CUB CHAIR

SUPER CUB CHAIR

PANDA

KINDER

KOALA CHAIR

down-home feel than many of the big Tahoe resorts. Nevertheless, there's plenty of good terrain all over the mountain, including numerous sick chutes and gullies and big hits.

Where to Stay

A variety of lodging options are available in Bear Valley village, about four miles down the hill from the ski area. Contact the **Calaveras Lodging and Visitor Information Center** at (800) CAL-FROG or (800) 225-3764.

The Mountain

Bear Valley's layout is entirely the opposite of most mountains: Bear Valley gets hairier the farther downhill you go. The frontside bowls on the mountain's lower half, known as Snow Valley and Grizzly Bowl, are solid black diamonds laced with cliff bands and chutes. The entire backside of the mountain is a well-groomed intermediate playground.

Freeriders

Hard-core freeriders will spend most of their time on the lower mountain, downhill from the midmountain lodge. The chutes and bowls off the West Ridge traverse (best reached by riding either the Bear or Kuma chair to the summit) include Infinity, Flying Serpent, and Other Half. These are great steep pitches on powder days. Below these, you'll find two big cliff bands in the throat of Grizzly Bowl. Another pair of cliff bands bisects Snow Valley, east of the Kodiak chair, and features chutes such as Hari-Kari and Renegade.

Also look out for the massive hits below the Kuma chair on the upper mountain.

Cruisers

Cruisers will hang on the backside on the Westworld, Bear Boogie, and other runs below the Hibernation and Pooh Bear chairs. These are wide, groomed trails with plenty of room to open up. A NASTAR course and several other cruising runs can be reached from the top of the Koala chair at the east end of the resort.

Freestylers

Bear Valley has had an experimental snowboard park, which they're planning to get shaped up by the 1996 season.

Grommets

The beginners' area fans out uphill from the midmountain lodge. Grommets will hang out on the Kinder, Panda, Super Cub, and Cub lifts, depending on their adventure level.

Nonbelievers

Bear Valley is a scenic place, without the bustle of the Lake Tahoe region. Cross-country skiing and other nonsnowboarding activities are available out of Bear Valley village.

June Mountain

P.O. Box 146
June Lake, CA 93529

Phone: (619) 648-7733
Snowphone: (619) 934-2224; (619) 934-6166 (Mammoth); (213) 935-8866 (Los Angeles); (714) 955-0692 (Orange County); (619) 231-7785 (San Diego)
Elevation: base, 7,545'; top, 10,135'; vertical, 2,590'
Lifts: 8 (2 quads, 5 doubles, 1 tram)
Terrain Variety: 20% advanced, 45% intermediate, 35% beginner

The Season and Hours

The mountain opens in November and operates through April. Lifts run 8:30 A.M.–4:00 P.M. during the week and 8:00 A.M.–4:00 P.M. on weekends.

Lift Tickets

All day—Adult/Teen (13–18)/Senior or Child: $35/$25/$18
Afternoon—Adult/Teen/Senior or Child: $25/$20/$13

(Prices are the same as they were during the Bush administration.)

Specials

Tickets for three, four, and five consecutive days offer escalating discounts. If you plan to spend more than eight days at the mountain during the season, look into the June Mountain Club Silver card, which costs $60 and entitles you to $25 lift tickets.

Logistics

June lies about ten minutes north of Mammoth on Highway 395. Take the Highway 158 exit to June Lake and follow the signs. See the Mammoth Mountain entry for directions on how to fly in.

JUNE MOUNTAIN

JUNE MTN.
10,135'

RAINBOW
10,050'

Base Elevation - 7,545'

CHAIR J4
CHAIR J6
CHAIR J2
CHAIR J1
CHAIR J5
TRAM

RUNS

1. Silverado
2. Bodie
3. Gunsmoke
4. Rosa Mae
5. Rainbow Ridge
6. Chaparral
7. Schatzi
8. Deer Bowl
9. Dave's Drop
10. Pro Bowl
11. Matterhorn
12. Baby Face
13. River Run
14. Surprise
15. Canyon Trail
16. Gull Canyon
17. Gull Ridge
18. The Face
19. Carson
20. Wall

The Local Scene

Snowboarders will make a long drive to ride at June. Because of its half-pipe (one of the best in the nation) and snowboard park built to go big, June Mountain has emerged as a snowboarding destination for top riders.

You'll get kind of a lost-in-space feel while you're riding June. The town of June Lake is small and quiet, yet the resort features a state-of-the-art aerial tram, good food in a clean cafeteria, and its own Pipe Dragon.

Some of these amenities owe to June being part of the McCoy/Mammoth empire. But the mountain is by no means an overflow hill. June has its own unique terrain, its own feel (friendly, laid-back, barbe-cuing-on-the-deck vibe), and its own attractions for snowboarders. The mountain sponsors several USSA events each year, but the snowboard-ing scene doesn't resemble the pants-at-your-knees, Bible-sized-wallet-toting bunch you'd find closer to L.A. June is kind of out there on its own, and we think that's a good thing.

Where to Stay

Like Mammoth, June has a number of property-management outfits that can help you find a hotel or cabin:

Big Rock Resort, (619) 648-7717

Boulder Lodge, Inc., (800) 4-JUNELK

Century 21 Rainbow Ridge, (800) 462-5589

Fern Creek Lodge, (800) 621-9146

Gull Lake Lodge, (800) 631-9081

Heidelberg Inn at June Mountain, (800) 426-6493

June Lake Motel and Cabins, (800) 648-6835

June Lake Pines Cottages, (800) 637-7705

June Lake Properties Reservations, (800) 648-JUNE

June Lake Village Motel, (800) 655-6545

Reverse Creek Lodge, (800) 762-6440

Whispering Pines, (800) 648-7762

Bum's Tip

Ten-dollar Wednesday lift tickets bring out the bum in everyone.

The Mountain

Even if June isn't your primary destination, there are reasons to check it out while you're at Mammoth. Because of its lower elevation and because trees cover the entire mountain, June doesn't get the gale-force winds that will shut down the top of Mammoth. It's also home to a groomer who dedicates his winters to building big hits in the snowboard park off Gunsmoke and keeping the pipe at the bottom of Surprise in pristine condition. You really will find no better pipe in the West.

The mountain can be divided between the runs above the lodge where the tram lets out, and the runs below. Most folks stay on the upper mountain, but those in the know will head down toward the trees on the bottom half to get into fresh snow weeks after the last dump. The upper half of the mountain features the board park on the left and some steeps to the right. You're committed to one side or the other because of the way the lifts are laid out, so your best bet is to session chair 4 for a while, go down to the lodge, then take chair 2 up to chair 7. After putting your time in there, give the lower mountain a try if you're into things like fresh turns, steeps, and playing in the trees.

Freeriders

The upper mountain off chair 7 presents a series of steeps that will give you a few good turns. Then the terrain flattens out a bit and you're just cruising back to the lift. Your best choice for finding the goods is to come down Surprise, near chair 3, and cut to the left on Wall Road (above the half-pipe). You have to unbuckle and walk for three or four minutes to get to the pitch that opens up into Carson. The terrain here is virtually untouched except by people who know to come here and who don't mind a little hike. Along the boundary line, you'll find the best snow on the mountain. Gull Canyon, on the other side of the lower face, sees a little more action, but again, because the lower half isn't as frequented, you'll be able to get fresh turns for a long time after it's been snowing. On the entire lower mountain, you'll be in for some good tree runs where hits, logs, and rock jumps abound.

Cruisers

Schatzi, off chair 7, is the best cruiser run, with a steep fall-line pitch to turn down. Sunrise is another good bet—not as steep, but wide and always nicely groomed. The runs off chair 4 that are easy cruisers are Bodie and Rosa Mae. You can hit the trees off these runs for a while, but things flatten out in a hurry and on a powder day you'll be swimming out.

Freestylers

Gunsmoke. Half-pipe on Surprise. Nectar. 'Nuff said.

Grommets

Learn-to-Snowboard packages include lesson, rental, and lifts and cost $68. A lesson consists of a morning and afternoon session that run from 10:30 A.M.–12:30 P.M. and 2:00–4:00 P.M.

Nonbelievers

All the skiers we saw seemed to be enjoying themselves. June has the charm of a smaller resort, and the folks who visit here are just out to have fun. It's not a glitz scene or a grunge scene. More like folks on vacation playing in the snow.

Mammoth Mountain

P.O. Box 24
Mammoth Lakes, CA 93546

Phone: (619) 934-2571 or (800) 832-7320
Fax: (619) 934-0603
Snowphone: (619) 934-6166; (213) 935-8866 (Los Angeles); (714) 955-0692 (Orange County); (619) 231-7785 (San Diego)
Elevation: base, 7,953'; top, 11,053'; vertical, 3,100'
Lifts: 31 (2 high-speed quads, 4 quads, 7 triples, 14 doubles, 2 gondolas, 2 surface lifts) covering 3,500 acres
Terrain Variety: 30% advanced, 40% intermediate, 30% beginner

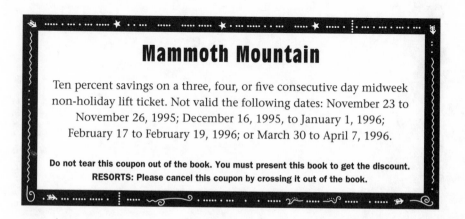

Mammoth Mountain

Ten percent savings on a three, four, or five consecutive day midweek non-holiday lift ticket. Not valid the following dates: November 23 to November 26, 1995; December 16, 1995, to January 1, 1996; February 17 to February 19, 1996; or March 30 to April 7, 1996.

Do not tear this coupon out of the book. You must present this book to get the discount.
RESORTS: Please cancel this coupon by crossing it out of the book.

MAMMOTH MTN.

EL. - 11,053'

Base Elevation - 7,953'

Mt. Lincoln

CHAIR 14
CHAIR 13
CHAIR 12
CHAIR 11
CHAIR 23
CHAIR 26
CHAIR 72
CHAIR 6
CHAIR 58
CHAIR 3
GONDOLA 2
CHAIR 18
CHAIR 2
CHAIR 10
CHAIR 21
CHAIR 5
CHAIR 22
CHAIR 10
CHAIR 4
CHAIR 16
CHAIR 17
CHAIR 7
CHAIR 8
CHAIR 9
CHAIR 25
CHAIR 15
CHAIR 24

RUNS

1. Hemlock
2. Felipe's
3. The Paranoids
4. Wipe Out
5. Cornice Bowl
6. Scotty's
7. Hangman's
8. Huevos Grande
9. Dave's
10. Dragon's Back
11. Dragon's Tail
12. Sunshine
13. Avalanche Chutes
14. Encore
15. Face of Five
16. Central Bowl
17. Wall
18. Agee's Run
19. Stump Alley
20. Jill's Run

The Season and Hours

Because of the incredible amount of snow that Mammoth receives, the season begins in early November and sometimes lasts through the Fourth of July. During the week, lifts run from 8:30 A.M. to 4:00 P.M.; on weekends, from 8:00 A.M. to 4:00 P.M.

Lift Tickets

All day—Adult/Teen (13–18)/Senior or Child: $40/$30/$20
Afternoon—Adult/Teen/Senior or Child: $30/$25/$15
Spring (effective April 24)—Adult/Teen/Senior or Child: $30/$25/$15

Specials

Tickets for two, three, four, and five consecutive days offer escalating discounts. If you plan to spend more than eight days at the mountain during the season, look into the Mammoth Club Silver card, which costs $60 and entitles you to $30 lift tickets. You can also find a deal in the lodging-and-lift packages that start at $58 a day based on a minimum of three days' lift tickets and three nights' lodging, midweek and nonholiday; call (800) 228-4947 for more information.

Logistics

Mammoth is located off Highway 395, on the eastern side of the Sierra. At the Mammoth Lakes junction, take Highway 203 west and follow the signs to the mountain.

Mammoth can also be reached by air through **TW Express**, which offers daily flights to Mammoth Lakes from Los Angeles, Orange County, San Francisco, Bakersfield, Monterey, San Diego, San Luis Obispo, and Santa Maria. Call (800) 221-2000 for flight information.

Once you're in Mammoth Lakes, a free bus service provides transportation to the mountain. If you plan to drive to the slopes, you'll be pleased to hear that Mammoth has recently installed a people mover to get you from the parking lot to the lifts.

The Local Scene

The town of Mammoth Lakes combines quaintness and alpine beauty with a local community of families and lift-ops. Mammoth Lakes is far more than a ski town: it's raising money to build a university, and the locals are already saying the town's getting too big. It's still a gem, though, situated on the eastern slope of the Sierra four hours away from any urban center.

The town has a lot to offer by way of après-boarding fun. Immediately after coming off the slopes, head for the **Yodeler** at the base of the mountain. There you'll find cheap beer served until seven. After dinner (the town's full of restaurants; take your pick), check out **Gringo's, Kegs 'n' Cues, Slocum's, Whiskey Creek,** or the famous **Goat Bar.** Each bar has its night, so ask around to find out what will be going off.

When it comes to board needs, you can visit the **Storm Riders Snowboard Shop,** (619) 934-0679, or the **Wave Rave Snowboard Shop,** (619) 934-AIR-1, on Main Street between Slocum's and Gringo's.

Getting around Mammoth is pretty easy on the free bus system. You'll have to put your time in waiting for a bus, especially in the afternoons, but they operate until midnight during the week and until 1:30 A.M. on weekends.

Overall, Mammoth is a friendly place. The town is laid-back and the folks are down-to-earth and easygoing. That's a broad generalization, but as our mothers told us, if you have nothing but good to say of something, then say a whole lot.

Where to Stay

Mammoth has a number of lodging reservation services. Here are a bunch of numbers. Maybe one can help you out.

Mammoth Accommodation Center, (800) 358-6262

Mammoth Country Reservations, (800) 255-6266

Mammoth Lakes Lodging Referrals, (800) 367-6572

Mammoth Lodging Connection, (800) 468-6386

Mammoth Mountain Inn, (800) 228-4947

Mammoth Premiere Reservation, (800) 336-6443

Mammoth Properties, (800) 227-SNOW

Mammoth Reservation Bureau, (800) 462-5571

Mammoth Sierra Reservation, (800) 325-8415

Ski Time Reservations, (800) 462-5584

Bum's Tip

The **Ullr Lodge** in Mammoth offers dorm beds that start at $15 a night on weekdays and $16 on weekends. A queen bed (shared bath) costs $29. There's a TV and fireplace in the main lodge, a sauna, and a community kitchen. Call (619) 934-2454 to reserve your bunk.

The Mountain

Mammoth lives up to its name. Encompassing thirty-five hundred acres, it's the largest single resort on the West Coast. Because of its location in the eastern Sierra, it gets thirty feet of snow in a pretty good year. Mammoth also logs around 70 percent sunny days, and in the spring its snow corns out to perfection.

The mountain is divided into upper and lower because of the strong winds that often close the upper mountain. On those days, you'll have to content yourself with the lower tree runs (groomed) and the numerous chutes coming down off Mt. Lincoln. When the top is open, you've got chutes and steeps galore.

It will take you at least a week to explore the mountain thoroughly, and the terrain makes it well worth it. The deep snowpack and variety of terrain will give every boarder a great big smile.

Freeriders

Without a doubt, Mammoth offers some of the best freeriding on the West Coast. The chutes on the upper mountain are steep, and if you hit them after some snow has fallen and the wind has packed it down tight, you'll be able to hold an edge in just about any situation. Chair 23 is a good place to start: go right, get in a tuck, and bomb downhill and then up the ridge. A chute called Felipe's is a fun steep descent, and there's usually good snow beneath it. Closer to chair 23, the Paranoids are always a good bet, along with Scotty's. Be sure to check out the conditions before you open it up; if you sketch out on ice, there's a good chance you'll slide four or five hundred feet before you can stop yourself. On the other side of the ridge, Hemlock Bowl requires a short hike, but you can almost always find some freshies coming down.

A ride up gondola 2 will allow you to scout the chutes on either side of the peak. They're steep, and they'll fire up the adrenal glands. Hangman's, Varmit's, and Warner's are a few of the chutes to the right. On the left you're up against Huevos Grande and Upper Dry Creek. You have to know what you're doing in these chutes, and know if they're filled with enough snow to really go off. If they aren't, there are a couple of drops to negotiate, and with a fifty-degree landing, one wrong move and you're doing a Raggedy Ann to the bottom.

You can find the best snow on the mountain by making a long traverse from the upper gondola over the Dragon's Back to Dragon Tail. Here, the trees hold the powder for a long time after a storm. It can be wind-packed and hard on the upper mountain and still loose and fresh on Dragon Tail.

The other spot that you should not miss is Mt. Lincoln. When the upper mountain is closed, Mt. Lincoln is the place to be. It's sheltered from the wind, and you'll find the best snow in the Avalanche Chutes

The Vegas Show

Every March, Ski Industries America (SIA) puts on its ski and snowboard trade show in Las Vegas. It's a manufacturers-and-retailers-only show, and gatecrashers risk taking on a formidable group of Sluggos posing as security guards. The show is closed to the public, but if you come up with some retailer credentials it's worth a visit. You can shell out some bucks to buy your entrance. Once inside you'll find yourself surrounded by more shaved heads, long sideburns, baggy pants, tattoos, and eyebrow rings than you can shake a big stick at. There's a wooden half-pipe out front where skateboarders and skaters fly high above the lips. There's live music and a table with free chips and peanuts. There can be no doubt—the SIA show is a scene.

The snowboarders have their own wing of the convention center, and the booths are constructed of school buses, helicopters, and all sorts of unclothed mannequins. At the 1995 show, snowboard-related manufacturers occupied half the booths. If snowboarding is the sport of the future, then the future is now.

At night, boarders become even more conspicuous as they flirt with Lady Luck in the casinos. There's nothing like seeing a group of bros and Bettys gathered around the craps table with the slickster Mr. Vegas types, hollering when they win, getting excited about money in a way that only those who don't have a lot of it around can get.

If you happen to find yourself in Vegas during the show, here's a short list of how best to prepare yourself for the weekend:

1. Talk to the guys at your local board shop and see if you can join their team so you can get a badge. This will enable you to receive all sorts of stickers and giveaways that the manufacturers heap on potential buyers.

2. Bring your skateboard. Las Vegas has more parking lots per resident than any other city on the planet.

3. Bring shorts, even if you're coming from the snow. Las Vegas is smack dab in the middle of the desert and it warms up during the day, especially when you're riding your skateboard.

4. Always hit a fifteen if the dealer's showing a seven or better.

5. Bring a backpack and fill it with beer before you walk in. Beer carts make the rounds in the foyer, but they charge a premium. If you hang out until the end of the exhibition hours, you can usually find a booth on the ski side hosting a reception. There's also a beer sponsor who throws a party on one of the evenings.

6. Leave your camera in the car. You have to register it with the conference organizers to take it inside, and to do that, you have to have press credentials.

7. Never take a hit if the dealer's showing a two through six.

8. Paste stickers you've collected on everything in sight. There was a guy bumming change with his dog at the 1995 show, just across the street from the convention center. He was literally pasted from head to toe with all the friendly pats the boarders were giving him. The dog had a few on him, too.

9. Remember that skiers are afraid of you, so be nice.

10. In spite of the scene, this is where the majority of business happens in the snowboard industry. Brace yourself to witness snowboarders cutting deals and making bottom-line decisions. It's scary to see your bros acting like their fathers, and even a shaved head and a pair of Arnets can't disguise it. Snowboarding's big business. Accept it and ride on.

(the Avys). Also, when you come down beneath chair 22, look for some nice boulder gardens that are fun to play in.

There's too much fun to describe it all. Besides, instead of reading about it, you'd be better off getting yourself to the mountain to find out for yourself.

Cruisers

When the wind blows at Mammoth, it's setting up the snow for perfect cruiser conditions. As soon as it stops blowing, take chair 23 to the upper mountain and check out the Noids. Steep, obstacle-free, turbo-powered cruising is what you'll be in for.

There are all sorts of good groomer runs. Here are a few you shouldn't miss: Glades coming down off chair 1; East Bowl beneath the upper gondola; anything off chair 5; and Downhill, which runs along the base of Mt. Lincoln.

Given the good number of alpine riders at Mammoth, you should have no trouble finding the runs where you can carve to your heart's desire.

Freestylers

Don't come to Mammoth looking for a jibbacious experience. There's too much good, natural terrain to ignore. There are also some great natural hits, with the best being underneath chair 4 and chair 16. The rock gardens beneath chair 22 will provide some good launches as well. In the late spring, once June Mountain has closed, Mammoth builds a terrain park, so you can actually ride a short board and carry around a Bible-sized wallet, at least for a couple of months.

Grommets

The one-day Learn-to-Snowboard package—which includes lesson, rental, and lifts—goes for $68. Learn how to ride as quickly as possible so you can get up the mountain.

Nonbelievers

Skiers love the mountain as much as boarders. A number of other activities are also available, among them cross-country skiing, snowmobile rental, bobsledding, tobogganing, sleigh rides, dogsled rides, and hot air balloon rides.

Sierra Summit

P.O. Box 236
Lakeshore, CA 93634

Phone: (209) 233-2500; (209) 233-0900 (lift ticket reservations); (209) 233-1200 (accommodations)

Snowphone: (209) 893-3311 (Sierra Summit area); (209) 233-3330 (Fresno area)

Elevation: base, 7,030'; top, 8,709'; vertical, 1,679'

Lifts: 3 doubles, 2 triples, 2 rope tows

Terrain Variety: 25% advanced, 65% intermediate, 10% beginner

The Season and Hours

Sierra Summit is open from November through April. Lift hours are 8:30 A.M. to 4:00 P.M.

Lift Tickets

Weekend, all day—Adult/Child: $30/$20
Midweek, all day—Adult/Child: $25/$15

Specials

For $49, the Sierra Summit Club card provides a $10 discount on all regular lift tickets. Club members are guaranteed a ticket on sellout days until 9:00 A.M.

Logistics

To get to Sierra Summit, take Highway 168 east from Fresno about forty miles.

The Local Scene

Sierra Summit is Fresno's snowboarding destination. It's a friendly, low-key, low-tech resort. Because it's so popular with valley residents, Sierra Summit limits lift-ticket sales on its busiest days (so make reservations if you're going on a holiday or busy weekend).

Where to Stay

Stay at the **Sierra Summit Inn,** (209) 233-1200, or call the **Shaver Lake Chamber of Commerce,** (209) 841-3350, to find out about lodging in Shaver Lake. Alternatively, you can check into one of Fresno's many roadside attractions.

The Mountain

Sierra Summit qualifies as a midsize mountain, which actually means it has a lot more terrain than most of the hills in the central Sierra. It's also extremely friendly to snowboarders. It offers a couple of half-

SIERRA SUMMIT

CHINESE PEAK
8,709'

Base Elevation - 7,030'

RUNS

1. China Bowl
2. Academy
3. The Face
4. Buck Horn
5. Dynamite
6. Waterfall
7. Boulder Alley
8. Copout
9. Avalance
10. Juniper
11. Ridge Run
12. Tollhouse
13. Peter Built
14. Easy Street
15. Huntington
16. Kaiser
17. Exhibition
18. Tamarack
19. Red Fir
20. Big Creek

CHAIR 2

CHAIR 4

CHAIR 5

EXPRESS

CHAIR 3

FIREBOWL T-BAR

T-BAR

ROPE TOW

pipes and a huge, well-maintained snowboarding park with a maze of slides, hits, kickers, and bonks. The mountain has enough steeps to dial in on big pow days, and the tree runs, though we wish they were better serviced by the lifts, provide the most fun riding we've found.

Freeriders

On powder days, freeriders will want to take the number 1 double to the area above China Bowl. From there it's a straight shot down the wide-open China Bowl through some trees to the area called the Face. While Avalanche and Juniper are the named runs on the Face, it's really just another huge, steep drop. Alternatively, you can ride chair 3 to the top of Dynamite. To the left of this chair are the mogul runs called Buck Horn and Dynamite. The trees next to these runs are outrageous cascades of big hit after big hit. Better yet, almost nobody rides these trees. Days after a dump, plenty of untracked powder lies waiting in here. The reason is simple enough: it's almost impossible to make it back to the chairlift without walking out. In fact, however, a well-groomed cat track at the bottom is easy to walk on, and it only takes a couple of minutes to mosey on down to the lift with a fat grin on your face.

If you ride down the Express run on the other side of chair 3, you can take a right turn over the cat-track lip above the Waterfall run and log some flight time as you drop in.

Cruisers

There are lots of long, wide, fast, groomed runs at Sierra Summit. Express, Ridge Run, Tollhouse, Kaiser, Tamarack, and Red Fir are some of the best. A racecourse is set up near the snowboard park just off chair 2. China Bowl on "packed powder" days is a huge carving face where you can pick your way through the mogul patches.

Freestylers

Jib heads will have a ball here. The snowboard park is challenging, with some monster tabletops, but it's built to accommodate most levels. Make sure you check out the gaps and flats before you hit, though. Skiers are not allowed in the park. Also, the edges of the trees off Buck Horn and Dynamite have some amazing hits where it's easy to stick 360s and other big airs.

Grommets

Sierra has a big school program. A T-bar and a handle tow near the lodge are used for teaching beginners. More advanced beginners move to chair 4 to hang out on the Academy and Easy Street runs.

Nonbelievers

Sierra Summit has a family-oriented take on the mountain, and skiers and snowboarders get along well here.

Ski Dodge Ridge

P.O. Box 1188
Pinecrest, CA 95364

Phone: (209) 965-3474
Snowphone: (209) 965-4444
Elevation: base, 6,600'; top, 8,200'; vertical, 1,600'
Lifts: 2 triples, 5 doubles, 4 surface lifts
Terrain Variety: 20% advanced, 60% intermediate, 20% beginner

The Season and Hours

Thanksgiving to April, 9:00 A.M.–4:00 P.M. weekdays, 8:30 A.M.–4:00 P.M. weekends and holidays.

Lift Tickets

All day—Adult/Junior/Youth/Child/Senior: $32/$23/$16/Free/Free
Half day—Adult/Junior/Youth/Child/Senior: $24/$18/$12/Free/Free

Specials

Beginners' packages are available. Tuesdays through Thursdays, adults get a two-for-one ticket. Also check with the local Save Mart supermarket for discounted tickets.

Logistics

Dodge Ridge is an easy drive from the East Bay area. From Oakland, follow I-580 east and take the cutoff to Manteca. Take Highway 120 past Oakdale, and where the road forks, continue on Highway 108 through Sonora. The ski area is about ten miles past Sonora, just off the highway.

The Local Scene

The snowboarding scene is just taking off at Dodge Ridge, with more and more snowboarders moving in. But the whole place still has a family-oriented feel and it hasn't fully transformed into a hard-core boarder park.

Where to Stay

Contact the **Tuolumne County Chamber of Commerce** at (209) 532-4212.

The Mountain

Dodge Ridge is a pretty easy mountain to figure out. Most of the "big" runs are on the left-hand end of the park serviced by the Prospector lift. Below here, you'll find a fair amount of steep terrain and some rideable trees. As you move right along the ridge, you'll come upon more and more open areas and groomed runs. Here's where you'll find the best hits and cruising.

Freeriders

Freeriders will tend to hang out on the Prospector chair and ride the Flume and Stagecoach runs. Below Stagecoach is the funnest freeriding area on the mountain, a wide tree glade known as Sun Bowl. Hidden in these trees is a big drop called the Wall.

If you cruise down the ridge along the Stamp Mill trail, most of the trees you pass on your right are rideable. Hidden in the woods between the Fool's Gold and Claim Jumper runs is a huge fallen tree that locals call the Nordy Log. Few can ride its length all the way to the big drop-off at the end.

Another nice tree glade is off the end of the Coyote trail, in an area called Cork Screw that ends up near the Mother Lode chair.

Cruisers

Cruisers will enjoy Dodge Ridge's big, open runs like Center Bowl, Waterfall, and Face.

Freestylers

Dodge Ridge has yet to install a boarders' park, but there are lots of good hits buried in the trees. We found some big cat-track launches and hits along the edges, especially under the Prospector chair, along the Stamp Mill ridge trail, and in the big Center Bowl.

Grommets

Dodge Ridge is a great beginners' area. Grommets will have nearly the whole right side of the mountain to themselves.

Nonbelievers

Dodge Ridge prides itself on being a family ski area.

Southern California

If you're not from this part of the world, you may be scratching your head at the prospect of snowboarding so close to Disneyland. Trust us, save the Mickey visit for later and head for the hills. The San Bernardino and San Gregorio mountains of Southern California stand over eight thousand feet high and receive more than ten feet of snowfall in an average year.

There's a confusion over which mountain is the closest to L.A., not that this is a big badge of honor. Both Kratka Ridge and Mt. Waterman make the claim, along with Mountain High, which is probably the quickest to reach because of the roads that take you there. If you decide to drive two hours instead of one, you'll find yourself in the San Bernardino Mountains, which offer Southern Californians the best choice for boarding destinations.

In Southern California you will encounter the highest density of snowboarders in the world. In the early and late parts of the season, it's not unusual to find 70 percent of the people on the mountain strapped into boards. The surf and skate cultures are strong in the south, and as a result there's a high percentage of jibbers in the mix. The resorts all embrace snowboarders, some more grudgingly than others. Because more people live and ski in Southern California than is good for anyone, mountains have been forced to micromanage their snowboarding programs to ensure that boarders don't drive away skiers, while giving boarders a quality place to ride. The upshot of all this is large mounds of snow shaped into hits and roped off from the main runs. Snowboard parks, while not a Southern California invention, have definitely found their home at the resorts; they're kind of like big day-care pens for riders.

Southern California receives about three hundred sunny days a year. Since it's not snowing a lot of the time, snowmaking becomes vital to generating a sufficient base. Once the temperatures drop, the resorts are blowing snow, and continue to do so as far into spring as the weather permits. Most mountains that stay open in the spring are able to do so because they cover over 80 percent of their runs with manufactured snow. While it's not that much fun to face-plant on, it at least allows the mountains to stay open an extra month, and keeps you from riding on dirt.

An hour from the city, up in the hills, some local spots provide the quickest fix for Angelenos jonesing for some turns. Their seasons are spotty, and they've got only two or three lifts each, but after a snow-storm you can find some good fun at these locations:

Kratka Ridge, 1 triple, 1 double, 1 rope, half-pipe, (818) 449-1749

Mt. Waterman, 3 doubles, (818) 440-1041

Snow Forest, 1 triple, 3 tows, (714) 866-8891

Bear Mountain

P.O. Box 6812
Big Bear Lake, CA 92315-6812

Phone: (909) 585-2517
Fax: (909) 585-6805
Snowphone: (619) 238-5555 (San Diego); (213) 683-8100 (Los Angeles); (909) 585-2519 (San Bernardino)
Elevation: base, 7,140'; top, 8,805'; vertical, 1,665'
Lifts: 9 chairs (1 high-speed quad, 1 quad, 3 triples, 4 doubles) and 2 poma lifts
Terrain Variety: 25% advanced, 50% intermediate, 25% beginner

The Season and Hours

The mountain begins operations in November, before Thanksgiving if enough snow has fallen or the temperature's been low enough to ac-commodate snowmaking, and stays open through mid-April. Lifts run from 8:00 A.M. to 4:00 P.M. during the week, and from 7:30 A.M. on weekends.

Lift Tickets

Weekend, holiday—Adult/Junior: $38/$21
Weekday—Adult/Young Adult/Junior/Senior: $38/$28/$21/$21
Half day—Adult/Junior: $24/$16

Specials

Lift tickets for two consecutive days are $66 ($34 junior); for three consecutive days, $99 ($50 junior). Young adults (ages 13–23) who can prove their age with a valid picture ID may board for $28 midweek. Children age six and under ride free. If you're not having a good time, you can exchange your lift ticket within an hour of purchase for a voucher good for another day.

Logistics

Highway 18 takes you to Big Bear Lake from the Inland Empire as well as from the backside of the San Bernardino Mountains. Once you get

BEAR MOUNTAIN

BEAR PEAK
8,805'

SILVER MTN. PEAK
8,560'

GOLDMINE MTN.
8,440'

BEAR PEAK TRIPLE

SILVER MOUNTAIN DOUBLE

SKIERS ONLY

CLEMENT

INSPIRATION TRIPLE

SUPER CUB POMA 1

SUPER CUB POMA 2

HIBERNATION

GOLD RUSH QUAD

GOLD MINE

BIG BEAR EXPRESS

SHOWDOWN

Base Elevation - 7,140'

RUNS

1. Rip's Run
2. Upper Claim Jumper
3. Lower Claim Jumper
4. Showtime
5. Marion's
6. Cascade
7. Gold Rush
8. Old Miners
9. Inspiration
10. Clementine
11. Geronimo
12. Bow Canyon
13. Deer Canyon
14. Gold Mine Canyon
15. Rim of the World
16. Grizzly
17. Expressway
18. Hidden Valley
19. Silver Connection
20. No Snowboarding Zone

to Big Bear Lake, look for Moonridge Drive. Turn away from the lake (toward the mountain).

The Local Scene

On any given day, you'll find a film crew or photographer shooting a group of pros in the Outlaw Snowboard Park. This playground is known worldwide as a place to go big, and with over three hundred days of sunshine a year, it's a photographer's dream. The mountain caters to snowboarders, having dedicated a full-time staff to maintaining the park. Skiers aren't allowed in the park, and never will be according to the snowboarding program supervisor. In town, every other shop seems to rent snowboards. Some full-service shops to check out are **Bro Boards,** the **Outback Snowboard Shop,** and the **Real Deal.** For libations try **Chad's,** a smoke-filled biker bar just across the street from the video arcade (huge), and the **Mountain Pub,** a sports bar and eighties-music hangout.

Where to Stay

If you call the **Big Bear Lake Resort Association** at (909) 866-7000, it can set you up with lodging. There are at least a hundred resorts, hotels, and condo complexes from which to choose. If you've got a group of twenty to forty-two people, consider the **Bavarian Lodge,** where your group will get its own building complete with pool table, kitchen, fireplace, and upright piano.

Say Cheese

Human nature is the cause of rubbernecking at a car crash and lining up thirty riders deep to session a hit that a photographer is shooting. Bear Mountain's Outlaw Snowboard Park has more snowboard photo shoots during the year than any other place on earth. Even if you're looking for a sponsorship, don't be a cheese. If you can ride with the big boys, chances are you'll win some contests here and there and get noticed.

The Mountain

The runs are spread out between three peaks, with a good amount of trees in between the peaks—making the mountain a freeriding paradise when there's fresh. At Bear Mountain, skiers have their own chair to Silver Mountain Peak. While snowboarders aren't allowed on the runs beneath this chair, they can work the trees to either side. It's okay to pop out of the trees at the bottom of Quicksilver as long as you're making a mellow entry into the run. It's also good not to get caught down in the gully at the bottom of Deer Canyon where it flattens out. The snowboarders have the Outlaw Snowboard Park, so everything's fair and square in terms of access.

Freeriders

When there's fresh snow, the trees are where you want to be. Off Bear Peak, Bow Canyon and Deer Canyon await on either side. The mountain's management calls this "off-trail snowboarding"—even though the canyons are within the ski-area boundary, they are not patrolled—so the caveat of at-your-own-risk is in effect. Although the Silver Mountain Peak chair is off-limits to snowboarders, you can traverse down Bear Peak and poach all the pow you want on the skiers' side of the canyon. Just stay off their runs unless you want to deal with a bunch of fist-shaking blue-haired skiers yelling, "You damn kids!" Once in the trees, it's up to you where to go. The locals would only tell us that there's nothing but goods in there in the form of rock jumps, logs, and stumps sprinkled throughout.

Cruisers

While Bear Mountain is not a real alpinist scene, if you've got your hard boots on, take the Express quad and come down Claim Jumper to get your turns in. Gold Rush is another good fall-line run, and off the Bear Peak chair you can tear big GS turns on Geronimo, a steep, groomed pitch that's usually not too crowded.

Freestylers

The number and size of hits vary in the Outlaw Snowboard Park, but you can be sure that the landings are designed for going big, bigger, and biggest. At the top is a snake course used for boarder-cross events, but you can also line up hits off it. You'll find tabletops, spines, gaps so big you get sick just looking at them, fun boxes, pyramids—basically whatever the groomers are in the mood for. The groomers are pros, and they're snowboarders. The Showdown chair services the board park. A Pipe Dragon comes a couple of times a season to shape the half-pipe, and the park and pipe have grooming machines run through them about three times a week. On the Cascade trail, a Pipe Dragon–constructed half-pipe awaits you. The pipe is four hundred feet long with ten-foot walls, or higher when there's enough snow.

Grommets

The New Snowboarder Program is a great deal if you're just learning. Lesson, rental, and beginner lift ticket go for $39. The lesson begins with a video orientation, followed by a truck ride to the top of the beginners' chair so you have a chance to come down once before negotiating a chairlift. A four-day learning package includes four days of lift tickets, three lessons (progressing through the skill sets), and three days of rentals—all yours for $117. The lift ticket on the first day is good for the beginners' area only, but after that you're free to ride. For the most part, you'll want to stay on the Clementine chair to work on your turns.

Nonbelievers

With their own chairlift, skiers will feel that their kingdom hasn't been totally invaded by the snowboarding hordes. Bear Mountain has a program called Share the Bear that emphasizes the need for every mountain user to display respect for the mountain and the people on it. There's good communication between the management and the users, with the result that everyone is usually kept riding hard and happy.

Big Air Green Valley

P.O. Box 8438
Green Valley Lake, CA 92341

Phone: (909) 867-2338
Snowphone: (909) 867-2338
Elevation: base, 7,000'; top, 7,470'; vertical, 470'
Lifts: 1 double, 1 poma, 1 surface lift
Terrain Variety: 45% advanced, 50% intermediate, 5% beginner

The Season and Hours

The season runs from mid-November through mid-April (weather permitting), with the lifts operating from 8:00 A.M. to 4:00 P.M. daily.

Lift Tickets

All day—Adult/Child: $27/$20
Half day—Adult/Child: $18/$14
Discounts are available on tickets purchased through Ticketmaster. Phone (213) 480-3232, (714) 740-2000, (805) 583-8700, or (619) 278-TIXS.

Specials

The Encourage-a-Codger special entitles you to a free lift ticket if you bring someone age thirty-five or older and that person takes a first-timer's package at the boarder school. It's a good way to get your folks on the mountain and scam a free ticket at the same time.

Logistics

Green Valley is located in the San Bernardino Mountains near Lake Arrowhead. From San Bernardino, take Highway 215 north to the "Mountain Resorts" turnoff (Highway 30) and follow the signs to Running Springs. Alternatively, take I-10 to Highway 30 to Highway 330. Go two miles past Running Springs to Green Valley Lake Road, turn left, and drive three miles to Big Air.

The Local Scene

After about fifty years as a ski area, Green Valley kicked out the skiers. It wasn't able to compete with the longer runs and faster chairs that the surrounding mountains offered skiers, so it built a big jib park instead. Now Big Air Green Valley is the largest snowboard park in the nation, and one of a handful of snowboard-only resorts.

The scene at Green Valley will make snowboarders a little giddy. You can check out a shovel and go build a hit. The owners of the mountain like to ride around with a camera taking pictures of riders, which they then put in a scrapbook that's on display in the main lodge. If you're a few quarters short for a lift ticket, chances are you can talk your way into a discount. The management just wants to see people out on the mountain having a good time.

Green Valley is one of those noble experiments that seems to be succeeding. While the mountain still lacks the snowmaking capabilities that would extend its season, it has captured the loyalty of a large number of riders who come to session the hits, go big for the camera, and hang out with other snowboarders.

Where to Stay

The majority of visitors stay in Big Bear Lake or Lake Arrowhead, but you can find a place to stay in Green Valley by calling **Green Valley Lake Cabins**, (818) 343-1747, for daily or weekly rentals.

The Mountain

What used to be one of the nation's smallest ski areas (forty acres) is now the nation's largest snowboard park (forty acres). The mountain consists of a single face with about ten lines to take down. Among these lines are rocks, steeps, a half-pipe, and some huge hits (yeah, yeah, really big!) off Line Drive. You can access the Outback, the mountain's forested region, by heading left off the Eagle chairlift. The trees back here are old growth, and you'll find some fallen logs, some rocks, and a few challenging steeps to keep things interesting.

Freeriders

You'll want to take a few runs through the Outback, a forest-friendly area that's been untouched by the chain saw and is full of natural hits. But the reason you come here is for the park, not for the free-riding. The runs are short, and you'll want to session the hits after a while.

Cruisers

Leave your alpine board in the car. Otherwise, you run the risk of feeling like a weenie.

Freestylers

Everywhere you look there are hits and bonks, rail slides, barrel bonks, death boxes, quarter-pipes, spines, and tabletops. The half-pipe below Spiritmaker has its own surface lift. The pipe was built around a tree, so watch out for flying bark. Big G and Line Drive, located in Green Valley's bowl, are where you'll find the big hits. Smaller hits and jumps are everywhere, so just go out and start hucking.

Grommets

The beginner package ($55) includes lift ticket, rentals, and a group lesson. A nice thing about Green Valley is that when the snowboard instructors aren't giving a lesson, they're riding the slopes, offering quick instructional tips to riders who might need them.

Nonbelievers

Skiers, don't even think about it.

Mountain High

25234 Highway 2
P.O. Box 428
Wrightwood, CA 92397

Phone: (619) 249-5808
Fax: (619) 249-3155
Snowphone: (714) 972-9242 (Orange County); (310) 578-6911 or (818) 888-6911 (Los Angeles); (909) 874-7050 (San Bernardino); (619) 294-8780 (San Diego)
Elevation: base, 6,600'; top, 8,200'; vertical, 1,600'
Lifts: 11 chairs (6 doubles, 3 triples, 1 quad, 1 high-speed quad)
Terrain Variety: 15% advanced, 65% intermediate, 20% beginner

The Season and Hours

The mountain opens in mid-November and operates through mid-April. Hours are 8:00 A.M.–5:00 P.M. on weekdays and 7:30 A.M.–5:00 P.M. on weekends. A night lift ticket is good from 3:00 to 10:00 P.M.

Lift Tickets

Weekend—Adult/Young Adult (12–22)/Child (under 12): $39/$34/$15
Midweek—Adult/Young Adult/Child: $39/$25/$15
Night—$27

Children age ten and under ride for free.

Specials

On Wednesdays, students with a valid photo ID get half off lift tickets. Mountain High also gives a $10 discount when you present any Southern California ski area frequent-skier discount card. Military discounts are available as well.

Logistics

The blessing that Mountain High bestows upon its visitors is major roads to the resort and no steep grades to negotiate. This is especially nice when it's been snowing. From Los Angeles or Orange County, take I-10 east or Highway 91. Follow I-15 north to Highway 138, and go west on Highway 138 to Highway 2. The ski area is three miles past the town of Wrightwood. From the San Fernando Valley, take the I-5 north to Highway 14. Follow Highway 14 east to Pearblossom Highway (Highway 138). Turn east on Pearblossom and follow the signs to Mountain High.

The Local Scene

You can see the local scene best at night when you ride up to the top of the mountain and look toward L.A.—that fuzzy glow in the distance. There are a couple of bars in Wrightwood where you might want to try your luck, but an overwhelming majority of visitors to Mountain High are on day trips. The one (only?) positive aspect of its being an L.A. destination is that the surf and skate cultures have made snowboarding very popular here. Half the mountain that had been closed to snowboarders opened up in 1993. Now a board park and half-pipe are situated at West, and everyone's buttering his or her bread on both sides.

Where to Stay

The best place to stay is on the couch in your friend's apartment in L.A. But if you're dead set on avoiding that eighty-minute drive, call (619) 249-5477 for the mountain's lodging information.

The Mountain

Mountain High is actually two mountains—East and West. The main lodge is at West, and that being the side where the snowboard park sits, you'll probably want to park there as well. In general, West's terrain is a little more diverse, while East has good, straight fall-line pitches. There are some tempting tree runs between the two peaks, but there's also some extreme avalanche danger and a $1,000 fine waiting for those who get busted, so don't be tempted.

Freeriders

Freeriders will want to stay mostly on West, which sports a number of tree runs and good rock jumps. If you hang toward the boundary line, on Six Gun, you'll spot some trees where there's almost always good snow. The locals tell us that they're not sure exactly where the ski-area boundary lies, but that if you keep chair 5 always in sight, you'll be doing okay.

Coming down off chair 6, you'll find some nice steeps, and the trees between the runs are well spaced for playing near-miss. Don't miss the rock jump at the top of Prospector off chair 5, and look for the side hits coming down both the Prospector and the Stage Coach runs.

Cruisers

East offers cruisers some really long, steep, nonstop runs and the mountain's only high-speed quad to get back to the top. If you're into laying out big turns, go to the top of the Mountain High Express and come down Goldrush. You can fork off into Stampede, which features a nice steep pool-and-drop section through Olympic Bowl. The fall line in Olympic Bowl runs down along the trees to your right, and the groomers keep it from getting bumped out. The Sundance run and Sepp's to Butch Cassidy Canyon are other good routes down from the mountain. Hard-boot riders will find some of the best turning in Southern California on a good corn day at East.

Freestylers

Mountain High's Ground Zero Snowboard Park is located underneath chair 4 below the Red Eye run. You'll find a good selection of rails, gaps, and tabletops, and a four-hundred-foot-long half-pipe. At the top of West, off the runs beneath chairs 6 and 5, look for hits along the sides and through the trees. You'll find that most of the riders stay on the West side, so you'll be able to pick up some lines that will lead you to the goods.

Grommets

Learn to ride for just $39.75 and use that quarter on one of the lodge's fine video games.

Nonbelievers

Skiers used to have exclusive privileges at East, but because they're slowly learning that snowboarding is not a crime, and the mountains are quickly learning that snowboarders buy lift tickets, the entire mountain is open to both skiing and snowboarding.

Mt. Baldy

P.O. Box 399
Mt. Baldy, CA 91759

Phone: (909) 931-4458
Snowphone: (909) 981-3344 (San Bernardino); (818) 877-3311 (San Fernando Valley); (619) 692-3311 (San Diego); (714) 547-3311 (Orange County); (310) 397-3222 (Los Angeles)
Elevation: base, 6,500'; top, 8,600'; vertical, 2,100'
Lifts: 4 doubles
Terrain Variety: 40% advanced, 40% intermediate, 20% beginner

The Season and Hours

Mt. Baldy is open Thanksgiving through April, conditions permitting from 8:00 AM through 4:00 PM.

Lift Tickets

All day—Adult/Student/Child/Senior: $35/$27/$21/$18
Half day—Adult/Student/Child/Senior: $24/$18/$14/$12

Specials

Ten-punch and twenty-punch cards are $210 and $375, respectively (good for two seasons). A book of ten tickets is $275. Group lessons, private lessons, and learn-to-ski packages are also available.

Logistics

Getting to Mt. Baldy from Pasadena is almost ridiculously easy. Take the I-10 to Mountain Avenue. Follow this to Shinn Road, turn left, and proceed until it runs into Mt. Baldy Road. Turn right and drive twelve miles to the ski lifts.

The Local Scene

Baldy is a hard-core, locals-only surf spot. Whoops, we meant snowboarding spot. All the Newport aggro, in-your-face, don't-drop-in-on-me-or-die attitude applies.

As our guide on the mountain, a wild-eyed, crazy-talking snow hermit named Black Dick Dog, put it: "It's not new school, it's not old school. It's more like dropped out of school."

This characterization particularly holds true for a well-publicized natural feature known as the Turkey Shoot. This quarter-mile-long natural quarter-pipe is such a perfect snowboarding ramp that Baldy has no need for a man-made terrain park. To ride the Turkey Shoot without getting harshed and harangued, you'll have to commit to your hits, go big, avoid scraping the lips, and stick more than you beef. It's advised that you sit at the top and watch the locals ride for a while before you drop in.

Where to Stay

Stay at the **Mt. Baldy Lodge**, (909) 982-1115, or stay in L.A. The lodge has cool cabin-style rooms with fireplaces and a great bar with pool tables and a restaurant. L.A. has girls in bikinis, smog, and freeways. Your choice.

Tell Your Friends

There are all kinds of out-of-bounds opportunities near Baldy. Locals will tell you all about the possibility of riding down the awesome-looking backside of Baldy, and may fill you in on some of the mountain's out-of-bounds secrets. Before you head for the backcountry, be clear about what you're getting into at Baldy. Because of the extreme warming and other unusual conditions that exist here, avalanches are a constant and serious threat. Bodies have spent entire winters waiting for recovery because of the danger.

A better-known secret is the Sierra Club cabin a couple of ridges over from the ski area. With prior arrangements, you can hike into this cabin and use it as a backcountry base camp.

The Mountain

Baldy is a big mountain by Southern California standards, but half the rideable area is often too bony to open. Snow depth is always a concern here. When it's deep, the mountain is made up of two peaks with the Notch in the middle. Below the Notch, many of Baldy's spookiest expert runs await. These aren't to be taken lightly, as cliff bands and other hazards line the routes down.

Freeriders

When there's a big dump and avalanche danger is minimal, an impressive amount of freeriding through trees and steeps is available. One of the best runs on the mountain is along the edges of Holcumac.

Cruisers

Because this is city boarding, don't expect to lay hundreds of miles of tracks in a day of riding. The best high-speed runs are on the east peak, including Robin's Run and Goldridge.

Freestylers

Baldy is a jibbers' park the way Pipeline is a surf spot. Turkey Shoot is the point break.

Grommets

The available space for beginners is fairly small. They'll hang out almost exclusively on the short run under chair 2.

Nonbelievers

While skiing at Baldy may not be the ultimate skiing experience, it beats not skiing. It's a pretty nice place to get away from the hustle of L.A., at any rate.

Snow Summit

880 Summit Boulevard
P.O. Box 77
Big Bear Lake, CA 92315

Phone: (909) 866-5766
Fax: (909) 866-3201
Snowphone: (310) 390-1498 (Los Angeles County); (818) 888-2233 (San Fernando Valley); (714) 972-0601 (Orange County); (909) 866-4621 (Inland Empire); (619) 294-8786 (San Diego County)
Elevation: base, 7,000'; top, 8,200'; vertical, 1,200'
Lifts: 11 (3 quads, 3 triples, 5 doubles)
Terrain Variety: 25% advanced, 40% intermediate, 35% beginner

SNOW SUMMIT

EL. - 8,200'

Base Elevation - 7,000'

RUNS

1. Timber Ridge
2. 7-Down
3. Perfect Pitches
4. Tommi's
5. Log Chute
6. The Bowl
7. Dicky's
8. Miracle Mile
9. Summit Run
10. Ego Trip
11. East Why
12. Half-Pipe
13. West Ridge
14. ZZYZX
15. Mainstream
16. Sundown
17. Skyline Creek
18. The Wall
19. Pipe Dream
20. West Ridge
    Freestyle Park

CHAIR 9
FAMILY SKI PARK (BOARDING RESTRICTED)
CHAIR 3
ALL-MOUNTAIN EXPRESS
CHAIR 1
CHAIR 10
CHAIR 8
CHAIR 4
CHAIR 6
CHAIR 5
CHAIR 11
CHAIR 7

The Season and Hours

The season runs from late November through April, with the lifts operating 8:30 A.M.–4:30 P.M. on weekdays and 8:00 A.M.–6:00 P.M. on weekends. Night boarding, on Wednesday, Friday, Saturday, and Sunday nights, lasts until 10:00 P.M.

Lift Tickets

All day—Adult/Child: $39/$20
Half day—Adult/Child: $24/$15
Night—Adult/Child: $24/$13

To keep lift lines and crowds on the slopes down, Snow Summit limits the number of tickets it sells. Reservations are suggested for weekends and holidays. Call the **Snow Summit Credit Card Reservation Service** at (909) 866-5841.

Specials

Join the Gotta Ride team and save $10 every day you ride Snow Summit, plus you'll receive a 20 percent discount on snowboard school, a half-price snowboard check, one free lift ticket to Sierra Summit, and a free hot wax at the Snow Summit Service Center.

Logistics

Snow Summit is located near Big Bear Lake in the San Bernardino National Forest. From San Bernardino, take I-10 West to 30 north. Highway 330 splits off to the left, and then becomes Highway 18, which takes you through the town of Big Bear Lake. When you reach Summit Drive, take a right and follow the signs to the area.

The Local Scene

Snow Summit hosts several USASA events and pro contests, and it sponsored Board Aid II in 1995. For competitive snowboarders, Snow Summit is one of the best scenes in the nation. Now that the resort has added a new half-pipe, a mile-long terrain park, and a high-speed quad that allows you to session both, you'll find the real scene happening at the base of the All-Mountain Express, where boarders mill about or lie on the snow or nose-blunt into the crowds waiting in lift lines.

It's not rare to spot some of the top pros (Brushie, Guch) riding through the park with the grooming crews, giving their expert opinions on where to tweak a certain hit or transition. The mountain has dedicated a large chunk of resources to creating a snowboarding program, from hiring snowboard patrols to recruiting a snowboarding staff that makes sure boarders have a quality experience.

If you find yourself with nothing to do at night and tired of the bars in town, check out the night-boarding scene on the mountain. Folks tend to gather at **Summit Inn's Bullwheel Bar,** located at the top of the main lodge, for a nightcap or two.

Where to Stay

The **Big Bear Lake Resort Association,** (909) 866-7000, will help you find accommodations.

The Mountain

The mountain has just gotten a whole lot easier to ride with the addition of the All-Mountain Express. This high-speed quad takes you to the top of Summit Peak, and from there you can access every run on the mountain. The lift lines get a little long, but they move quickly.

On weekends and holidays, the runs off chair 9 are closed to snowboarders. The reason is to give the families a place for a relaxing cruise. Nothing is really lost by not being able to use the chair—the runs are easy, wide-open, and just not that exciting. What is exciting is the West Ridge Freestyle Park, a mile-long terrain park that features a wide variety of tabletops, gaps, spines, rails, quarter-pipes—basically, if it can be made out of snow, you'll find it there.

Freeriders

The mountain is mostly cut runs, with a few stands of trees in between, but nothing to really get lost in. Still, on a powder day you'll find some good pitches off chairs 6 and 7. This side of the mountain features the Wall; it's usually bumped out, but after a snow the bowl fills up with the best snow on the mountain. If you stay near the boundary, you can get in some good tree turns coming down the Ridge. Be careful not to get caught beneath the chair, though, or you'll have a harrowing hike out. Hits are sprinkled throughout the tree bands, but for the most part this is a jibbers' mountain.

Cruisers

The Timber Ridge and the Log Chute runs coming down from chair 7 are groomed fall-line pitches where you can lay out some nice turns. The middle section of the mountain, while nicely groomed, is usually packed with skiers. Nevertheless, you can bomb down underneath chair 1 until you hit the potato patch near the bottom that can send you tumbling. Playing near-miss with beginning skiers is good practice for both your turning and your negotiating skills, so be the best you can be.

Freestylers

A mile of snowboard park! A friggin' mile! The hits vary, and you can't go big everywhere, so do your scouting first. Then go have some fun.

Grommets

The lesson program at Snow Summit features a league of instructors and even more people learning how to ride. Beginner packages ($49) include a two-hour lesson, rental, and a beginners' lift ticket.

Nonbelievers

Because Snow Summit is a Southern California mountain, you will most often find more of an urban experience on the mountain than in your quiet abode. As a result, skiers are used to snowboarders being around, and snowboarders know the penalties of displaying too much vibe. Folks have learned now to just get along, and at Snow Summit this is evident.

Snow Valley

P.O. Box 2337
Running Springs, CA 92382

Phone: (909) 867-2751
Fax: (909) 867-7687 or (800) 680-SNOW
Snowphone: (909) 867-5151 (San Bernardino); (714) 972-0611 (Orange County)
Elevation: base, 6,700'; top, 7,841'; vertical, 1,141'
Lifts: 13 chairs (5 triples, 8 doubles)
Terrain Variety: 30% advanced, 35% intermediate, 35% beginner

The Season and Hours

The mountain opens in mid-November and operates through mid-April. Lifts run from 8:00 A.M. to 4:00 P.M. daily, and night skiing lasts from 4:00 to 9:00 P.M.

Lift Tickets

All day—$39
Half day—$24
Night—$26

Snow Valley offers something called an Option Pass, which is a point-valued lift ticket. You buy points (250 for $37; 375 for $50), and every time you ride a chairlift you're debited a certain number of points. For children and riders just getting started, 250 points will stretch out over two days pretty well.

SNOW VALLEY

SLIDE PEAK
7,841'

Base Elevation - 6,700'

RUNS

1. East Slide
2. Shake Run
3. West Slide
4. East Run
5. Wine Rock
6. Quickie
7. Race Peak
8. West Run
9. Bear Canyon
10. Lake Run
11. Mambo Alley
12. The Ladder
13. Big Bowl
14. Show Off
15. Little Bowl
16. Monster Pipe
17. The Face
18. Stemptation
19. Ego Flats
20. Thunder Mtn.

CHAIR 11
CHAIR 10
CHAIR 9
CHAIR 8
CHAIR 5
CHAIR 4
CHAIR 2
CHAIR 1
CHAIR 3
CHAIR 6
CHAIR 7
CHAIR 13
CHAIR 12

Logistics

Snow Valley is twenty miles north of San Bernardino. Take the Highway 30/Running Springs exit off I-10 and follow the signs to Running Springs. Snow Valley is five miles east of Running Springs on Highway 18.

The Local Scene

Snow Valley aims its marketing at families coming up for a day or two, and as a result it's not nearly the scene you'll find at Big Bear. The locals say this is nice, though, because when the snow falls there's not a pack of everywhere-you-look grabbing up all the fresh. The mountain is just off Highway 18, and there's not much nearby that would count as nightlife. You'll have to go to Big Bear, or make the trek back down to the valley for some of that.

Where to Stay

The closest bed base is Lake Arrowhead, where lodging-and-lift packages are available from $139 for two people. Call **ABC Mountain Accommodations** at (800) 550-5253. If you don't mind a little drive, Big Bear has thousands of beds available in a wide range of room rates. Call the **Big Bear Lake Resort Association** at (909) 866-7000.

The Mountain

In the big storms, Snow Valley catches more snow than the Big Bear resorts. With 230 acres of terrain, it's also the largest resort in Southern California. The mountain features a long series of minipeaks that stairstep up to the summit. As a result, the chair rides are numerous, but not too long. Another feature is a number of drainages that form folds and gullies across the faces. With a little creativity and a little more speed, you can really work these ridges that run mostly perpendicular to the fall line.

Freeriders

On powder days, you'll find nothing but the goods at Snow Valley. If you stay to the left as you come down from the top of the mountain, you'll encounter some nice trees all the way to the top of chair 5. Here you'll want to cut right and hit the rock on Wine Rock, and then cruise down the steeps in Big Bowl, Show Off, or Little Bowl. Race Peak has some nice open trees, and East Slide is probably the steepest pitch on the mountain, although you'll have to skate out of the bottom of the bowl. The best strategy is to keep to your left, near the boundary, and find the rocks and stumps that await the daring shredder.

Cruisers

The runs on the mountain don't follow the fall line because of all the ridges that they cross, but you will find that this makes for some interesting turning. Coming down underneath chair 1 on Bear Canyon and Little Bowl is a good choice, as is Lake Run. You won't find too many alpine riders here, mostly because the steeps get bumped out pretty quickly. The wide cruisers are relaxing and all, but not the nose-dragging fun that Euro-carvers seek out.

Freestylers

The Monster Pipe is aptly named. It will chew you up and spit you out. Well, not really, but it's a good-sized half-pipe. You'll find that most snowboarders hang out on the East Run and Bear Canyon underneath chair 5. These offer some nice sidewall hits, and you have the option of continuing down to the *monster* pipe if you dare. The terrain park is located at the top of chair 5. The groomers are still perfecting the design, but Snow Valley receives enough snow to pile up a couple of ferocious hits. Just below the park, in the trees between Lake Run and Mambo Alley, you'll find a number of snow-covered rocks that make nice launching pads.

Grommets

Snow Valley is a good spot to learn the sport. The lower runs closest to the lodge make up a large beginners' meadow. The snowboarding beginners' package ($49) includes two hours of instruction, rental, and beginner lifts.

Nonbelievers

Cross-country skiing is located on Highway 18 five miles east of Running Springs, across from the Snow Valley ski area.

Safety, Comfort, Competition

Backcountry Safety

You've seen the videos of Valdez and Mt. Rose and you're champing at the bit to hike up and drop into the backcountry. There's no doubt that backcountry boarding is where you'll find the finest powder and lay the freshest tracks. However, backcountry snowboarding is a potentially deadly sport. Avalanches, trees, cliffs, even big patches of harmless-looking powder can and have killed snowboarders. Here's how.

Avalanches

Avalanches require a trigger. Usually this is the weight of new falling snow, but the weight of a person on a snowboard, rain, a loud noise or concussion, or even the heat of the sun can trigger a slide. Consider the fact that almost no one buried more than three feet under an avalanche has lived to talk about it. The survival rate of those buried under even small amounts of snow in a slide is not very high—about 50 percent. This is because many people caught in avalanches are slammed into trees and rocks, and frequently get their necks broken.

Trees

Trees are one of the biggest killers at ski areas around the world. People go too fast, get out of control, and hit their head and die. For snowboarders, a real hazard is falling into a tree well upside down. A boarder can get seriously, completely trapped in this position.

Cliffs

Cliffs look like fun to jump off and they can be. But hit a submerged rock or a patch of ice, and you may suffer from broken bones, or far worse, compression fractures (crushing) of the spine that can paralyze or kill you. Check your landings extremely carefully before you leap and remember that landing on your back or head will seriously hurt you, no matter how soft the powder.

Deep Powder

Snowboarders have died by landing head first in powder. With your arms pinned to your sides and your feet strapped together, there is nothing you can do but suffocate if friends aren't there to dig you out.

Weather

Even more than avalanches, weather is a threat to the backcountry boarder. If you get caught in a whiteout or a blizzard, you can easily die of hypothermia. Learn how to protect yourself from cold by getting out of the wind and building a snow cave if necessary (this is taught in avalanche safety classes).

Things to Know

Backcountry boarding doesn't have to be deadly. Here are some things to know that will help you avoid a tragic fate:

1. *Don't ride alone.* The number-one rule when in the backcountry is to go with friends. While it won't save you from crashing into a tree, having a friend along is your only chance of rescue if you do auger into a snowbank or break a leg jumping off a cliff.

Riding with a friend means staying in visual contact all the time. The best way to do that is to make a lot of noise when you're in the trees—holler at each other constantly—and to switch leads often so that one person never gets too far ahead.

Beyond that basic precaution, the rules are really based on an understanding of what causes avalanches and how to rescue someone who gets buried.

2. *Learn how avalanches work and arm yourself with a beacon.* Avalanche safety is a science that can be learned with good instruction and careful practice. Most mountaineering schools offer courses in avalanche awareness, and part of the course usually includes the use of avalanche beacons. A beacon is a small transceiver (both a transmitter and a receiver) that you wear on your body when you're in the backcountry. It only works if you're with one or more friends who also have them and know how to use them. If you're buried, the signal from your beacon penetrates the snow and is picked up by your rescuers' receivers. The closer they get, the louder the signal becomes. Because it's not as simple as following a pointing arrow, you need to spend at least a couple of hours practicing with a beacon before you'll be able to rescue someone using it. If an avalanche beacon (about the price of a snowboard without bindings) seems lavishly expensive, consider the alternative.

3. *Carry safety equipment.* In addition to beacons, you should carry a pack with collapsible poles, which double as probes, and a shovel, in case you need to dig someone out or dig a snow cave (a snowboard makes a fair substitute). It's also a good idea to have some food, water, first aid, and an emergency "space" blanket in your pack.

4. *Check with the local Ski Patrol.* The Ski Patrol is typically in charge of keeping avalanches from happening at the ski resort, but by monitoring snow conditions daily, the Ski Patrol's avalanche personnel know exactly what local conditions are like and will be able to advise you on whether it's foolhardy to venture out. Some states post regular avalanche updates that warn of dangerous conditions. (California has cut this service from its budget.)

5. *Check the weather reports.* The most common cause of dangerous avalanches is wind loading of snow. If the wind is blowing or new snow is falling, the avalanche danger significantly increases. Also, don't rush out into the backcountry the minute a storm clears. Snow generally stabilizes and bonds as it sits, so the avalanche danger is likely to decrease as time passes after a new dump.

Responsibility Code

Here it is, the National Ski Areas Association's Responsibility Code, which after twenty-eight years has been updated to include snowboarders. The message is the same as it always was, but the words were changed to protect the innocent.

Your Responsibility Code

Skiing can be enjoyed in many ways. At ski areas you may see people using alpine, snowboard, telemark, cross country and other specialized ski equipment, such as that used by disabled or other skiers. Regardless of how you decide to enjoy the slopes, always show courtesy to others and be aware that there are elements of risk in skiing that common sense and personal awareness can help reduce. Observe the code listed below and share with other skiers the responsibility for a great skiing experience.

1. Always stay in control and be able to stop or avoid other people or objects.

2. People ahead of you have the right of way. It is your responsibility to avoid them.

3. You must not stop where you obstruct a trail, or are not visible from above.

4. Whenever starting downhill or merging into a trail, look uphill and yield to others.

5. Always use devices to help prevent runaway equipment.

6. Observe all posted signs and warnings. Keep off closed trails and out of closed areas.

7. Prior to using any lift, you must have the knowledge and ability to load, ride and unload safely.

KNOW THE CODE. IT'S YOUR RESPONSIBILITY.
This is a partial list. Be safety conscious.

This message brought to you by the National Ski Areas Association.

Equipment Notes

Literally hundreds of equipment and apparel manufacturers have burst onto the scene in the last few years. As a result, a lot of advertising dollars are being spent, but there's not a lot of information that accompanies the full-page pitch. Many times, you'll find yourself favoring a board because of its graphics (such as Lib Tech's Litigator), the pro who rides it, or the price. All these are important, but so is a general knowledge of a board's attributes and how to choose one that best suits your style of riding.

Similarly, you wind up spending your money better when you've got a specific idea of what you're looking for in a jacket, pants, boots, mittens, and gloves. Below are some general suggestions that will help you better navigate the snowboard shop. The best resource by far is the snowboard shop employee, whose sometimes surly manner disguises a wealth of information. These are the folks who see equipment sold, and then see what comes back in for repairs or returns to the factory.

Every year brings a number of innovations to board, boot, binding, and clothing design. Boards, boots, and apparel designed specifically for women have finally appeared. A step-in binding system for soft boots is upon us, as well as the Mighty Morphin backcountry snowboard that converts to cross-country skis. Technologies and styles are constantly being updated, but here are some general guidelines for choosing and using your gear.

Clothing

Dry means warm. Although it sounds simple, staying dry is really an act of virtue. Much like Odysseus trying to navigate between Scylla and Charybdis, your ability to layer clothing with precision will determine whether you stay dry and warm or become the human bath mat.

Socks

Snowboarders' socks come up over the calf to prevent them from bunching up beneath the cuff of your boot. Most boots have insulated liners, and in this case you'll want to wear a silk or polypropylene sock liner underneath a single pair of socks. Don't wear anything on your feet with over 20 percent cotton in the blend—your toes will sweat no matter how cold it is outside, and cotton will retain this moisture.

Underwear

Thermal underwear and synthetic undergarments come in handy when the wind is howling and the temperature's hanging in the teens. The one bit of advice we feel qualified to offer about your underwear is, when in doubt, leave the extra layer in the car. This is the opposite of what the Boy Scouts or your mother will tell you, but the reasoning's pretty simple. Your car is a quick walk from the mountain, not a daylong hike through the woods. If you're getting cold, just go back to the car at lunch and layer up. A lot of times when you're getting dressed in the morning, your body's internal heater hasn't been stoked hot enough and you might be tempted to wear all sorts of layers onto the snow. Once you start moving, though, you'll be looking for a place to ditch granny's sweater, which, if you lose it, will get you in a mess of trouble. So it's up to you—the extra layer will keep you more comfortable on the lift, but it could also cook you by the end of your run.

Mittens

We encountered very few snowboarders this winter who wore gloves. The reason for this, besides being a fashion choice, is that snowboarders are smarter than your average bear and know that mittens keep the hands warmer. They also protect the fingers from getting caught in the snow, and they facilitate getting the hand around the board on a grab. The best mitten designs come high up the arm—midforearm or so—to keep snow from slipping in at the wrist. When buying mittens, also look for elastic or straps around the upper sleeve that you can tighten to form a good seal.

Most mittens are insulated, and all you do is put them on and ride. Your other choice is to buy a mitten shell (usually made from Gortex or coated nylon) that will disguise a pair of gloves underneath. These are usually cheaper, and they give you the option of layering different glove liners underneath. In the case of gloves, it's always good to have a pair of polypropylene liners in your pocket. This runs contrary to the underwear advice, but gloves are easy to take on and off, and carrying an extra pair doesn't significantly add weight or bulk.

Insulating Layer

What you wear on top of your underwear (if you're wearing any) should depend largely on how dry your shell keeps you. If you own good waterproof outerwear, you're okay wearing a cotton sweatshirt underneath. If you're still getting your money's worth out of a nylon parka, you should layer in pile and wool. At the start of the season, pay attention to the wind and temperature readings, and each time you go for a run, experiment with layers to find your comfort zone. Everyone has a temperature that makes him or her happy, and that's why it always seems ridiculous to ask other people what they're going to wear onto the snow. If cold hands bother you, beef up your mittens. If you find yourself sweating all the time and fogging your glasses, cut down on a layer. Be true to your furnace.

Shell Layer

The most important clothing purchase you make will be the shell layer. This is the difference between staying dry and warm and being reduced to a damp, shivering, clammy human being. It's also the difference between looking stylish and nondescript. There's an inverse correlation between looking stylish and staying dry. The farther south you go, the more you'll find pants that ride at a boarder's hips and top layers that resemble casual wear more than winter jackets. Up north, you'd either get laughed off the slopes or driven off by the wet snow that would make you feel like you'd just jumped into a swimming pool.

Before we go any further, we want to emphasize that there's no "right" way to dress. Southern California averages around three hundred sunny days a year, so riders down there don't need to rely on a good powder skirt or a warm hood. Up in northern Washington, the sky dumps heavy wet snow every few days and it's important that your shell be waterproof. This could mean going to the Wal-Mart and buying one of their Gorton Fisherman rain suits, or coating everything you own with Scotchguard every few days, or paying many dollars for the fancy waterproof/breathable materials they've designed for space travel. Low on style points but high on functionality is the way of life up there.

Take a look around you. Figure out where you live. Then buy your shell according to the types of conditions you think you'll be riding in.

When you're shopping for a jacket or pants, you'll see all sorts of labels dangling from the garments that advertise the waterproof and/or breathable properties of the fabric. Some jackets are sprayed with a coating (Supplex, for example) that promises to offer both, but somehow we always found ourselves dripping by the end of the day. The moisture was coming through the fabric, but from the inside. When your body comes into contact with a fabric that can't breathe at the rate you're creating water vapor, condensation forms on the inside, and pretty soon you've got a steam sauna going on inside your clothes.

If you're making a long-term investment in a jacket, think about shelling out the extra dollars for Gortex or Entrant GII. These two high-tech fabrics create a one-way membrane that water can escape but can't enter. The price of the jacket goes up 20–40 percent when you get into this material, but if you live in a wet climate and you plan to spend a few days on the snow, the money will be well spent. Some other features to consider include a hood, powder skirt, taped seams, zippered pockets, and Velcro at the wrists to seal the cuffs. Shop around, pick a jacket you like, then look at the price. If the sticker doesn't cause blood to retreat from your extremities, buy it.

The breathability of pants isn't quite as necessary because the main heat of your body gathers in the upper regions. But make sure you've got something waterproof on your legs—your knees and butt spend a lot of time in contact with the snow. Also, cover up the plumber's crack. A long jacket will accomplish this, as will a pair of overalls. If you keep your crack dry, you'll be happy. If it gets filled with snow, you'll be unhappy. Simple as that.

Hats

Let your conscious be your guide. Depending on how old you are, something that worked for you in third grade should be making the cycle again.

Eyewear

When the sun's out, you need a good pair of sunglasses to prevent your retinas from getting burned out by the glare off the snow. When it's snowing, you need goggles to keep the ice crystals that form a snowflake from gouging your eyes like a thousand tiny hurtling stars. When it's overcast, it's up to you.

As a general rule, don't bring wire-frame shades to the mountain. One face-plant and they've lost their shape for life. Also, make sure the glasses offer at least 98 percent UV protection. Although cheap sunglasses are the coolest thing since sliced bread because you can break them and not get bummed out, if they don't offer UV protection you're facing possible eye damage. The lens filters out light, which causes the pupil to dilate, but if the lens doesn't filter UV rays, then the pupils become that much more vulnerable. Another general rule involves sunglass karma. You lose sunglasses and you find sunglasses. That's the way the world works. But if you see someone leave his shades on the lunch table, it's your responsibility to scream at the person that he forgot his shades. This way, if you ever forget your glasses somewhere, you've got a chance of getting some of the dharma back.

Before we start talking about goggles, we'll just say that sometimes they're more trouble than they're worth. When it's dumping and your goggles are fogged out and you don't have a backup pair, you might as well kiss off the rest of the day. You won't be able to see a line, not to mention all the little swells and bumps you'll be riding over. Some good rules to live by when using goggles are: (1) never take them off unless you're inside or protected in some way from falling snow; (2) always carry a backup pair; (3) don't wear them too tight on your head; and (4) own a good chamois. When your goggles fog up, most of the time it's from water vapor rising off your skin. This occurs when you're exerting yourself without any air cooling. Leaving your goggles on your face while swimming out of a drift is a good way to fog them up.

Once you've found exothermic harmony between your face and your goggles, you're in heaven. They keep your face warm, keep the wind from blowing snow in your eyes, keep all the pointy twigs from scratching your cornea when you're in the trees, and make any snowboarder look just like a Greek god.

When choosing goggles, be aware that the lenses come in various colors, which are designed for a wide range of conditions:

Yellow/gold. If you own only one pair of goggles, this is the lens to have. These colors work best for flat light, which occurs when the sun is blocked by clouds and its light becomes diffused. As a result, the terrain becomes almost two-dimensional, and when you're moving fast you can't see any of those bumps or rolls that can send you over the handlebars. If you happen to be above the tree line, sometimes you don't even know if you're moving fast or slow. When it's snowing or overcast, a light lens with a yellow tint will help bring the terrain to life.

Rose/brown/gray. These lenses work best when the sun's out and you need protection from the glare. The advantage of wearing goggles instead of sunglasses is that they keep your face warm, and many times the clear skies that accompany high pressure will be accompanied by cold air masses.

Clear. If you're a night boarder, a clear lens will keep your face warm without sacrificing visibility. This lens offers no UV protection, but who needs it at night? Also, try a clear lens if your yellow lens doesn't give you enough light when it's snowing hard.

Boards, Bindings, Boots

We can't give you any real advice when it comes to choosing your board, boots, or bindings. The only way to know if a particular setup works for you is to ride on it. But here's some general information about the different pieces of gear to choose from:

Boards

This is by far the most important equipment choice you'll make during a season. Every year board shapes are changing, the construction moving from sandwich to mono-hull or capped, the sizes getting longer, or extremely short, and the overall weight of a board seemingly dropping every year because of new construction techniques. When you buy a new board, make sure you've got at least a one-year warranty that your shop will honor even if the manufacturer can't (with over three hundred board manufacturers, chances are the industry will thin out over the next few years). Then think about the type of riding you do, borrow or rent an appropriate board to test it out, and finally, inform your family of the early Christmas present that you're wishing for. Below we describe three major styles of boards, although there are more and more crossover designs that allow riders different combinations of performance.

Freeriding boards are longer (170 centimeters or more), with a longer nose scoop that helps the board plane out on top of the snow when you're descending deep powder. The rise at the tip and tail is more gradual, and the boards are stiffer and built to withstand big cliff jumps and the occasional trunk thwack. As a result, you'll find them heavier than other boards, with a swing weight that spinners might find prohibitive. On the positive side, the heavier, stiffer board drives like a Cadillac, powering through crud and chunky snow, and reaching top speeds with minimal chatter. Freeriding boards are designed to go anywhere on any mountain, and as the sport continues to move toward the all-mountain/backcountry/extreme approach, you'll see more and more longboarders in the lineup. A longer board allows you to stick a bigger landing. With folks doing tricks off bigger and bigger hits, you'll find that overall board lengths are growing.

Freestyle boards run a little shorter (140–165 centimeters). You should use your height and weight to determine the length you need to keep you moving over fresh snow. The shorter length is compensated for by sharpening the nose and tail kick, which creates a longer effective edge with less total length. Freestyle boards are also slightly wider to allow the shallower stance angle that freestyle riders prefer for fakie riding. Other attributes include light weights that allow riders to get airborne and spin with greater ease, and a generous flex to make landings more forgiving and also accommodate the numerous flat-snow tricks (wheelies, nose blunts) that snowboarders seem obligated to perform as they near the lift line. If you find yourself lining up hits, sessioning the pipe or park, or wanting an all-around board that's easy to handle, the freestyle board is the one of choice.

Alpine boards are built for speed. If you're into racing or just carving some big half-moons down a slope, an alpine board is the key to riding cheek-to-cheek with the snow. The alpine boards are built for performance, and they have a long, flat side cut that keeps the maximum amount of edge in the snow. As a result, you can crank high-speed turns without sketching out. The boards are narrower, with low noses and no tail kick, and you ride with an extreme stance angle—forty-five degrees or more—using hard boots and plate bindings. Lengths run from 145 to 175 centimeters, depending on the type of turning response you require. Many alpine boards come in an asymmetrical design that further enhances the heelside effective edge. If you have any Euro-carver in your veins, you know that there's joy to be found early in the morning on a groomed slope, cruising at full throttle.

Bindings

Bindings are the weak link in snowboard technology, and it may be a while before we see a binding that's both durable and easy to get in and out of. Because the bindings are subjected to a tremendous amount of torque every time you turn, and even more when you fall, the plastic straps frequently break, the backs crack, the base plates pull out from the board, and your only option is to skate down the mountain (a pulled groin waiting to happen) and find a new strap or piece of hardware somewhere—which, depending on where you're riding, might result in a thirty-minute drive to a board shop.

This said, the great thing about snowboard bindings is that they don't release when you crash. As a result, snowboarders don't have to collect the yard-sale items after they bail on a jump. A lot of times you can just tumble back up on your board and keep riding like it was all part of the move. The nonreleasing system also saves the knees by always keeping them in a fixed relationship to your feet and to each other. So while we complain about the occasional strap blowing out, the very nature of snowboard bindings allows riders to catch the big air and stick the big hits, and ensures that they'll have functional knees well into old age.

Bindings come in an assortment of styles, but the two-strap *freestyle binding* is what you'll find on 90 percent of boards. One variation of this is the *baseless binding,* which eliminates the bindings' base plate. The pros of this construction are that it reduces weight and gives you a better feel by putting your boots in direct contact with the board. If you've got big feet with toe slop that hangs over the edge, the baseless binding puts your toes that much closer to the snow and might not be a good choice. Another problem is that some baseless designs put a lot of torque on the screw inserts, increasing the chances of a blowout. Another variation that will be available in late 1995 is the step-in binding. The advantages are: no sitting in the snow to buckle in and easy in and out when you're hiking the half-pipe.

The other major type of binding is the *plate binding* that hard-boot riders wear. Burton is manufacturing a step-in plate binding that makes getting in and out of their binding as quick for boarders as it is for skiers. Depending on what you plan to do with your board, here are a few things to consider when selecting a binding.

Hole pattern. Look at the hole pattern on your board. The manufacturers have started to standardize with a four-by-four hole pattern, but there are still a few holdouts. When you're replacing a pair of bindings, take your board into the shop to make sure you've got the hole pattern and hardware to hold them on.

Straps. Two straps are the standard. A third, top strap is found on some high-back bindings. This gives you greater edging control and more overall stability. The top strap can interfere, though, with certain tricks that require you to bone out. Any strap or cam can blow out without notice, so keep an inventory of spares in your truck or inside one of your big pockets.

Backings. Low backs are best for freestyle riding. They give you greater flexibility to bone out and change your body position on top of the board. A high back will give you greater heelside edge control because it provides more leverage for initiating a turn. Some riders are getting rid of their backings all together. This provides the maximum flexibility, which comes in handy when you're twisting around up in the air.

Materials. Bindings are being constructed from high-strength plastic and aircraft aluminum, with predrilled patterns or insert disks for adjusting stance angles. Talk to the binding guru at your board shop to find out which designs have been holding up the best for the money.

Boots

Snowboarding boots alone are reason enough to snowboard. When the sport began a decade ago, riders usually wore the Chuck Conners. This improved to a pair of Sorels, on which the modern boot is now based. A combination of fashion and function, they're more comfortable than plaster-cast ski boots, and with regular duct taping they'll last for years. Like boards and bindings, boots are designed to accommodate different styles of riding.

Freestyle boots are basically insulated, waterproof basketball shoes with no-skid treads on the bottom. They provide substantial ankle support while allowing enough flex to facilitate all the bone outs and tweaks of your favorite moves. They give you the best feel for your board, and as the lightest boot they're the choice for riders who are into moves and spinning. The downside is less ankle protection and reduced edge control at high speeds.

Freeriding or extreme boots are constructed with an ankle-supporting bladder that greatly stiffens the uppers. What you lose in feel, you make up for in edge control and stability. If your style of riding includes sticking some big hits or tearing down faces at high speed, this type of boot provides solid ankle support while allowing enough flex to get in some good midair contortions.

Hard boots are used by the Euro-carvers and racers to provide maximum edge control. Because the boots have very little flex, each weight shift transfers directly to the board. This speeds up the board's response to minute positioning and alignment changes. You can ride an alpine board without hard boots, but you're not able to drive an edge into the slope or crank a turn with the same authority. The snowboarding hard boot evolved from a ski boot, and you can ride an alpine board with a pair of ski boots. A lot of crossovers from skiing prefer this approach because it saves them from having to fork out hundreds more dollars for a new pair of boots. The advantages of buying hard boots designed for snowboarding are that they have more flex than ski boots and their forward lean is designed for a boarder's stance, not a Lange poster girl.

Notes on Competition

We talked to some riders who have been with the sport since its early days and were down on competition. Their arguments varied, but the underlying message was: snowboarding isn't about winning or losing; it's about fun. And who can argue with that? Other riders, who didn't really harbor dreams of getting sponsored, said that competition brought out the best in them, and that they found themselves pushing harder in front of judges or a stopwatch or a crowd. You can't argue with the adrenaline rush you get from going bigger or faster than ever before, either.

So there is no argument. If you're riding for a soul session, then ride away. If you like pushing yourself in a competitive situation, then pay the ten bucks and go big. For those who dream of snaring one of those lucrative sponsorship gigs, the best way to get noticed is to enter contests and win them. If you only care about fresh powder, then hike up a ridge away from everyone else and get the freshies. Human natures are different; goals in riding are different; and to say, for example, that snowboarding in the Olympics is good for the sport, or bad for the sport, is to assume that everyone's coming from the same perspective. Snowboarding *is*. It exists above and beyond individual riders and manufacturers and resorts and advertising budgets. If you're having fun, then you're doing everything exactly right.

If you are a competitor, you'll be happy to know that the number of contests has been increasing every year. This is due in large part to the increasing coverage that snowboarding has been receiving in such outlets as ESPN, MTV, and numerous general-interest magazines. With greater coverage come more sponsorship dollars, and more competitions.

USASA

By far the most important contributor to the development of the sport has been the United States Amateur Snowboard Association (USASA). Since 1986, the organization has nurtured U.S. snowboarding through the creation of an amateur contest system. What started as a series of grassroots competitions has blossomed into an organization that establishes the standards of competition for amateurs and promotes the sport on the local level. The USASA has gained the support of the snowboard manufacturing industry by adopting a nonexclusive stance regarding intra-industry sponsorship that provides equal access and recognition to all concerned. What this means is, they haven't gone corporate. In addition to promoting the sport at the local level, the USASA has implemented programs such as the scholarship fund for snowboarders. Traditionally, school and snowboarding have been at odds with each other. Now you have to keep up in your classes to stay on your school's snowboard team. This just proves that anything is possible.

The USASA divides the nation into thirteen regions that stage roughly 125 amateur snowboard competitions each season. The West Coast series is staged in the following regions: Alaska, Pacific Northwest (Washington and Oregon), Northern California/Nevada, and Southern California. Using a point system, each region ranks competitors in the disciplines of Half-pipe, Giant Slalom, and Slope Style, all leading toward the USASA Amateur Nationals. Additionally, the contests often feature such nonsanctioned events as Moguls, Boardercross, Obstacle Course, Super G, Downhill, and Big Air contests.

The USASA is the International Snowboard Federation's (ISF) exclusive national governing body in the United States for amateur snowboarding. This is an important thing to know if you hope to compete at the top amateur level. Right now the ISF and the Federation of International Skiing (FIS) are engaged in a conflict over who chooses the national team, whether riders can compete on both circuits, sponsorship and advertisement issues, and a whole lot of organizational hoo-ha that has absolutely nothing to do with snowboarding and a whole lot to do with business and the mighty dollar. Unless you're planning to go for the gold in Nagano, this situation shouldn't keep you up at night.

USSA

The United States Ski Association (USSA) began sanctioning snowboard competitions in 1990. The plan was to increase the program to the international level and to field the United States' first Olympic team. The plan has worked, and the USSA will manage the U.S. Snowboard Team as it gears up to compete internationally. The U.S. Snowboard Regional Race Series divides the country into seven regions, with West Coast series in the Pacific Northwest region (Washington, Oregon) and the Far West region (California, Nevada). The USSA stages half the number of events that the USASA puts on, but its regional series also culminate in two holy grails—the U.S. Snowboarding Championships and the North American Youth Snowboarding Championships—that include the disciplines of Slalom, Giant Slalom, and Half-pipe.

Judging

When you are competing, there are usually three or four judges, with each in charge of one category of the judging. They use a 1–10 point system to score riders on the following criteria:

1. Amplitude: distance between the lip of the pipe or hit and the closest part of the rider and his or her equipment to the lip.

2. Execution: the fluent style of the maneuvers performed without fault by the rider during his or her run.

3. Variety: total number of different maneuvers from the start to the finish of the run. Four different categories of maneuvers must be presented to achieve the maximum points for variety: vertical rotation (i.e., inverted aerials), horizontal rotation (i.e., 180, 540), upright jumps (with hand grabs), and lip tricks (including handplants).

Each judge enters only one score for each run. The scores are then added up, and in case of a tie each of the riders with the same points is ranked in the same place. When four judges are present, two judges split the Variety category into rotation and nonrotation subsections.

The above is the official word from the USASA. A smart rider will know what the judges are looking for, especially by way of variety, and try to cover all the bases. But if you don't have that much variety in your back pocket, we know of a few cases where consistently going huge was enough to bring the points in.

International Snowboarding

The trouble in snowboarding lies in its management of international competition. The current conflict began with a decision by the International Olympic Committee (IOC) to declare snowboarding a discipline of skiing. The IOC then gave the nod to the FIS, rather than the ISF, to govern the selection of the Olympic snowboarding team. Because of its affiliation with U.S. Skiing, the FIS has given the selection process for U.S. Snowboarding to the USSA. All this sounds confusing, and it is.

The ISF's disappointment over the IOC's decision is for good cause. The ISF has been with snowboarding from the beginning. Its work to attract sponsors and establish international standards of competition hasn't been recognized. With the FIS circuit now featuring matchups between future Olympians, the advertising dollars have to make a decision between the two circuits, and it appears the riders do as well. While riders can be members of both FIS and ISF tours, FIS riders can't race in nonsanctioned events. If a rider races an FIS race, then an ISF race, and then a second FIS event, another rider could protest and the rider who raced in different series could be disqualified.

Another dispute arising out of snowboarding's entrance into the Olympic arena orbits around sponsorship deals. In the latest contract with its riders, U.S. Skiing gets the exclusive rights to use the athlete's name, likeness, picture, image, voice, and snowboard performance for endorsements, publicity, advertisements, and such. This conflicts with riders' sponsorship deals with their manufacturers. It's like the Dream Team warm-up suit conflict when the most important issue was what brand warm-up suit the players could drip their hamburger juice on.

All of this is a jumble of politics and behind-closed-doors meetings. While it doesn't affect the average rider, it does threaten to tear the sport apart at its top level. Riders have staged protests and walkouts over these governing body conflicts, and the equipment manufacturers who hold several riders under contract are being drawn into the fray. Everyone involved is committed to promoting the sport, but who can do it best and who deserves to do it are the two questions that haunt the deliberations.

The Olympic spirit has pushed snowboarding into a bureaucratic labyrinth, and while some folks try to save its soul, others are trying to squeeze out the golden egg. This rant isn't about competition anymore, so that's all we'll say for now.

Schedules

Contact these offices to get a schedule of events for the upcoming season:

United States Amateur Snowboard Association
18 Corporate Plaza
Newport Beach, CA 92660
(714) 644-8769

United States Ski Association
P.O. Box 100
Park City, UT 84060
(801) 649-9090

International Snowboard Federation
P.O. Box 477
Vail, CO 81658
(303) 949-5473

Federation of International Skiing
P.O. Box 100
Park City, UT 84060
(801) 649-9090

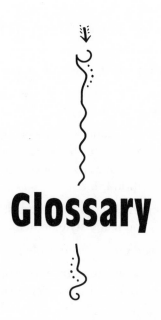

Glossary

We're hesitant to define the vernacular of the snowboarder, mostly because it's highly regional and has the lifespan of a tsetse fly. The language has roots in surf culture, the skateboard scene, and mountain-speak, as well as in the Rastafarian religion, country-western music, and the Weather Channel. Probably more significant than the words are the inflections that accompany them. Rising, falling, undulating, and shotgun inflections can bestow a wide range of meanings on a single word. The most important thing you can do to speak like a snowboarder is to ride harder and go bigger than everyone else. Pretty soon folks will be talking like you.

Aggro. An aggressive, in-your-face, no-fear, amped-up attitude.

Asymmetrical design. When the side cuts of a board do not parallel each other or the core is not shaped symmetrically. This feature is found most often on alpine boards, which you won't be taking fakie.

Avalanche. The release of snow on a steep slope preceded by a degeneration of bonds between snow layers; very often triggered by a hapless skier or snowboarder who doesn't know how to read snow conditions; something to be avoided.

Backside. A jump, spin, or trick performed in counterclockwise (for regular-foot riders) fashion.

Bail. Landing a big air with survival taking priority over style. Usually done on the face, side, or back.

Base. The bottom of your board; P-tex covered by wax.

Big air. Air is said to be big when the rider has the time to contemplate exactly how high up he or she is.

Boarder-cross. With roots in Rollerball, the boarder-cross is a no-holds-barred gate race where up to six racers try to cross the finish line first. There are rules against blatantly knocking someone down, but fiercely jockeying for position is legal.

Bone out. Straightening the leg to its full extension while in the air. A good bone out will win you many style points.

Bonk. To bang your board off a nonsnow object.

Bowl. A terrain feature characterized by a wide-open, steep wall between ridges that the wind fills with powder. A cornice usually occurs at the top of a bowl.

Brah. *See* Bro.

Bro. A fellow snowboarder (male or female).

Broform. Like proform, but more out of friendship than for business reasons.

Butt-checking. A tribute to the common monkey, whereby a snowboarder's butt makes contact with the snow upon landing a jump in order to maintain the rider's balance and allow him or her to continue down the slope. If monkeys could snowboard, they would tail-check.

Camber. The arched shape of a board. If you lay your board flat, the middle will curve up from the ground, like the flex of a bow. Camber allows you to pump speed, among other things.

Carving. To initiate a turn using the edges of the board, as opposed to sliding into a turn.

Chatter. The sound your board makes as you're losing your edge on an icy slope.

Climax. What a slope is said to do when avalanche debris falls from top to bottom of the slope.

Corduroy. A term used to describe well-groomed snow.

Cornice. An overhanging snow mass that usually results from wind.

Corn snow. A granular snow created by a melt-freeze cycle that occurs when sun hits the snow during the day and partially melts it, followed by freezing temperatures at night. Corn snow is most common in spring. A snowboard cooks on corn.

Dad. Appellation used to address a fellow snowboarder, or suffix added to a bro's name, for example, Sean-dad, Jaime-dad, Betty-dad.

Death box. *See* Fun box.

Death cookies. Chunks of avalanche debris that have the shape and consistency of large rocks and will surely hurt you if you try to ride over them.

Dialed, dialed in. In the zone.

Effective edge. A measurement used to define the actual length of the edge that comes into contact with the snow.

El Niño. A mass of warm water in the Pacific Ocean that moves north, creating unusual weather patterns for the West Coast. Hurricanes, floods, locust swarms, volcanic activity, and spontaneous love have been ascribed to the little boy.

Emma Peel. One of the Avengers.

Ernie. *See* Kook.

Euro-carver. A hard-boot rider who likes to carve perfect half-moons at high speed. He or she has usually studied a foreign language, smokes imported cigarettes, and knows where to find good espresso.

Face-plant. A painful union of face and snow.

Face shot. Occurs in deep powder. The loss of vision due to nectar snow conditions.

Fakie. Riding with the back foot forward.

Fall line. The path by which gravity pulls an object down a hill. If you dropped your snowboard from the top of a mountain, it would travel straight down the fall line until it killed someone.

Firn snow. Snow that has not melted during the summer.

Freshies. First tracks down an untouched slope. Whoever hikes the ridge first gets the freshies.

Frontside. A jump, spin, or trick performed in clockwise (for regular-foot riders) fashion.

Fun box. A wooden or plastic box or half-barrel planted in the snow so that riders may bonk off it. It makes a nice hollow sound when you thump it good.

Gap. A jump where you must clear a recession or gap in the snow in order to land safely. It's good to know about the gap ahead of time.

Gnarly. Synonym for hairy, scary, or sick.

Go big, go fat. Flying high or far off a hit, lip, or cornice.

Going through the car wash. Riding through tight trees.

Goods. The pleasing features of a mountain; also, the story or facts on a particular subject.

Go off. A section of the mountain is said to be going off when conditions (wind, sun, snow) have allowed it to display its maximum potential for fun. For example, a chute goes off when snow fills it to the optimum level, a rock goes off when the landing is filled and uncompacted, and a bar goes off when it's filled with people.

Goofy-footed. Riding with the right foot forward.

Grinds. Food.

Half-pipe. A ditch in the snow patterned after the trail an earthworm leaves in the mud, except bigger.

Heelside. Backside.

Heli. Helicopter. Something that all snowboarders want to ride. If a friend has been on a heli trip, they will be saying heli-this, heli-that all season long. You won't know what to say.

Hit. Snow mass that you launch off.

Huck. To fling yourself into the air.

Jib. A word that's used for just about anything, but usually refers to flat-snow tricks: little spins, grabs, and other trick-oriented maneuvers.

Jibber. A somewhat derogatory or diminutive term referring to a snowboarder who spends his or her life on a short board doing tricks in the snowboard park.

Kick a trail. To create a series of steps in the snow that lead up a ridge.

Kickers. Banks on the sides of groomed runs created by snowcats pushing snow to the sides. They function as perpetual quarter-pipes and are a good thing if you're looking to break up the monotony of simple turns.

Kook. A derogatory label for someone who pays more attention to the people on the mountain than to the mountain itself.

Lift-op, liftie. A lift operator. Ninety percent of the time, the lift-op is a snowboarder who might share some local knowledge of the mountain if you ask nicely.

Line. The path you take down a pitch or run. An interesting line is one that maximizes the terrain's potential, thereby showcasing a rider's skill and creativity.

Lunch trays. Short boards with minimal effective edge used for jibbing.

Mailbox. U.S. postal worker employer. Also, a rounded, oblong aluminum tube that snowboarders like to bonk off of.

Method. A grab behind the heels. A big, fat method will score you many points in a competition.

Mug down. Suck face.

Oatmeal. Warm breakfast cereal that gets chunky when it cools. Also, warm Pacific Northwest snow.

Over the handlebars. A pitch forward that results from getting your body weight too far forward, or the tip of your board buried in snow or otherwise obstructed.

Pineapple Storm. A weather system that blows up from the South Pacific, usually causing the snow level to rise above the highest peak of the highest mountain. As a result, rain falls on the snow, compresses it, causes avalanches, and exposes rock, and then transforms the base into a rock-hard substance that only resembles snow.

Pipe. *See* Half-pipe.

Pipe Dragon. A grooming tool used for shaping half-pipes with flawless transitions and vertical walls. If a mountain owns or rents a Pipe Dragon, it will also have a nectar pipe.

Posthole. To break through the crust while walking through snow. Postholing out of an area can sometimes take hours and is seldom fun.

Pow-pow. Powder.

Proform. A discount given by a manufacturer to snowboard instructors, hot local riders, and distant relations. A proform deal usually allows riders to buy gear for cost plus a certain percentage.

Pump speed. To compress then decompress the legs coming out of a turn or transition in order to generate speed.

Purl. A surfing term used to describe the tip of the board becoming buried in the water. Applies to snowboarding in oatmeal, where purling will send you over the handlebars, and to riding in powder, where putting your weight forward will cause the nose to dive.

Pyramid. A type of manufactured snow obstacle that resembles a pyramid in shape and allows riders three working faces to hit.

Quasimodo walk. *See* Skating.

Rock garden. A series of boulders on a slope that provide the opportunity for drops and hits.

Scrub. To purposely sideslip in the middle of a carve in order to control speed.

Session. To work something. To session a hit means to hit it, unbuckle, hike back up, hit it again, unbuckle, etc. You can session, or sesh, anything from a hit to a particular line down a slope, a bowl, a section of trees, or the local Taco Bell.

Shredder. The 1980s term for snowboarder.

Sick. Scary or excellent—often both.

Side cut. The curve built into the sidewalls and edges of a board to enhance turning characteristics.

Skating. To push yourself across the snow with the unbuckled rear foot.

Sketchy. Marginal conditions, often characterized by ice, rocks, or crud hidden under a thin layer of snow.

Skiboarding. Dorky name for the sport from the early days of snowboarding. The term is still used by some old-fart skiers in an attempt to claim the sport as a discipline of skiing.

Spine. A long mound of snow with transitions on either side; usually found in a snowboard park. It provides a continuous face that you have the option of hitting frontside, hitting backside, or jumping over.

Starfish. To roll down a slope at high speed, with outstretched arms and legs in a painful ballet that invokes images of the sea creature.

Steeps. Steep sections of a mountain.

Stick a hit. To land a fat air.

Stiffy. A maneuver where the rider grabs the board during a jump with both legs locked straight out in front.

Switchstance. Going off a hit fakie.

Tabletop. A type of jump usually found in a terrain park where the top of a mound of snow has been leveled off. It's best to clear the tabletop and land on the downward transition, although coming up short is not nearly as painful as with a gap jump.

Tail. The rear of the snowboard.

Tip. The front of the snowboard.

Toeside. Frontside.

Transition. A slope that connects a flat area to a vertical or near-vertical wall.

Turn. To make a turn; also used as a synonym for riding, as in, "It was good turning with you, dude."

Tweak. To adjust, as in a binding or stance angle, or a small flutter of the board performed in concert with a bone out; also to injure, as in a knee, wrist, or shoulder.

Ullr. Norse god of winter.

Underage. Used to describe a trick yet to be perfected; also, the vast majority of snowboarders.

Vert. Short for vertical and verticilaster (an almost circular flower arrangement formed by a pair of clusters facing each other on the stem, the flower arrangement preferred by snowboarders.

Vibe. To send positive or negative energy. A place can vibe you good; a kook can vibe you bad.

Wire. To get a trick wired means to practice it until it becomes second nature or instinctual.

Yard sale. To deposit pieces of gear on the snow as you starfish down. Skiers put on the best yard sales, sometime spreading their skis, poles, and hats over hundreds of vertical feet.

Zone. A place beyond rational thought that, upon entering, a rider is empowered with the ability to ride in fluid concert with the terrain beneath him or her.